D1833242

SOME ECONOMIC ASPECTS OF
BRITISH RULE IN INDIA

SOME ECONOMIC ASPECTS

OF

BRITISH RULE IN INDIA

By

G. Subramania Iyer

© **Author**

All rights reserved. No part of this work may be reproduced, stored, adapted, or transmitted in any form or by any means, electronic, mechanical, photocopying, micro-filming, recording or otherwise, or translated in any language, without the prior written permission of the copyright owner and the publisher. The book is sold subject to the condition that it shall not, by way of trade or otherwise, be lent, resold, hired out, or otherwise circulated without the prior publisher's written consent in any form of binding or cover other than that in which it is published.

The views and opinions expressed in this book are author(s) own and the facts reported by them have been verified to the extent possible, and the publishers are not in any way liable for the same.

ISBN : 978-81-212-0147-6

First Published in 1903

Indian Reprint in 2018

Published by

Gyan Publishing House
5, Ansari Road
Daryaganj, New Delhi-110002
Phone: 011-47034999, 9811692060
www.gyanbooks.com
E-mail: books@gyanbooks.com

Printed at: G. Print Process, Delhi.

"*For whom should I work if not for the people? Born of the people, trusted by the people, I will die for the people.*"

CHARLES BRADLAUGH,

in Bombay, 28th December, 1889.

"*The government of a people by itself has a meaning and a reality; but such a thing as government of one people by another does not and cannot exist. One people may keep another for its own use, a place to make money in, a human catte farm to be worked for the profit of its own inhabitants.*"

JOHN STUART MILL.

PREFACE.

IN the following pages I have put together the results of my studies during a pretty lengthy period of my journalistic career. Since I gave up my connection with the *Hindu*, I have been able to make a special study of Indian financial and economic questions, and my impression has been strengthened that the time has come when our public men should distinguish between the different branches of politics and devote themselves to their study with a due sense of proportion as to their relative importance. The great bulk of the Indian press mainly concerns itself with what may be called administrative politics. But it must be admitted that, while this branch has its own importance, what may be called fiscal and ndustrial politics, as involving the wider and the more permanent interests of the country, demand a clo er and a more regular study. Questions of the latter character are no doubt taken up by the Indian press and public bodies as they arise from time to time and are disposed of from the Indian point of view, which is not always the point of view of the Government. When new taxes are imposed or new proposals concerning the public revenues of the country are made, public opinion no doubt declares itself either for or against them. Similarly, in regard to industries of the country, there has been a general and vague complaint that the policy of British rule has been destructive in its effect in the past, and is unsympathetic in its attitude at present. But neither the fiscal nor the economic questions of India have been systematically studied in view to a consideration of the applicability to Indian conditions of the theories and conclusions of the economists of the Western countries, of those of England more especially.

I do not forget that there are worthy exceptions to the generality of our public men, like Mr. Dadabhai Naoroji, who for a long time stood alone among educated Indians as a student and expounder of Indian economics. The late Mr. M. G. Ranadé has also left valuable records of his views on the same. And latterly Mr. R. C. Dutt, by his 'Economic History of India' and other writings, has placed the Indian people under obligation. I may mention Mr. D. E. Wacha, and the Hon: Mr. G. K. Gokhale among other Indians who have thrown light on economic and fiscal questions by their various public utterances and writings. Still, in my humble opinion, these questions should be more generally studied by our politicians and journalists than is the case at present; and their views should be more largely diffused among the classes that take an interest in public affairs. In the following pages I endeavour to make a small contribution towards this end.

With the greatest diffidence do I place before the public my views on some of the most important questions considered in this book. There is no pretence whatever to originality or scientific treatment. Most of my veiws are those that are held by my educated countrymen in general, and some of them have been expressed by me in the columns of my weekly journal, *United India*. All that I have done is to collect these views together in regard to some of the more important questions and place them before the public in, I hope, a popular form. The invaluable book of Mr. Dadabhai Naoroji 'Poverty and Un-British Rule in India' and Mr. William Digby's equally invaluable book 'Prosperous British India', are a storehouse of information indispensable to every citizen, and my book is by no means intended to supersede them.

Being quite inexperienced in book-making, I have allowed many defects in the arrangement of the book. It was written at intervals during a course of a rather busy life and in spite of continued ill-health. Some subjects are treated too summarily while others, like the foreign trade of India, receive a treatment which may be considered rather lengthy. In the present state of public information on Indian politics, however, I think it is an error on the right side to indulge in profusion rather than brevity. Should I be so fortunate as to see my book reach a second edition, I expect to be able to introduce improvements in several portions of it.

CONTENTS.

APPENDIX.

CHAPTER I.*

The Present Economic Situation.

AT the Provincial Conference, it is the practice to include in the programme of business only such subjects as are connected with the interests of the province. These nterests are neither unimportant nor narrow. Questions connected with legislation, taxation, judicial administration, land revenue administration, education, &c., arise, involving the well-being of millions of people. It is therefore very proper that these questions should receive special and exclusive attention from their representatives and that their conclusions should be pressed on the attention of the Local Government, while other questions of wider and higher interest, governing the broad current of the nation's destiny, should fall within the scope of the deliberations of the national assembly which is constituted by the representatives of the various provinces, and which appeals, not to provincial authorities, but to authorities at the helm of the Indian Empire, and over and above them, to British Imperial statesmen. But on this occasion, while we are

* This Chapter is a reproduction with slight changes of my Presidential Address at the Provincial Conference held at Cocanada, June 11th, 1902.

primarily concerned with provincial questions, we are conscious that these are only a branch of the more serious and more momentous national problems, on a right and liberal solution of which depends the administrative and the economic well-being of the province as well as the Empire. I have no doubt that you, gentlemen, come from different parts of the Presidency with local experience and knowledge, will debate the local questions that will be brought up before you with thought and reason, and will formulate correct conclusions. It would be presumptuous on my part to anticipate these conclusions by any remarks I may make in this inaugural address. The responsibility of choosing the subjects for discussion and of framing the resolutions on them for adoption at the Conference, properly belongs to the Subjects Committee, which you will presently elect, though, through the alertness of the Reception Committee, all of us have had a foretaste of the scope and nature generally of these subjects. Meanwhile, you will pardon me if I draw your attention to some important and pressing problems which mark the situation of the country as a whole at present, and which, throwing as they do direct light on the provincial problems immediately to engage your attention, will be of help in the direction of your deliberations. I propose to dwell at some length on some of the more serious of these problems, which are more and more prominently coming to the surface of Indian politics, and are destined to affect the immediate future of our people for weal or woe.

Of these problems, gentlemen, I need not say that the one most prominent at the present moment in the minds of us all, and one which, I dare say, has filled them often and anon with sad reflections and with despair, is the increasing frequency of famine, and the growing intensity and extent of its deplorable evils. Our rulers have declared that famine is the visitation of Providence, the result of the caprice of nature, and that all that can be done to relieve the people from its disastrous effects, is to organize to perfection measures of relief during its career, and to adopt certain palliative measures. We quite appreciate the benevolent motives of Government and the sense of responsibility which actuates it. But we are far from satisfied that this attitude meets the full requirements of the situation. In the opinion of a large number of competent men, if the Government were to discharge its whole responsibility and give full scope to its benevolence, it should go further than these temporary and palliative measures, and devise means, after a full and competent investigation of the economic condition of the country, to prevent these appalling afflictions which have of late occurred with greater frequency, and have wrought worse disasters, than in former years. This great question has recently engaged the attention, as you know, of a large number of public men in England, and in order that it might be brought to a definite issue before the British Parliament and public, our stuanchest and most valued friend,

Sir William Wedderburn, with the help of other well-known friends, has organized a society, called the Indian Famine Union, in London. At a public meeting recently held under its auspices, steps which should be taken, from our point of view, for the prevention of famine in this country, were pointed out in a series of resolutions, which I need not reproduce at length in this place. But you will remember that the first and most important resolution adopted, postulated, as the basis of its demand, the continued prevalence of famine throughout vast regions in India, the permanent poverty of great masses of the people, the wide-spread indebtedness of the agricultural population and the lack of precise official information regarding the foundation causes of agricultural distress, and that it pressed for a detailed local enquiry into the economic conditions of typical villages in famine areas. On the facts ascertained during this inquiry were to be based preventive and remedial measures suited to the various provinces. Now, gentlemen, I have not the slightest doubt in my mind that you entirely approve of this resolution, and in my opinion, this Conference should record its entire concurrence with our friends that met in London. Other subsidiary resolutions were also adopted, asking for a more lenient and elastic system of land revenue administration, for local experiments in the establishment of agricultural banks, for a more liberal expenditure than hitherto on irrigation, and for the stimulation of industrial education throughout the country with a view to increase the productive power of the people. On these important topics, I hope and believe that the Conference will express its opinions after due deliberation.

THE ATTITUDE OF GOVERNMENT.

Gentlemen, you must have noticed, as others have, the lamentable attitude of Lord George Hamilton towards the Indian Famine Union. In taking up that attitude, I think you may believe that he had the concurrence of his own Council and of the Government of India at Calcutta. Now, so long as representatives of British rule in India, charged with awful responsibility for the contentment and prosperity of millions, remain satisfied in their own minds that, about the economic condition of the millions of the poor cultivating classes, living an obscure and humble life in remote villages, quiet, voiceless and ignorant, they, *i.e.*, the representatives of British rule, living amidst the sweet amenities of fashionable and luxurious lives in inaccessible hill stations, know everything that is worth knowing, and that no light outside their own charmed circle can illumine their minds, so long as this is the attitude of our rulers, there is not much chance of criticisms, even from men of the highest weight and authority, producing favorable impression on the official hierarchy, or shaking its complacent self-confidence. It is therefore incumbent upon us to maintain a ceaseless agitation of the question, placing irrebuttable facts before our rulers and exposing the fallacies of their arguments. Nothing can be dearer to us than the happiness of the millions of our poorer classes, who, in normal periods, poor and under-fed, in times of famine " die like flies," to use Sir Antony MacDonnel's expression. There is no more important or worthy object to which we, who represent the political sense of the community, can devote our best energies and resources.

THE PITCHED BATTLE.

The stoutest champions of the official view do not deny that there is frightful poverty among the people; but while we contend that this poverty is growing wider and deeper as the result of certain economic and political causes, the officials maintain that this poverty is diminishing and the people are making more than fair progress along the path of prosperity. So far as this controversy could be settled by a war of words, it has been within the past few months waged to exhaustion on either side. But, naturally, either side claims the victory; and we are not nearer to a practical solution than we were at the time when Mr. Romesh Chander Dutt started the campaign. Only an impartial, competent and full enquiry, such as suggested by the Indian Famine Union, can put an end to the controversy.

The pitched battle was fought on the floor of the House of Commons between Lord George Hamilton and Mr. W. S. Caine. Mr. Caine's indictment was fierce and merciless, and consisted of arguments and statements verified from official figures, whereas Lord George Hamilton's reply was feeble, and self-contradictory, and consisted mostly of mere assertions. Mr. Caine did not speak as the mouth-piece of the Congress party or as that of the Indian Famine Union. He spoke for himself, as a friend of India, and it is remarkable that his arguments, facts and conclusions are in entire accord with those put forward by the non-official pessimist school.

ENORMITY OF THE ECONOMIC EVILS.

Imagine the loss of life and property that has occurred to the people during the last two famines, and you will have an idea as to the enormity of the economic evils that have made such awful and general calamities possible. According to official figures, the property lost to the agricultural community of Western India is estimated to be no less than £50,000,000, and the loss in Central India is calculated to be £20,000, 000 ; and 70 millions in these two provinces alone. If the loss in other parts of India, in Ajmere, Rajputana, &c., be included, the total loss of agricultural property may be safely put down at £100,000,000. This enormous loss occurred during the last famine. If the loss of property at the end of the previous famine of 1897 be taken to be half this amount, the total loss of property during the decade, on account of famine and scarcity, may be put down at £150,000,000. To this figure should be added the amount which the famines cost to Government in the way of direct expenditure on relief, of the loss of land revenue, the loss of revenue from other sources, other direct and indirect losses, because the Government can meet its expenditure on famine relief as on other objects, only from the tax ation of the people Supposing this last item amounted to £50,000,000, the total loss of money and property to the people amounts to 200,000,000 sterling. Then, about the loss of life, it is calculated, from the difference between the census figures of 1891 and 1901, that the deaths due to famine causes, to starvation and diseases arising therefrom, were 19 millions. Such a terrible loss of population, apart from the humanitarian side, has its economic side also. In so far as the loss consisted in the death of the old and infirm, who were only consumers and were neither producers nor wage-earners, it is a gain to the surviving population who will get more food and earn higher wages. To the extent that the lives lost were those of children, there is also gain, because there will be fewer mouths for the available food-stock of the country to be distributed among. But among the 19 millions, women as well as men, there must be a very considerable number, who were neither children nor old and infirm and who were producers and wage-earners. And, then, when the number of the children and unmarried persons that died and that would, if they were alive, reach marriageable age, married, they would have themselves contributed their share to the wealth of the country and their addition to its population. Their death and the reduction in the normal rate of growth in the population, must tell on the extension of cultivation. I do not know that any calamity that ever befell a people in any part of the world either in ancient or modern times, from causes natural or human, caused the death of so many human lives and loss of so much property. Yet, hardly has such a calamity stirred any strong indignation or contrition among the people of Britain. Responsible statesmen, attributing the calamity to the anger of Providence, are content to sit with folded arms and wait on events till the anger of Providence is appeased.

THE ROOT EVIL.

The root evil of the whole economic condition of India is the extreme, and we may say hopeless, poverty of the agricultural classes who form more than three-fourths of the population. This problem of poverty has received unusual attention of late years, and has been subjected to a good deal of scrutiny by officials and others, both in India and England, and in my opinion, all that can be said on both sides, on the strength of available data, has been said. I need not traverse here the same ground, except to point out the fallacy of certain statements made by Lord George Hamilton in Parliament and by the Government of India in their Council at Calcutta. I select a few of these fallacious statements from Lord George Hamilton's speech in the House of Commons, in reply to Mr. Caine, which was intended to be also a reply to the Indian Famine Union, and a full and exhaustive disposal of the contentions on the side of the non-official pessimistic school, represented by Messrs. Dadabhai Naorojee, Digby and others, and by the Indian National Congress generally.

LORD GEORGE HAMILTON'S FALLACIES.

Lord George Hamilton said in the House of Commons that the weight of taxation which India bore under British rule was the lightest of any country in Asia—he used to say formerly, of any country in the *world*. Well, light taxation can only mean that it admits of a margin for safe increase in critical times. If this is the meaning, why did Government resolve in 1893 not to increase taxation, but to tinker with the currency? One official witness after another said, before the Currency Committee, that to increase taxation would be dangerous, and that an indirect addition to it by means of a false currency was preferable because the ignorant people of India would neither know nor feel it. In this indirect way, and not quite in a spirit of straightforwardness, have Government added to the public burden since 1893, an amount reckoned by some to be 36 crores of rupees a year, and have brought to the brink of ruin the producing classes. I may remind you here what the Treasury wrote to the Secretary of State in 1879 on this subject: "In the present case, the object of the Indian Government appears to be to increase the amount they have to receive from their taxpayers. The Government scheme may relieve the Indian Government and others who desire to remit money to England, but this relief will be given at the expense of the Indian taxpayer." A minority of the Currency Committee itself pressed this view in their separate report. But, the Government of India had reached a state of bankruptcy when a desperate remedy was immediately called for, and at such a time Government did not think of rendering the *lightest* system of taxation a bit less light! Why did they not?

NO MORTAL POWER COULD PREVENT FAMINE.

2. "No doubt, if you could elevate the people to a higher standard, there might be less distress and greater power of resistance to drought when it comes; but even if the Hon. Member were to carry out all the schemes—mad schemes I will call some of them—he has mentioned to-night, if you bring the people of India to a standard of comfort such as no European nation has ever attained, if for ten years no more rain fall than the recent average, no mortal power could prevent India from suffering from famine." So says Lord George Hamilton. Let us examine this. The first part of the above sentence contradicts the second part. If the Indian people were raised to the European standard of prosperity, there would be a large number of non-agricultural industries, which will absorb millions now subsisting on agriculture. There would be plenty of money, the only effect of the failure of rain would be increased prices and not scarcity of food. There might be a pinch, but there would be no famine. There would come into existence a prosperous agricultural middle class, capital would grow, manufactures and arts would flourish, and there would be wealth and contentment in the land.

3. "The reports show that the people who were on relief during the famine of 1876-77, were of a higher social standing than those who sought relief during the recent

famine, and that far more land went out of cultivation than has recently been the case. Therefore, I think I may fairly contend that, as far as famine is concerned, we have conclusive evidence that the people are better able to sustain the terrible infliction imposed on them by drought than they were before." This is not true ; just the contrary is the truth (*vide* Lord Curzon's celebrated Circular of December 1899). Something may be due to the fact that people are getting more accustomed to famine and aware of the sure relief from Government, and that, accordingly, there is now less panic and less dislocation of society than there were in previous famines. But, as a fact, the ruinous effects of famine are reaching the higher strata of society.

4. "Every branch of revenue is improving; the powers of consumption and production are steadily increasing; the exports and imports—particularly those which relate to the masses—are increasing in volume. Is not this a clear and indisputable evidence that, on the whole, the economic condition of the Indian people is *slightly* (mark the word) improving?" No. Mr. Caine and his school of critics have repeatedly proved from official statistics that the powers of consumption and production have not increased; and the imports of articles, chiefly consumed by the masses, have not increased. For instance, cotton manufactures, grain and pulse, brass, copper and lead, sugar, umbrellas—these have not shown a uniform tendency to increase. Nor is the improvement in the revenues an indication of prosperity.

5. "The unpleasant feature concerning the indebtedness of the agriculturists in India is that it does not arise from over-assessment or too heavy land revenue; it results from light land revenue. If we had so taxed the agriculturist that he could not get a livelihood out of his holding, the money-lender would not advance large sums on a security that was of little value." This is a most extraordinary argument that has recently come into vogue. If the holding of the ryot would give him no livelihood, why should he ever cultivate a holding at all? The argument is the same as saying that, if a man had no palate, he would not eat unhealthy food. If the holding were to give the ryot a livelihood, including not merely his bare physical sustenance, but his ability to meet other wants also, such as clothing, domestic and social expenses, why should the ryot borrow at all? It is absurd to imagine that the Indian ryot iso differently constituted from other human beings that he would borrow and entangle himself into the meshes of indebtedness, when there is no need for doing so. It is because the ryot's holding gives him some livelihood though scanty, and because the deficiency of the yield from his holding—a deficiency caused by excessive taxation—can be made good by borrowing in the absence of other help, that he borrows. In fact, he borrows because he is poor, but not because he is an extravagant spendthrift. If, then, taxation is so light as to bring on this stupendous evil of rural indebtedness, it is quite open to Government to issue an *ukase* declaring such an increase in the tax as would make his holding yield no livelihood, and thereby get rid

of indeptedness altogether! Why should Government pledge themselves—as Lord Curzon pledges himself—to further leniency in future?

6. "They (the ryots) had incurred these debts for dinner parties on the death of various members of their families, for dowries and other marriage expenses . . . . In no instance was Government assessment even mentioned as a cause of the debt." To this, our answer is in the words of the Deccan Riot's Commission. The Report of that Commission says (page 19, para. 54): "The results of the Commission's enquiries show that undue prominence has been given to the expenditure on marriage and other festivals as a cause of the ryot's indebtedness. The expenditure on such occasions may undoubtedly be called extravagant when compared with the ryot's means; but the occassions occur seldom, and probably in a course of years the total sum spent this way by any ryot is *not larger than a man in his position is justified in spending on social and domestic pleasure.*" Here is a body of chosen experts, appointed by Government to investigate this very matter, charged with official responsibility for their conclusions, deliberately recording their opinion, on evidence collected, that the charge of extravagance cannot be brought against the Indian ryot. Yet, Lord George Hamilton, who must be aware of this opinion recorded by the Commission, prefers to mislead the uninformed House by quoting the opinion of a single officer whose opinion is his own opinion uncorroborated by evidence.

Those that glibly talk of the extravagance of the ryots are not aware of the peculiar customs obtaining among the peasantry with regard to marriages. One of these is—that the relations and friends who assemble at the marriage give what they call "Katnams" or cash presents to the bride or bridegroom, and in most cases the expenses connected with the ephemeral part of the programme are covered by the presents received. In other words, it means that the expenditure is met, without any loss of self-respect, by a general subscription raised among the relations and friends of the parties. Is it possible to conceive a more practical way of meeting such extraordinary expenditure? After all, the major part of the expenditure consists in the feeding of relations and the poor; and an institution which leads to the distribution of wealth in this form ought not to be deprecated in this country. "I have seen a number of marriages among the ryot families in this part of the country, and my wonder has always been that even a well-to-do ryot spends so little and not so much in proportion to his circumstances on marriage and other festive occasions. He sets an example in this respect which the upper classes will do well to follow." *

It may not be out of place to recall in this connection the results of the enquiries of the Deccan Riots Commission, as the causes of the ryot's indebtedness are more or less the same all over the country. Before this Commission submitted its report, the prevailing notion about the causes of the Ryot's indebtedness was, that the ryots were

* Mr. G. Venkataratnam, in "United India," April 29, 1902.

idle spendthrifts and extravagant in their marriage and other expenses, and that the Sowcars were inordinately oppressive. and exacted usurious interests. These two causes were always urged by the apologists of the Government as satisfactorily accounting for the ryot's misery and helplessness. The Commission's report, however, most effectually exploded this theory. The Commission found the ryot to be a simple, well-disposed peasant, contented with hardy fare and scanty clothing. His recklessness in incurring debts was held to be apparent only and to be really the result of sheer necessity; his extravagance was only occasional, and his improvidence no greater than that of other people in the same low scale of civilization. They held that undue prominence was given to the expenditure attending marriage and other festivals, and that this expenditure was not the cause of his indebtedness, which was due to the smallness of his disposable margin of profits and the constantly recurring debit items of food-necessaries and seed and Government assessment. As regards the money-lending classes, the Commissioners found that their profits were not extravagant, and that on the whole they were not higher than were warranted by the nature of the business, precarious, unpopular, and even dangerous. Of the human and preventible causes, the Commissioners recognized two classes of agencies for which Government was more or less responsible—the action of the revenue system and the action of the Civil Courts. Among the fiscal causes all the Commissioners agreed in finding fault with the rigidity of the rules and the suddenness of the enhancements, while a very strong majority of the Commissioners directly charged the enhanced assessments and the defective working of the survey system generally, as being chiefly responsible for the ryot's wretchedness. The Hon'ble Mr. Hope, who introduced the Deccan Agriculturists' Relief Bill, 1879, in the Supreme Legislative Council, admitted that "to our revenue system must in candour be ascribed some share in the indebtedness of the ryot" and that "it seems likely that indebtedness arising mainly from other causes, normal or special, may have been aggravated by our rigid system." He proposed that relief might be given by modifying the mode by which the land revenue was assessed and levied—by changing the periods of the instalments and by abolishing eviction for default in the payment of assessment. The Hon'ble Sir Robert Egerton, however, went further and touched the very heart of the question when he pointed out that it was scant justice and bad policy for Government, while not abating a jot in its own rigorous methods of levying its dues from the ryots, to intervene to the prejudice of private creditors, and he insisted on the necessity of requiring the Bombay Government to lighten its burdens, which had the chief hand in driving the ryot into the hands of the Sowcar. The Hon'ble Sir A. Arbuthnot, thereupon, gave the assurance that the views of the Government of India were at one with those of Sir Robert Egerton on this point. The Hon'ble Mr. Thomson also emphatically recognised the fact that legislative relief was but a small part of the remedies demanded, and he enlarged upon the heavy responsibility which rested upon the Bombay Government to meet the claims of the case by liberal administrative changes. The Hon'ble Sir J. Strachey admitted that the assessment, though moderate, still presses with extreme severity in bad seasons upon the ryots. Lastly, His Excellency the Viceroy remarked, that, what "My Hon'ble friend, the Lieutenant-Governor, pointed out to us yesterday is, I am afraid, only too true, that this state of things exists, not indeed in the same degree of intensity, yet more or less potentially as it were, throughout the greater part of India, where a comparatively slight aggravation of existing circumstances might not impossibly produce results scarcely less distressing than those which it is our present object to mitigate in some parts of the Deccan." This confession on the part of Lord Lytton has a significance in the fact that the depression of ryots is general over the greater part of India, and that the causes of such depression are the same all over the country. Lord Lytton vouchsafed the assurance that the Government of India were in no sense indifferent to the gravity of the case for fiscal reform, and he expressed his belief that the rigidity of the revenue system did require, and admitted of, relaxation both in the methods of collection and of assessment. Instead of carrying out the promised fiscal reforms, however, the Government have gone on enhancing the taxes and collecting their revenue with increased rigour consoling themselves that their land revenue policy was not the cause of the ryots' depression, but their own social customs and domestic usages were the only cause.

7. "Food in India is extraordinarily cheap, and, during the worst famines and during the recent famine relief in the Central Provinces, a man doing a good day's work could be kept in good condition on a penny a day when the price of food was at its normal rate. . . . . . Any one in receipt of three pence a day and being the head of a family consisting of not more than four, could give himself and his family every day three meals of rice and millet, and fish and butcher's meat once or twice a week. But there would be no milk or butter or cheese for the children." This is a most audacious assertion. Three pence or three annas a day would at this moment in Madras barely buy rice of the coarsest kind to give two meals to a family such as Lord George Hamilton mentions, and unless an additional amount is earned for condiments, fuel, etc., the family must necessarily reduce the quantity of meals. Compare with this estimate the estimate which Sir Charles Elliott made when he was Settlement Officer in the North-Western Provinces: " One pound of flour is sufficient, though meagre, sustenance for a non-labouring man. That a labouring adult can eat 2lbs. I do not doubt; but he rarely, if ever, gets it. But take the ordinary population in a family of five, consisting of the father, mother and three children. The father will, I would say, eat a little less than 2lbs., the mother a little more than 1lb., the children about 3lbs., between them; altogether

7lbs. for five people is the average with after much inquiry I am inclined to adhere to." In the North-Western Provinces and Oudh, the average price of wheat in the District of Mirzapur during the five years ending 1900 was about 1 seer, or 22½lbs., per rupee. And according to Sir Charles Elliott, 7lbs. being the daily requirement of a family of five, or 6lbs. for a family of four, the cost of food for Lord George Hamilton's family would be not 3 as. but 4 as. 3½ ps. But this makes no allowance for fish or butcher's meat, for condiments or for fuel, not to speak of primitive comforts, illness, social or spiritual requirements. In other words, on 4 as. 3 pies a day, Lord George's family would be below the line of what Mr. Rowntree calls "primary poverty."

The Poor in Europe and in India.

If the frightful poverty that prevails in India is lamentable, it is no less lamentable that our official class should have grown so callous as to apologise for it by a reference to the poverty that prevails in other parts of the world. Most officials deny there is excessive poverty, and assert that what apparently is poverty from an absolute point of view, ceases to be such when it is viewed in relation to the wants of the Indian people. These wants are extremely few and simple, and, therefore, the pittance of 6 pence, or even 6 pies a day, is all that an Indian of the poorer classes wants for his bare sustenance. This is an extremely narrow, if not a heartless, view to take of the life and prosperity of the millions that constitute the working population of India. Nor can it be any consolation to these people to be told that they are not the only people suffering from poverty, but, in other parts of the world, there are people who are in a worse condition. We have heard a good deal of this argument of late. Mr. J. D. Rees and Mr. Pennington may be named among other Anglo-Indians. "It seems to be generally forgotten," writes Mr. Pennington in the last number of the Asiatic Quarterly Review, "that the proportion of those who never have enough to eat does not differ so widely all over the would (except, perhaps, in America). Ten per cent. of the population of India account for nearly 30,000,000, and there are more than 10 per cent. even in this country (England) *who never have enough to eat*, or depend on "famine relief" in the shape of the poor-law, and suffer more misery in winter than the poor in India ever do." Here, Mr. Pennington institutes a comparison between the United Kingdom and India, not in respect of poverty, but in respect of destitution, that is, steady under-feeding; and in this respect, he says that the United Kingdom is worse than India. He also asserts the Poor Law of England operates in the same manner on the poorer population as the famine relief of Government does in times of famine. There is another assertion made, namely, the poorer classes in England suffer more misery in winter than the poor in India ever do. This last we shall leave out of our consideration, because winter is not an economic cause. Confining ourselves to the other two issues, more especially to the one relating to destitution, we shall presently show that Mr. Pennington, Mr. Rees and others speak without their book, and employ vague generalities calculated to mislead uninformed people. Now, Mr. Pennington says that, in England, there are more than 10 per cent. of the population *who have never enough to eat.* This is not a fact. When people talk of poverty in European countries, they mean a different thing from what we mean when we talk of the same in this country. There poverty in its ordinary sense is used to signify a standard of living which includes a condition considerably above want and at which it is not impossible to provide for the working men facilities for *improving* their physical and mental condition. Whereas, in India, poverty is used in reference to a state which consists in destitution, steady under-feeding, disease, shortened life, and continued deterioration of the body and mind. In a recent publication by Mr. B. S. Rowntree, which received considerable attention from economists when it was published some time ago, the author calculates that from 25 to 30 millions of the town population of the United Kingdom are living in poverty, and that "some seven-and-a-half millions of people are at the present moment in England living below the poverty line, in other words, in a state which "does not allow of any thing but the primitive wants of the human animal—food, shelter, light and warm clothing." Mr. Rowntree does not say that there is any considerable proportion of the population whose condition does not allow of even these. Probably, a large proportion of the so-called poor population have to be content only with these "primitive wants." What Mr. Rowntree means by "poverty line," is explained by him as follows: "A family living upon the scale allowed for by the estimate must never spend a penny on railway fare or omnibus; they must never purchase a half-penny newspaper or spend a penny to buy a ticket for a popular concert. They must write no letters to absent children, for they cannot afford the postage. They must never contribute anything to the church or chapel, or give any help to a neighbour which costs them money. They cannot save nor can they join sick club or trade union, because they cannot pay the necessary subscription The children must have no pocket money for dolls, marbles, or sweets. The father must smoke no tobacco and drink no beer. The mother must never buy any pretty clothes for herself or for the children, the character of the family wardrobe as of the family diet being governed by the regulation. Nothing must be bought but that which is absolutely necessary for the maintenance of physical health, and what is bought must be of the plainest and most economical description. Should a child fall ill, it must be attended by the parish doctor; should it die, it must be buried by the parish. Finally, the wage-earner must never be absent from his work for a single day."

From this it is plain Mr. Rowntree does not write of poverty that does not allow of these "primitive wants" even. It will be admitted that, in India, when we talk of poverty, we do not keep in view such a high standard.

Mr. Pennington says that, on 6 pies a day, an adult Indian of the peasant class can live "without any fear of starvation." This is not Mr. Rowntree's standard. His definition of poverty includes food, shelter, light and warm clothing. His seven-and-a-half millions are not people who have, in ordinary times, "never enough to eat." But, even without the application of Mr. Rowntree's comparatively high standard, but applying the lowest standard of the brutes, namely, the mere keeping of the life in the body, experienced Anglo-Indian administrators calculate that "more than half the agriculturists of British India—a few favoured localities excepted—are now in about as miserable a plight as human beings, not officially designated slaves or serfs, can be." "To the sympathetic discernment of the disinterested statesman, —the man who considers producers as well as production--India contains not one atom, but three hundred millions of units, each a struggling atom of humanity, lying prostrate and bleeding under the wheels of the Jagannath car called progress on Western lines." "Behind all is the discouraging fact that for more than 70 millions of the sufferers it is too late for any change of system to be beneficial." What a fierce indictment by a retired official who held one of the most responsible posts in the Indian service and who had exceptional opportunities of knowing the exact economic condition of the whole province of the Punjab ! We do not know that any critic of the working classes of the United Kindom has ever brought an indictment of this dismal character against those who are answerable for the condition of these classes, or has ever written in a strain of such deep despondency about their future.

Far from there being any ground for such a despondent view in the United Kingdom, the progress made by the working classes during the last fifty years has been so remarkable that their future is full of hope. The statesmen of Europe are not disposed to neglect the interest of the labouring classes; on the other hand, in proportion to their advancement in general education, they are invited to exercise a substantial influence on the Government of the country. They are no longer the dumb, helpless and downtrodden multitudes that they were at the beginning of the nineteenth century. They have grown to a full consciousness of their rights and power; they have been educated and know how to co-operate, organise, and save. As the result of the marvellous changes that have taken place in the conditions of the poor, we find at the bottom of the social scale an almost continuous decrease in the proportion of paupers since 1855. The wages of almost all classes have greatly risen; and their purchasing power is greater. The savings banks deposits and depositors show a progressive increase, which is striking. The houses in which the masses of the people live are better, and continually increase in value; the conditions of life are more healthy and refined, and continually tend towards improvement. The hours of labor are much less and tend towards further reduction; the conditions of work have been greatly improved; and education, amusement, and recreation are provided for the people on a greatly extended scale. Nay, at last, we have the rising school of orthodox political economists in England already beginning to question whether poverty itself may not be abolished, and whether it is necessarily any more a permanent human institution than was slavery.

The above are the words of Mr. Benjamin Kidd ; and what a contrast between the hopefulness of the orthodox economists referred to above and the despondency of Anglo-Indian administrators like Mr. Thorburn ! Mr. Mulhall summarises as follows the changes that have taken place in the condition of wage-earners, in the United Kingdom, during the last hundred years :

1. Three pounds will now buy as much in England as four pounds would a hundred years ago.

2. Wages in England have doubled since 1780, and working-men can buy 44 per cent. more of food than they could then, notwithstanding the enormous rise in beef and butter.

3. The house-rent having trebled in the same interval, the advantages to workmen in cities are sensibly reduced.

4. The peasant's earnings, measured in grain, are 60 per cent. higher than in the eighteenth century.

5. Farm wages, compared with grain product, are 18 per cent. in the United States, 25 per cent. in Great Britain, and 44 per cent. on the Continent.

Such is the record of progress in the condition of the working classes in the United Kingdom. The progress is no less marked in France and Germany, and in Russia itself. Let those that compare Indian poverty with that of other countries, of the United Kingdom in particular, produce a record of achievements such as British history can show, and then defend or apologise for the state of the submerged half of the Indian agricultural population. Pauperism at the bottom of the social scale in Britain is steadily diminishing—that is the verdict of British statisticians like Sir Robert Giffen. Pauperism at the botton of the social scale in India is steadily increasing—that is the verdict of Anglo-Indian administrators like Sir James Lyall.

THIRTY RUPEES A YEAR.

According to Lord Curzon's own calculations, the annual income per head of the people of India, including both agricultural and non-agricultural incomes, does not exceed 30 rupees a year. His Excellency's calculations are based mostly on surmises, and as regards the figures he quoted it would not be difficult to show that they are erroneous. In his process of calculation it can be shown that many faults of commission and omission occur. Still, supposing his Lordship's conclusion is right, does it not point to a most lamentable state of things in India under British rule? It is true that he admits that the result is neither very brilliant nor satisfactory. But, as a fact, the result is most lamentable and, far from warranting the optimism of officials in general and the dangerous policy of drift based on that optimism, it calls for the most earnest and effective measures of permanent relief to the depressed and suffering people. What does an income of Rs. 30 a year mean? It means an income of one anna and four pies a day—exactly the wage earned by a famine coolie in the Government relief camp. Now, this wage of one anna and four pies paid to the famine laborer is a wage fixed for mere sustenance, to enable life to remain within the body. It makes no allowance for healthy nourishment and much less for luxury. The Government of India emphatically maintained that, in times when millions had to be fed at public expense, the interests of the general taxpayer had to be duly protected against extravagance and waste, and that this obligation on their part required a careful limitation of public relief to the mere saving of the people from starvation It was on this principle that the measure of relief was determined and did not exceed one and one-third anna a day per head Now, even supposing that the poorer classes of the Indian population get this income, in a short time they will necessarily deteriorate in their physique and will be exposed to diseases of all kinds. But, as a fact, this pittance is only the average, the richer classes with large incomes being taken into calculation as well as the poorer classes. It follows, therefore, that there must be millions upon millions of people who support themselves on a smaller pittance than one anna and four pies. Can it then be untrue that a large proportion of the population—one-fifth according to the late Dr. W. Hunter, and one-third according to

Sir Charles Elliot—go through life without knowing what it is to have their hunger fully satisfied? In addition to the testimony of Government officials, there is the testimony of Christian Missionaries, who have lived among the poorest of the poor and who can have no motive whatever to exaggerate the evil or indulge in statements calculated to impair the prestige of British Government in this country. And what is this testimony? The Rev. J. S. MacNair, of Cuddapah, writes: "I think the most trying experience I ever had was a three weeks' tour in September of last year, in a part of the country where our people are specially poor, and where they have had no proper crops for several years My tent was surrounded by day and night, and one sentence dinned in my ears perpetually—'We are dying for lack of food.'" Another Missionary, the Rev. G. H. Macfarlane, writes: "The grain which each householder is usually able to lay in store has this year been very meagre. It can serve only for a few weeks at most. After that, comes the period of no work and gradual starvation. It is the tiding over of this period—till June or July when rain may begin again—that is the difficulty. We cannot present harrowing tales of starvation and death as yet. But *people are living on one meal every two or three days.* The poorer classes in India are always prepared for this. As one of our Christians said: '*If we can eat food once in two days, we will not ask for more.*'" Is this a state of things on which any civilized Government can contemplate with indifference or equanimity? Yet, it is neither temporary nor local. It is the normal condition of millions of people living over wide areas. It is not like the condition of the poorer laborers of European countries occasionally driven to starvation in special seasons when they can get no work to do. It is the normal condition of people living in rural areas and drawing their subsistence from the produce of the soil. Most of these suffering starving classes are not day-laborers—though the condition of these is sad enough in all conscience,—but agricultural laborers accustomed only to work in the fields and obtaining their means of subsistence at long intervals in the year. There is some difference between starvation in cold countries and starvation in a hot country like India. In cold countries people enfeebled and rendered sick from starvation, do not live : they simply die sooner or later, so that they soon cease to be a burden on the general community and seldom leave behind them a progeny of weaklings too feeble to work and unable to earn their own livelihood. But in India people can live on food hardly better than water, and, while weak and sickly, they drag on their miserable life, begging or stealing, and leaving to posterity the most unwelcome legacy of weak and diseased children. It is no wonder that in the last famine, and in the famine that preceded it, it was the general complaint of the officials that the laborers would not work to earn their full wages. The reason was not so much their laziness as their want of physical ability for exertion. There cannot be a greater misfortune to a community than the existence of large classes, comprising millions of people, who are weak and sickly, with no muscle to work, no stamina for endurance, no sense of responsibility, no hope or prospect in life. . . . When millions of people have to be content with a farthing a day, the evil is bound to grow at a geometrical ratio ; and though the evil does not excite general attention nor create alarm at present, yet it will soon grow to a dimension which by its very magnitude and danger will compel attention and bring under requisition all the resources of British statesmanship. The great British nation will then open their eyes and discover with disappointment and dismay that, in regard to their so-called brightest jewel in their diadem, they were living in a fool's paradise and imagining prosperity and contentment where there were impoverishment and despair.

THE LAST TWO FAMINES—SIGNIFICANT DIFFERENCES.

The last MacDonnel Famine Commission call attention in the first part of their Report to certain differences between the earlier famine of 1896-97 and the later famine, which suggest significant inferences. The officials, including the Commission themselves, have drawn inferences favourable to their side ; but what inferences impartial outside critics will draw deserve not less to be considered. I myself think that the facts recorded by the Commission strongly point to a melancholy deterioration in the resisting power of the people, who, without resources or moral stamina, resign themselves to their fate at the first attack of adversity, and are more ready, than they used to be in former years, to resort to Government relief camps to which their former aversion has now become much weaker. There is, in the first instance, extreme indigence; and this and the despair brought on by it have blunted their feeling of caste prestige and self-reliance, and have altogether worked a most lamentable demoralisation among the poorer classes. The population affected by the Famine of 1896-97 was about 18 millions and the number of persons relieved throughout the period amounted to over 300 millions, whereas during the next famine, which appeared within the short interval of two years, these numbers were respectively 27 millions, and 1,100 millions. The increase in the number of people relieved in the year 1899 was, thus, out of all proportion to the increase in numbers inhabiting affected tracts. Commenting on this fact, the Commission say: "We are by no means prepared to accept the view that the number of persons relieved is the only or proper measure of the pressure of a famine, because it is obvious that these numbers may be affected by many considerations, such as the attitude of the people, or the laxity or stringency of the terms on which relief is administered." This is only the *opinion* of the Commission, which is entitled to weight as much as and no more than the opinion of others. The attitude of the people at the appearance of a scarcity or famine is well-known. They do not rush to relief camps at once. They wait on events, struggling as best as they can against the thickening calamity, and prefer privation and starving to deserting their homes and wandering abroad in search of a livelihood. This is the usual attitude of the people and was noted as a remarkable feature in former famines. If, in the famine of 1899, this kind of honourable feeling showed itself to a less extent, the inference is obvious, that the fact was due to an increased pressure of the famine. As regards the laxity or leniency of the terms on which relief was administered, it is well-known that the whole spirit of the administration of the last famine was that of stricter economy than was enforced in the previous famine. In Lord Curzon's well-known circular issued so early as December 1899, he emphasised the need for wages which would not too readily attract the people to relief camps.

The Government of India expressed their alarm at the sudden and large influx of relief-seekers at the very first stage of the famine, and warned the Local Governments against excessive liberality in giving relief, which was bound to attract to the relief camps even those individuals and those classes that had resource enough left to maintain themselves. Surely, in the famine of 1899, there were proportionately far more paupers in need of relief, belonging to classes who were not accustomed to resort to public support, than there were in the previous famines.

In consequence of this circular, the conditions of relief were stiffened. Far from the people rushing to relief camps, in Bombay at all events, "large numbers of people who probably did not begin to work till their stength was low, earned less and less, until they got a pittance of two annas or less in a week, and many accordingly left the works, and others were deterred from coming to them." Surely, there was no leniency here, which could have attracted unusual crowds of working men to the relief camps.

The Famine Commission of 1878 were of opinion that, in famine, the proportion of the total population likely to be in receipt of relief in the worst months would not exceed 15 per cent., and for the whole period, would not exceed 7 or 8 per cent. In the famine of 1896-97, this proportion was fairly maintained, though in some tracts it was exceeded.

But, writing in December 1899, the Government of India say of the famine of that year: "Already the ratio of persons relieved to the total population in a number of districts exceeds the proportion of 15 per cent. laid down by the Famine Commission of 1878 as the maximum for the worst months of the year." "When this is the case at the very outset," wrote the Government of India, "it is impossible to predict to what height the numbers may rise in succeeding months. The question necessarily arises whether there are not undue prodigality and profusion in the relief at present being dispensed, and whether proper care is being exercised to confine it to the absolutely destitute section of the population. . . . In no other way can there be any assurance that we may not have half the population on our hands, attracted, as otherwise they would be, by facile opportunities for earning at their very doors a daily wage for a nominal task."

In some places the maximum percentage of the total population on relief was nearly 50 per cent. The Commission do not suggest that this increasing pressure of successive famines, which can indicate nothing but the decreasing vitality and staying power of the people, was due to a corresponding laxity or leniency in the administration of relief—a suggestion that would be against actual facts.

"In former days", this remarkable circular pointed out, "the difficulty was to induce the people to avail themselves of the relief offered in unfamiliar forms. On the present occasion, their experience in the recent famine has made the people only too ready to expect relief and to accept it on conditions to which it is subject. The difficulty is to discriminate between the really necessitous and those who can support themselves or obtain support from others." In the Viceroy's Council, in January 1900, the Hon'ble Mr. Ibbetson observed: "There seems to be reason to fear that in many places (to quote the words of the Bombay Government) *destitution has reached, or will reach, a higher stratum of society than has ever been affected before, or since the country came under British rule.*" The italics are ours. What a flat contradiction of Lord George Hamilton's confident assertion! The circular from which we have quoted above, was sent, in the usual course, to the Secretary of State, who, in reply to a question, said, in Parliament, that the circular suggested that care should be taken not to allow the revenues of India to be expended for the benefit of persons who were not actually in need of it. At the time that this circular was issued, nobody questioned the fact—for a fact it was—that the destitution had reached classes higher than those usually affected by famines in past times, and that the fear expressed by the Government of Bombay was well-founded. But exception was taken by the public opinion to Lord Curzon's gratuitous insinuation that the Indian people had become demoralised, they had lost their old self-respect, cast aside their religious and caste scruples, and that, in order to add a few annas to their hidden resources still left to them, they did not scruple to mix in the motley pauper crowd and bring shame on their family and caste. That these more respectable classes were driven to relief camps by the sheer force of destitution, but that they were not demoralised at the prospect of an easy and undeserved relief, was the contention of the public, a contention which was subsequently accepted by the Government.

Another distinctive feature of the recent famine was the steady and unbroken rise in most provinces in the numbers relieved. In other famines, it is observed by the Commission, the harvesting of the spring crops led to a permanent or temporary departure of large numbers from the works ; but in the recent famine the *rabi* harvest had no effect whatever. In other famines, again, on the outbreak of the rains, the people were quick to resume their ordinary avocations ; but in the recent famine, the numbers relieved, particularly in the Central Provinces, instead of falling on the commencement of the monsoon, continued to rise, and reached their maximum during the rains after the demand for agricultural labor had set in. This remarkable fact the Commission attribute to a laxity of tests in the administration of relief which made the charity of Government more attractive and the cause of much demoralisation. If this were a fact, it would follow that the agricultural classes thought that they would be better off on relief camps than in their villages. They must have thought that to go back and resume their agricultural operation would be less paying than to work at the relief camps—a state of things strikingly significant of the depletion of village resources and the moral depression of the people.

The Commission calculate that this famine will in the end have cost the State not less than fifteen crores of rupees or ten millions sterling. This expenditure far exceeds that incurred in any previous famine. The Commission are of opinion "that a good deal of preventable expenditure was incurred on relief in the last famine and that, without the least departure from the humane policy of famine relief laid down by Government, the object in view can be attained at a moderate cost and with little demoralization, if prudence and foresight be duly exercised, and if means be properly adjusted to ends." Well, we know what prudence, foresight and the rest of it mean in a famine campaign constantly hampered by a regard for economy. They often mean starvation of the labourers. Sir Antony MacDonnel tells us that this need not necessarily be the case. How far economy based on prudence and foresight, and a humane policy of relief, are compatible with each other, we shall know at the next famine whenever it might come. So many calculations and prophecies of Famine Commissions have proved to have been made on data too optimistic and too much derived from imagination than from knowledge.

ADDITIONAL DIRECT TAXATION SINCE 1886.

Far from taxation in India being the lightest of any country in Asia or in the world, the burden on the backs of the taxpayers has swollen by constant additions of late. The Indian taxpayer at this moment, pays more than 6 crores of additional taxation over and above what he paid before 1886, and will soon pay practically 21 crores as the result of the currency reform.

During the year that the exchange was in an unsettled condition, a series of additions were imposed on the burden of the people, and they have not been since taken off, although the exchange has been made steady by the legislation of 1893.

These latter taxes were—

		Rx.
I.	Income Tax (including that in Burma) ...	1,800,000
II.	Duty on Petroleum	155,000
III.	Enhancement of Duty on Salt	1,600,000
IV.	Increase of Duty on Imported Spirits	100,000
V.	General Import Duties (including additional Duty on Petroleum and Duty on Silver)	1,600,000
VI.	Import Duty on Cottons	900,000
VII.	Increase of Kohat Salt Duty	50,000
VIII.	Re-imposition of the Patwari Cess in the North-Western Provinces	200,000
	Total ...	6,405,000

(1.) The income-tax was imposed in 1886, replacing a provincial license tax, which yielded in the last year of its operation about a third of the yield of the income-tax in the first year of its operation.

(2.) A duty was imposed in 1888 on imported petroleum, and the duty was doubled in 1894; non-illuminating petroleum, which had always been exempt, being also taxed at 5 per cent. in that year.

(3.) The salt duty was raised in 1888 in India from Rs. 2 to Rs. 2½, and in Burma from 3 annas to 1 Rupee per maund.

(4.) The rates of duty on imported spirit were raised in 1890.

(5.) An import duty of 6 annas per maund was levied on salted fish in 1893.

(6.) The import duties generally were abolished in 1882, only arms and ammunition, liquors, opium, and salt being retained on the list of dutiable imports. As stated above (4), the duty on spirit was raised in 1890, and in 1894 the whole of the customs duties taken off in 1882 was re-imposed, with the addition of a duty on silver.

(7.) The excise duties on spirit were raised when the duty on imported spirit was increased, and in every province additions have been made to the rates from time to time since. An excise duty has also been imposed on malt liquor.

(8.) The Patwari Cess in the North-Western Provinces was repealed in 1882, but was re-imposed in 1888.

(9.) No remissions or reductions of taxation can be noted as a set-off against the taxation which has been imposed since 1886. The additional taxation would not have been necessary but for the fall in exchange.

[*Mr. O'Conor's statement submitted to the Currency Committee*, 1898.]

RECENT SURPLUSES AND REMISSION OF TAXATION.

During the last five years successively, the financial statements of the Government of India have shown a surplus.

1898-99		£2,657,873
1899-1900		£2,774,623
1900-1901		£1,670,204
1901-1902		£4,672,900
1902-1903	(budget)	£873,700
	Total surplus	£12,61,3,300
		or Rs. 18,91,99,500.

Two questions have to be considered in regard to these large surpluses. How did these surpluses arise, and what use was made of them ? There can be no doubt that they are due to the large savings that have accrued from a rise in the exchange value of the rupee. The Government of India having to pay every year nearly 18 million sterling to meet the expenditure incurred by the Secretary of State in London, the equivalent of this sterling amount has to be raised in rupees in India, and in proportion as the rupee falls in value, the number of rupees required to make up this equivalent, increases. When the rupee was equal to 2 shillings, 180 millions of rupees would have sufficed to meet the demand of 18 million sterling ; but when the rupee gradually came down to 13*d.* or a little over one shilling, which it did in the year 1894-95, the Government of India had to raise, by taxation, to pay up the same 18 millions sterling, nearly 360 millions of rupees. This enormous increase in the rupee revenue which the Government of India thus wanted, could be raised only by resorting to additional taxation, which the Government of India, in a spirit of undaunted courage, piled up on the enduring back of the people, until at last no more pile could be added without serious consequences, political and economical. Bankruptcy stared Government in the face. Mr. O'Conor said in so many words before the Currency Committee that " The additional taxation would not have been necessary but for the fall in exchange." In 1894-95 the rupee went down to the lowest level, nearly 13*d*., and yet Government managed in their estimates to make up a surplus of 70 lakhs of rupees. Since that year, the currency reform of 1893 has begun to bear fruit and the exchange value of the rupee to rise steadily. In 1895-96 the average rate of exchange realised was 13·64*d*., and the surplus realised was 1½ crores. In the next two years, 1896-97 and 1897-98, the average rate of exchange was 14·45*d*· and 15 3*d*. respectively; but they were both famine years; and 1897-98 a costly frontier war was added to famine, and both years closed with a dificit But for these extraordinary charges, both the years would have closed with substantial surpluses. In 1898-99 exchange established itself in the neighbourhood of 16*d*., the average being 15·98*d*. and the year closed with a balance of 3·96 crores, after providing a crore for military expenditions on the frontier. Since, and including that year, our estimates have every year shown a surplus Now, the question arises, the additional taxation 7 crores having been imposed to meet the expenditure on account of low exchange, and, even when the exchange was at the lowest level, as it was in the years 1894-95 and 1895-96, the Government having been able to secure surpluses, what need is there, now that exchange has reached the high level of 16*d*. the rupee, for maintaining the same level of taxation, which low exchange—and low exchange alone—rendered necessary in former years? Since the year 1894-95, when the rupee was equal to 13 1*d*., and a surplus of 70 lakhs was realised, Government have been able to save on every rupee spent on exchange nearly 2½*d*., which for the whole Home Charges of 18 millions sterling yields a total saving of over 3 crores. If only the expenditure were reduced to the level of that year, apart from other improvements in the receipts and disbursements, there would be, under the item of expenditure on exchange alone, an annual surplus of 3 crores. It should be remembered that the two years, 1896-97 and 1897-98, did not yield surpluses because of famine and frontier wars ; but normally they would have been years of surplus. It follows therefore that either the currency reform of 1893 might be modified and the rate of exchange fixed at 13*d*., in which case the evils of an artificially inflated rupee, which, in the long run, must prove disastrous to Indian producers, would be considerably reduced ; or, on the present basis of exchange, 16*d*. per rupee, a remission of taxation to the extent of nearly three crores a year ought to be possible in normal times. Besides this regular savings from improved exchange, Government have had within recent years many windfalls. The saving in military expenditure on account of the absence of a part of the Indian garrison in foreign countries, improvements in the opium revenue and in receipts from Railways, and a few other items, have tended to improve the financial position of Government

What has become of all this excess of money ? Why, apart from expenditure due to famine which has twice devastated large portions of the country, and has cost, in the way of direct expenditure on relief, about 12 crores of rupees including 1897-98, the rest has been spent on increased allotments for army services and railways. The expenditure on armyservices was nearly 14 millions in 1889-90 and was a little over 15 millions in 1894-95, whereas the accounts of the last three years including the current one show £15,082,799 ; 17,135,300 ; and 17,664,700. The expenditure under Railway Revenue account was, in 1889-90, 12½ millions, and in 1894-95 it was 14½ millions. But since then the expenditure has steadily increased, and the figures under this head during the three years included in the last budget, are £17,968,505; 18,592,400; and £19,654,500. Under both these expensive headings, the standard of expenditure showed in the accounts of 1894-95, has been exceeded, but if it had not been exceeded, there would have been, as I have pointed out above, an average margin of 5 crores a year, out of which a considerable remission of taxation could have been made.

Nor has there been any necessity of a particularly pressing nature for thus exceeding the standard of 1894-95, even at the risk of maintaining the high standard of taxation, which, during all the years that low exchange was driving Government to their wit's end, the public were assured, was warranted and justified only by the disastrous consequences of the vanishing rupee. No serious consequences would have ensued if the expenditure on Railways had been limited to a maximum of 14½ millions, and if certain portions of military expenditure had been met from borrowed funds instead of from current revenues. Said the Finance Minister in March last: "It must b remembered that India is defraying from revenues the cost of undertaking both re-armament and the reform of military re-organization in important departments. I believe that this is an undertaking which has not been attempted by other countries without the assistance of loans in some form or other. Even in England, extraordinary military requirements for fortifications and barracks have been met by loans for short terms of years payable by instalments out of revenues. If, profiting by a period of political tranquillity, we can accomplish this task without the raising of a loan and the imposition of a permanent burden on future generations, I think we shall be able to congratulate ourselves on having done that which even the richest nations of Europe have not considered it advisable to attempt." The Hon'ble Mr. Gokhale was quite right in protesting strongly against the folly of India boasting of financial feats which the richest nations in the world have not dared to attempt. Even after all this excessive and unnecessary expenditure, even after performing feats which are beyond the power of England or Germany, Government have disposed of a total surplus of nearly 19 crores of rupees during the last five years. Such an extraordinary performance can be possible, as Mr. Chesney observed in the *Nineteenth Century* recently, only when more taxes are wrung from the people than are right, necessary or advisable.

CHAPTER II.

Land Revenue and Famine.

IN the elaborate Resolution published some months ago by the Government of India on the land revenue system, it is maintained that the theory of half the net produce as the standard of assessment is followed and that the actual share of Government is less than this percentage.

The Government of India Resolution says : " It is now nearly forty years since the alternative standard of half the net produce was introduced in Madras, the reason being that the gross produce standard, while it favoured the most fertile, pressed with extreme severity on the poorer lands. But even the standard thus adopted has not been worked up to in practice. There and elsewhere the net produce has been valued at much less than the current money rates, the out-turn per acre produced from crop experiments has been notoriously under-estimated, and liberal deductions have been made for unprofitable cultivation, distance from markets, vicissitudes of season, so that the rates in actual use for assessment are considerably below the nominal share. The truth is, the assessment of land revenue is subject to so many complicated and varying conditions that any attempt to reduce it to an exact mathematical proportion either of gross or net produce, would not only be impracticable, but would lead to the placing of burdens upon the shoulders of the people, from which, under a less rigid system, if sympathetically administered, they would be exempt." It is added that the influence of the personal equation should not be ignored. The settlement officers, it is observed, coming into close contact with the people, acquire exceptional sympathy with them and are loth to aggrieve those "among whom they spend some of the most laborious years of their life."

Now, let us examine this statement in the light of practical experience. As for the sympathy of the settlement officers or of the Local or Supreme Government, I shall leave it alone. I shall proceed to show that the principle of the 50 p. c. of net assets, as the instruction to settlement officers, holds good in theory, while in practice no such principle is followed. Said Sir Louis Mallet in 1875: "In truth, the fifty per cent. of the net produce has been a mere paper instruction, a fiction which has had very little to do with the actual facts of the administration, and in practice the rates levied have often absorbed the whole rental, and not unfrequently, I suspect, encroached on profits also." Sir George Campbell, in his minute on certain proposals made by the Madras Government in 1874, said: "According to the Govornor, they (the Settlement Department) are to be supposed to be elaborately carrying out, under explicit instructions from home, a system of valuation and assessment on the basis of half net profits ; but practically the rate of assessment is decided by very different and simpler considerations the most important of which is that no cultivator is to pay more than he paid before, *plus a very small percentage*" A very small percentage, indeed! What a travesty of truth! In the more recent re-settlements of Tanjore and Trichinopoly, the increase on the old assessments was 25 per cent. and 33 per cent. respectively, increases, which were really reductions made by Government in the original proposals of 45 per cent. and 70 per cent. made by the settlement officer, whose sympathies with the ryots and whose reluctance to aggrieve them Lord Curzon so grandiloquently praises. The District of Malabar is now undergoing a revision of settlement and the increase proposed for the whole is 80 per cent., and in certain Taluks in which the settlement has been completed, the increase is, in certain cases, 100 and even 200 per cent. Leniency, indeed! In this connection, it may be worth while noting that Mr. R. K. Puckle, C. I. E. had obtained the sanction of Government to the lands of the Salem district being assessed at rates favourable to the ryots. Mr. Goodrich, who was entrusted with the duty of introducing the settlement rates, succeeded soon after in getting Government to reconsider its decision and consent to impose higher rates. Whether Mr. Goodrich or Mr. Puckle was right, may be judged from the fact that, in the famine of 1876—78, the mortality was the heaviest in the Salem district, next after Kurnool and

Bellary, amounting to 18·7 per cent. of the population. The fact is, the Madras Government has said, in so many words, that the reasons for increase at each revision are, not the paying capacity of the ryots, but "the exigencies of Government" and "the re-adjustment of taxation in the interests of the general public." This latter is a fiction pure and simple, because in no single instance in recent settlements was the tax reduced on deteriorated property to equalise the weight of incidence of the tax on the poor and the rich proprietor alike. The first reason is the true reason. Far from issuing instructions in favour of leniency, the Supreme Government has given its sanction to these large enhancements, and the Local Government's proposals in regard to Malabar have also been sanctioned. The truth is, the Local Government and the Supreme Government share the land revenue between them, and both are interested in pushing it up. The Finance Minister wants to bring up a prosperity budget, and the Local Government wants for its expenses more money than the Supreme Government would allow in its quinquennial contracts. Between the two, the ryot's last pie is squeezed out of him.

As for the methods adopted in arriving at the net assets of the cultivator, which the Resolution puts in such roseate colours, far from their effect being lenient, it is just the contrary. The calculation of the cost of production, the estimation of the out-turn per acre, the deductions made for unprofitable cultivation, and the commutation of the produce into money, are all done in a manner which proves ruinous to the poorer class of cultivators. In the first place, as Mr. Dutt points out, the cost of cultivating an acre of good land is estimated at Rs. 14, the allowance for inferior soil is only Rs. 6 an acre, whereas it is notorious that the inferior soil costs more to cultivate than good land. A number of Madras authorities have pointed out this unnatural method of estimating the cost of cultivation. Moreover, many of the elements of cost are calculated unfavourably to the ryots; the estimates are inadequate and some omissions are also made.

Not only are the estimates of the cost of cultivation low, but the average produce of the fields is over-estimated. If the produce is over-estimated, and the cost is under-estimated, it can be seen how fictitious the Government's half share of the ryot's asset will be. Under such a system, as Sir Louis Mallet observed, the rates levied often absorb the whole rental and even encroach on the profits. Mr. Digby has in his book opinions communicated to him by various Indian gentlemen of Southern India regarding this important question. Says the Madras Government: "These calculations of the produce and expenses of cultivation have never been pressed to their full conclusion and the exact rates employed are much below those which the "half-net produce" principle would justify." But this is flatly denied by experienced and respectable Indian gentlemen holding extensive landed property.

Dewan Bahadur Ragoonath Row, for instance, says: "The Government are said to get out half of the net produce which is never less than 25 p.c. of the gross. This is only in theory, actually they receive on an average more than 50 p.c. of the gross. On paper it is shown to be between 25 and 30 per cent. of the gross by over-estimating the gross produce." Mr. Ragoonath Row gives further particulars. A village measuring 305 acres of wet land has been assessed on the estimated gross produce of 8557 to 9000 *kalams* (=12 Madras measures), while it never produced more than 6000 on an average. The yield since the years of the re-settlement has been, *fasli* 1303, *kalams* 5,300; *fasli* 1,304, *kalams* 5,275; *fasli* 1,305, *kalams* 5,224; *fasli* 1,306, *kalams* 5,329; *fasli* 1,307, *kalams* 5,760; *fasli* 1,308, *kalams* 5,108; *fasli* 1,309, *kalams* 1,813. According to the theory and spirit of the Government order, the assessment of this village should have been up to *kalams* 1,612 or Rs. 1,674. The fixed assessment is *kalams* 2,262 which raises the percentage to 37." "If there is any doubt in this case," adds Mr. Ragoonath Row, most emphatically, "I am prepared to hand over the village to Government, if I may be allowed to draw from the Government treasury annually the sum of fixed assessment perpetually."

Another correspondent of Mr. Digby's mentions the significant fact that in a memorial forwarded to Government of which, among others, Sir V. Bashyam Iyengar—a gentleman, this correspondent very rightly adds, who would never put his signature to any document unless he was satisfied that the facts were absolutely correct—was one of the signatories, the cost of cultivation was estimated at Rs. 36-8 per acre (not including anything for the subsistence of the cultivator and his family) whereas the Government estimate is Rs. 11-11-5 and Rs. 10-10-5. It may be added, that the cultivation expenses, as calculated by Government, do not include any subsistence for the cultivator's family; nor interest on the money sunk by the ryots in the purchase of bullocks, &c. Nor have the cultivation expenses been regularly made in recent settlements. These are now taken to be the same as have already been determined in neighbouring settled districts. Why not, then, the ryots relinquish their holdings, it may be asked? The question is answered by Mr. Digby's correspondent:—"The rise in prices since the seventies has acted as a providential set-off to the iniquitous figures of the Settlement Department." But the prices are bound to go down sooner or later under the operation of the currency reform.

Land Revenue Collections and Remissions.

Next in importance to the question of settling the equitable principles of periodical settlements of land revenue, is the question of the methods of its collection, and its remission and suspension in times of drought and scarcity. As I am not acquainted with the practice in other parts of India, I shall confine myself here to the Madras

Presidency. The *Madras Mail* said resently that the Board of Revenue had called for the opinions of certain Collectors and others in regard to the improvement of the present system of land revenue collections and of granting suspensions and remissions in seasons of famine or severe and prolonged scarcity. The latter inquiry, it was added, is on account of the recommendation made in this respect by the latest Famine Commission. The former, that is, the inquiry as to how the present system of land revunue collections can be improved, is the outcome, perhaps, of the requests made by the ryots in more than one place visited by Lord Ampthill in his recent tour. No doubt, the system is capable of considerable improvement. The revenue is collected at present in four monthly instalments beginning from December, whereas, prior to the year 1896, the instalments were eight in some districts, while in other districts the number of instalments and the months when the instalments were due, were different. Now the system of four instalments obtains in all the districts of the Presidency, no allowance being made for the variety of conditions prevailing, not only in the districts, but in the different taluks and even villages of each district. There is a difference of opinion regarding the number of instalments. In the replies which the Governor made to the addresses he received, he expressed himself in favour of the existing system. There were objections to the former system of eight instalments when it prevailed, and it was after a due consideration of these objections, that the present system was substituted. Now, to go back to the former system, sufficient reasons should be shown. I am not sure that the taxpayers would like to be troubled by demands for eight months in the year successively or that the risks of default would not be greater under that system than under the present. If the ryots could command the necessary funds, it would be on the whole more convenient to them to have done with the trouble by payment in as few instalments as possible. As a fact, however, the ryot's money-box is never full, and on the little that he can command at a time, whether his own or borrowed, there are frequent demands of a more or less pressing nature, which consume his money and leave him helpless when the next instalment is due. Against this contingency the ryot has to be protected. In this view, the system of four instalments seems to be better than that of eight instalments. As Mr. Alexander Rogers observed in a communication to *United India* in April last, if possible a rebate may be given on money paid by the ryots in advance of instalments, which is one of the most practical means of encouraging habits of thrift. But whether four or eight instalments be the system, the main principle to be kept in view is to so adjust the dates of the demands as to suit the convenience of the ryots. They should be called upon to pay exactly at the time when they can pay most conveniently, with the least loss, and without resorting to money-lenders, if possible. The Famine Commission of 1880 laid down that the instalments should correspond to the main crops raised, and the dates on which these crops ordinarily came to maturity, and to the relative weight and value of the harvests. They also pointed out that, where one crop was reserved for food and another raised for sale, the larger collections should be made on the latter crop, and that time should be allowed to the ryots to realise their crops without undue haste so as to avoid the risk of glutting the markets. Now, if the principle recommended above by the Famine Commission were to be adopted in the fixing of the dates of instalments, it is obvious that a uniform system for the whole Presidency would not do. Regard must be had to the months when the harvests are reaped in different districts and localities; to the time when the crops raised for sale rather than for consumption are reaped; and to the months when the grain markets are not glutted and money is not dear. As an able writer in the columns of the *Madras Mail* pointed out last year, the subject should be considered on broad and general lines, but also in its bearings on every village separately. Only when this is done will the ryot be enabled to carry on his business with efficiency, and only then will all the danger of undue pressure from land assessments be avoided.

Then, coming to the second enquiry regarding how suspensions and remissions can be granted, there is one important point which deserves to be carefully considered, and that is, the advisability of granting remissions straight way off in times of famine and severe and prolonged scarcity, instead of postponing the demands, of which eventually only a small portion is recovered after a good deal of harsh coercion, and the larger portion has to be written off. This latter system should be adopted very sparingly, and shonld not be adopted at all when there is no prospect of a second crop. Mr. Alexander Rogers, Mr. S. Thorburn and other experienced Anglo-Indian officers have expressed their disapproval of this system of tying a white elephant round the neck of the pauper ryot. Arrears are usually recovered from the first bumper crop. When a peasant has lost seed-grain, labour, cattle, and owes money for food, it takes, as Mr. Thorburn says, not one but several bumper crops to put him on his legs again. But hardly does he feel a sensation of relief at his bumper crop from the protracted affliction that has almost killed him and made him a homeless wanderer, when the inexorable demand of the sircar confronts him and throws him again in the throes of depression and despair. No situation can be more sad. What is the ryot to do? Is he to retrieve his lost position, rebuild his house, replace his dead cattle, and procure the other requirements of his occupation, purchase new utensils,—is he to do these from the proceeds of his bumper crop, or is he to meet the demands of the relentless sircar, not the demands of the current year, but the arrears of two or more years during which he was in the hell of a famine? What happened in Bombay during the last famine has happened in other provinces also. Every means of coercion was applied in Bombay* to squeeze the last pie of the revenue from the ryots, and even after doing so, the Government found it necessary to remit nearly a crore of arrears. In Madras the same thing happened recently. If the original postponements had been substituted by the remissions which had eventually to be granted, the ryots would have been saved a good deal of worry and borrowing.

Agricultural Improvement and Government's Apathy.

We recently read a paragraph in the papers that the Government of the United States have established an Insular Bureau of Agriculture in the Philippine Islands, in order to remedy the deplorable condition of agriculture there, and an accomplished botanist has been appointed

* Since this was written, the Bombay Government have admitted the faults of their revenue system and have placed before the Government of India a scheme of reform, according to which, in bad times, assessments will be suspended or remitted, as the case may be, on the recommendation of the District officers, without the invidious process of individual inquiry. The suspended amount will be partly or wholly collected in the subsequent year if that be a good year. " A scale liberally graduated for the different parts of the Presidency in accordance with the nature of the harvest, has been submitted for the consideration of the Supreme Government" and Lord Northcote has given the assurance that " under no circumstances will debts for assessments be allowed to hang indefinitely around the necks of the poorer cultivators." Suspensions would be general ; and remissions would be granted, in case the Government of India approved of the proposals, to all *bona fide* agriculturists whose cases might require them in the event of the recurrence of bad years. We may add that at present there is no system of suspensions and remissions in ordinary years in Bombay. The terms of the Famine Code give Collectors ample powers of suspension in the case of an abnormal failure of the harvest causing a total or almost total destruction of the crops over a considerable area, and direct that such suspension should be eventually followed by an enquiry into each case as to the desirability of remission or collection. This discretion, however, vested in the Collectors by the terms of the Code, has been taken away by the executive orders of the Bombay Government.

Chief of the Bureau with headquarter at Manila. In those islands, as in India, the methods of cultivation are primitive and ineffective; the ordinary vegetables, notwithstanding the fertility of the land, are small and poor, and the stock is evidently run out and has to be renewed. Many grains which are unknown to the people can undoubtedly be raised. They live chiefly on rice, and raise less than they consume. The main object of the Bureau is "to promote the development of the agricultural resources of the islands," and it will take charge of and conduct the model farms and experiment stations which were established in a number of provinces under the Spanish *régime*. This is what the Government of the United States are doing for their new protectorate, the Philippine Islands.

We shall see what the British officials directing the Government of Egypt are doing or propose to do in that country. Mr. W. Willcocks is an Indian Engineer, and his services were lent to Egypt soon after the occupation. His reputation is now so high that he is regarded as one of the most distinguished irrigation Engineers in the world. Mr. Willcocks believes that the British rulers of that country have already performed memorable feats in irrigation, but that these would pale into insignificance before the colossal system which would be inaugurated within the next few decades. He sees a time when the Nile will be controlled from its source to its mouth. A gigantic series of weirs and dams will supply perennial irrigation to the country which has been turned into a smiling garden. Great steamers will run all through the year to Khartoum and beyond. Mr. Willcocks pictures to himself a very paradise on earth in the cultivated lands of Egypt, inhabited by a prosperous and contented peasantry, 50 years hence. Fifty years hence is a period too far ahead, and none can be sure of the most sanguine predictions being fulfilled in the beneficial results hoped for. In India, only so recently as 25 years ago, the rapid construction of railways, it was said, would so cover the country with a net-work of communications that agriculture would be stimulated, trade would expand, money would pour into the pockets of the producing classes, and famine would once for all disappear from the land. Of course, none of these things have happened, and the economic condition of the country is now as bad as it was at the period when, instead of the 25,000 miles of railways now traversing the length and breadth of the country, there were no more than 10,000 miles. Though irrigation is a more efficient protective measure against famine or scarcity than railways, still neither the one nor the other is alone enough to blot out poverty from the face of the country and plant prosperity in its place. India pays away nearly one-third of her total revenues to England as her price for the blessings of civilized rule, and Egypt pays to her foreign creditors 45 per cent. of hers. No country with this drain of its life-blood can possibly prosper.

My immediate purpose here, however, is to point out the contrast between the Government of India and the Government of other progressive countries, in their attitude towards the great agricultural interests. The serious attention paid to irrigation works and the large sums spent on them by the Government of Egypt, and the comparative neglect of such works in India, form an important point of contrast. But the Government of Egypt, according to Mr. Willcocks, does not mean to be satisfied with the building of great dams and weirs to regulate the Nile. After doing this, it does not mean to sit down and expect the peasant and the landowner to do the rest unaided. No passages in the lecture, which this Engineer has recently published, are more interesting or convey a greater lesson to India than those relating to the duties of the Ministry of Agriculture, which Mr. Willcocks would see presently firmly established as the necessary complement of the Irrigation Department. The Agricultural Department will not only establish experimental farms to deal with manures and methods of cultivation, but will introduce agricultural banks among the village communities. It will have a weather bureau, forecasting seasons and weathers and disseminating information with the aid of wireless telegraphy. There will be a bureau of animal industry improving the breed of cattle and "studying compositions of butter suitable for hot countries," a bureau of plant industry, introducing useful fertilising insects and destroying harmful ones, and a bureau of soils, mapping the soils of the whole Nile Valley. Forestry, of course, will be considered. But what Mr. Willocks lays special stress on, is the bureau of foreign products. "Its trained agents will be travelling over the whole world, and forwarding to Egypt from every quarter of the globe grains and plants which give promise of being useful in the Nile Valley." This bureau will introduce labour-saving machines of every kind, it will study the world's market and instruct the country in profitable and unprofitable crops. Another section of the Agricultural Department will study pisciculture. Finally, the collection of statistics, which are essential to the proper distribution and growth of agricultural products, will be entrusted to trained experts. In a word, says Mr. Willcocks, the Agricultural Ministry will be full of courage and initiation, and will look with a single eye to the wealth of the country, without any design on the purses of its inhabitants.

How different is all this to what is being done by the Government of India? Very little is being done by the State here to add to the ryot's knowledge of agriculture or to protect it from those afflictions due, not to natural causes, but to other preventible ones. We shall not refer here at length to the Government's neglect of irrigation works. It is clearly its duty to keep them in good order, because on them the prosperity of agriculture depends, and on their assumed normally good condition are the assessments based. But when the assessments are levied to the last pie, and the irrigation works are in a state of disorder,

—appeals to the Public Works or Revenue authorities from the ryots ordinarily proving to be of little avail,—the hardship to the taxpayers may be imagined. But the ryot's misfortunes do not consist solely in deficient rainfall or in neglected irrigation works ; often they are due to other evils. In Gujarat and other parts of the Bombay Presidency, for instance, the evils arising from insufficient rainfall were aggravated by rats, locusts, grasshoppers and other insects, which continued to ravage many districts, and contributed to the unfavourableness of the season. Now, it is reasonable to complain that Government have made no provision for responsible and steady efforts being made to place agriculture above these evils. In other countries, as we have seen, large sums of money are spent by the State, through a well-organised and thoroughly-equipped Agricultural Department, to keep agriculture sufficiently protected against evils of this kind. The Hon'ble Mr. Perrazu, at a meeting of the Madras Legislative Council, complained that, while in small countries like Switzerland large sums were spent for the benefit of agriculture; in India, with more than 200 millions depending for their subsistance on the produce of agriculture, the amount spent was a trifle. The Hon'ble Mr. Nicholson made the same complaint in the Viceroy's Council in 1898. Still, the public have been kept in a state of suspense under promises yet to be fulfilled. Not to speak of other countries which afford material aid to the people in this direction, there is the example set by the Government of Bengal in respect of the sugar and silk industries, which there is no reason why other provincial Governments, under the direction of the Supreme Government, should not follow. A recent report of the Agricultural Department of Bombay has a section headed " Entomology"; and what is the amount of " entomology" the Department did ? Writes the *Times of India*: " Of what passes for Entomology in the Bombay Agricultural Department, the following is an authentic instance. Rewards at the rate of half-an-anna per *ser* for all locusts destroyed, and of three annas per *ser* for locust eggs, were granted. This may be a very wise administrative measure, but we fail to see the Entomology of it. We mention the matter here to show how insufficiently equipped our Agricultural Department is in respect of functions which, in other great agricultural countries, are considered to belong legitimately to it." There are several other ways in which the Government might render help to the cultivators. The Indian cultivators' knowledge of agriculture as an occupation subject to operations of science is little. The time-honoured *mamul* is their only guide. In regard to the breeding of cattle, variety of crops, the selection of seed, manure, the nature of the soil suited to particular crops, and in a score of other matters, the ryots' knowledge is primitive. The Government of India is in a position to collect a vast amount of extremely valuable information on all these matters from the publications issued by the Governments of other countries and from other sources.

Ever since Lord Mayo's time, during the last 30 years, the question of an Agricultural Bureau being established at Calcutta, if not in Provincial capitals also, has been talked of, and, now and again, whenever the latent consciousness of Government regarding agricultural interests is galvanised into transient activity. we have Conferences, Reports, Resolutions, regrets aud promises,—all in abundance. But, anon, the subject is dropped, and other more powerful interests capture the Government. Meanwhile the colossal engine of taxation goes on grinding the very face of the unfortunate agriculturists. Their burden steadily increases ; but their lord, to whom alone they can look for help, is absorbed in the consideration of more weighty matters, and has no time to pay heed to the cries of the humble ryots !

THE PEASANT'S MILLENNIUM.

Mr. Thorburn, in his speech at the Famine Union Conference, described the establishment of Agricultural Banks as the 'millennium of the peasant.' I do not know whether it will really be his millennium, or whether the Indian peasant will ever experience a millenium in the near or remote future. Though, in all countries, agriculture is the basis of national prosperity, still a nation depending on that alone can never be prosperous. Agriculture yields food for the population, but food alone does not complete the physical requirements of man. Comforts and luxuries are wanted, and these should be supplied by manufacturing industries. This was what the Finance

Minister of Russia, M. De Witte, meant when he said that as long as that country remained a purely agricultural country, it would not get rid of periodical famines and general destitution. India is worse than Russia in this respect. We shall never be prosperous so long as eight-tenths of our population depend upon agriculture, and the rest mainly on cooly work or trivial unproductive occupations. The essential condition of India's prosperity is that, in addition to the food that her soil yields, she should provide herself with her own comforts and luxuries, and, by selling to other countries what excess of these she may produce, should enjoy the profits and add them to her capital. At present, there is no scope for the labouring classes except agriculture, all the labour, which in other countries the local manufactures and non-agricultural industries afford to the poorer classes, being lost to India on account of her raw materials being taken away to foreign countries to the great benefit of the capitalists and the labouring classes of those countries. Until this serious anomaly in the economic condition of India is redressed, the millennium will not arrive either to the peasant or to other classes. The present dead level of poverty will not be removed. The establishment of agricultural banks will no doubt be a relief to the peasant, because these banks will make borrowing less ruinous to him. But they cannot raise him altogether above indebtedness, and make him a solvent individual We are not by any means disposed to undervalue the usefulness of those institutions. When they are established and prove successful, the peasant will find it possible, to some extent, to avert the serfdom to which his present indebtedness to the *Sowcar* often reduces him. But let us not forget that in Italy and in other European countries, where agricultural banks have long been established and worked successfully, the peasantry is by no means a contented or prosperous class. Because, there, the Government has, in pursuance of Imperial ambitions, imposed heavy taxes on the cultivating classes, and industries are not in a flourishing condition. Thus, while the agricultural banks will afford to the Indian ryots a welcome relief, the millennium will not arrive until other conditions I have referred to are satisfied.

PETTY HOLDINGS IN INDIA.—AN ECONOMIC WARNING.

From the latest issue of agricultural statistics published by the Government of India for the years 1896-97 to 1900-01, we make out the following statement, showing certain particulars of small holdings held from Government under the ryotwari tenure :—

Small holdings held separate and direct for the years 1896-97 and 1900-01.

		Assam.	Bombay.	Central Provinces.	Madras.
No. of estates ...	1896-97	740,467	1,127,442	31,448	3,198,415
	1900-01	813,871	1,144,325	29,128	3,328,468
Number of holders or shareholders ...	1896-97		1,127,442	25,946	5,556,560
	1900-01		1,144,325	27,352	5,900,520
Gross area ...	1896-97	2,498,851	27,130,046	1,950,204	22,911,305
	1900-01	2,463,741	27,350,007	1,406,864	23,047,118
Average area of each estate ...	1896-97	3·37	24·07	17*	7
	1900-01	3·02	23·9	48	7
Average assessment of each estate ...	1896-97	6·46	28·17	7	14·2
	1900-01	6·06	29·42	8	14

* In 1897-98 it was 41.
„ 1898-99 „ 46.
„ 1899-1900 „ 51.

It will be seen from this table that in the four Provinces where the ryotwari tenure prevails, while the gross area occupied has but moderately increased in Madras and Bombay—and in Assam and Central Provinces, it has actually decreased—,the number of separate estates (except in the Central Provinces) and the number of shareholders in all the Provinces, have increased. The average area of each estate has, at the same time, diminished or remained the same, and the Government assessment on each estate has increased or remained undiminished. Each and every one of these features has its significance in the economic condition of the agricultural classes. The population having multiplied faster than the extension of cultivation has taken place, the pressure on the produce of agriculture has increased. In other words, the same land has to support more people, who have to be content with less nourishment. The number of estates having increased and the average area of each estate having decreased or remained stationary, cultivation, so far as this change has taken place, cannot be carried on with the same efficiency as before, which means diminished produce. To this has to be added the increase in the assessment in Central Provinces and Bombay.

As a set-off against these features showing considerable backsliding of the agricultural condition, there has been no corresponding increase, on the whole. in the estimated area or in the yield under crops. In the year 1892-93 the total area of rice cultivation in the three rice-growing provinces of Bengal, Madras and Burma, was 48,358,707 acres. There has since been a good deal of variation, slight increase in the area; and in the year 1901-1902, the area was 49,620,326 acres, which was less than the area in some of the previous years, namely, in 1894-95, 1897-98, 1898-99 and 1899-900. As regards the total yield, in 1892-93 it was 420,282,625 cwts. This increased slightly in the succeeding two years; decreased in the next two; increased in the next three years; and decreased again in the years 1900-1901 and 1901-1902; in the last the total yield, under rice, being

395,329,247 cwts. Again, in regard to wheat, the variation in the extent of cultivation is more unsatisfactory. It was 27,033,172 in 1891-92 ; it increased in the next three years ; and has decreased since 1895-96 ; and in the year 1901-1902 the area of wheat cultivation, all wheat-producing provinces taken together, was only 23,308,992 acres. The yield shows similar variation, which was 6,442,760 tons in 1891-1892 and 6,010,899 in 1901-1902. Taking the non-food marketable crops, it will be tedious to go through the figures. It is enough here to state that, in regard to cotton, there has been a steady decrease in the area since the year 1893-94 and the yield too may be said to have shown the same tendency. Linseed also shows an unprogressive variation. Rape and mustard, sesamum and jute show considerable improvement, while indigo has gone down during the last ten years both in the area and the yield of the crops. Earthnut and sugarcane have gone through unfavourable vicissitudes. We have given here a brief summary of these figures, but a detailed study of them will be found to be instructive. The last ten years have not only been disastrous in the provinces which were afflicted by the two severe famines; but of the whole Empire the material progress has been arrested and pushed back.

To one serious feature in the statement printed above, I wish to draw special attention in this place. It will be seen from this statement that, in all the four provinces, the average area of ryotwari estates shows a steadily decreasing tendency.

So far as the Madras Presidency is concerned, this tendency is very pronounced. We pointed out that the ryotwari holdings in the year 1900-01 consisted of 3,300,000 in all, of which 2,2,34,000 were single, and 10,06,000 were joint holdings. Thirty years ago, the total number of holdings was 2,126,000, of which 1,864,000 were single, and only 262,000 were joint. The increase in the number of holdings by more than 50 per cent., and the increase in the number of joint holdings by nearly 400 per cent., are far in excess of the increase in the extent of cultivation or in the growth of population. The increase in the extent of cultivation in the Madras Presidency has been, since the great famine of 1876--78, only 1·93 million acres or about 2 millions. (During the last ten years, the increase has been almost nominal). This, in itself, is very significant, because the increase in the extent of cultivation has been far too short of the increase in population, which, between the years 1881-1901, has increased from 30,827,113, to 38,208,609, or nearly 27 per cent. This increase in the population must have brought about extreme pressure on inferior lands of which the increase in the area of cultivation must consist. But the extreme sub-division of the fields and the increase fourfold, within 30 years, in the number of joint holdings, must have led to a deplorable aggravation of the evil. If, in the case of the other three provinces where the ryotwari tenure prevails, similar figures can be obtained, their analysis must yield instructive results.

The *Madras Mail* quoted, some time back, the remarks made 28 years ago by the Board of Revenue on this question of the continued parcelling out of landed property into minute shares. "The ryotwari system and the Hindu law of inheritance," the Board remarked, "make the minute sub-division of holdings and the existence of joint holdings inevitable. The sub-division often proceeds to such an extent that the holder is a man of no substance, gaining his livelihood almost entirely by day-labour. When misfortune comes, he is ruined at once, and his land is sold in arrears." During these twenty-eight years, we have seen how the evil has increased. Over three millions of holdings distributed among an agricultural population of 20 millions is a serious economic situation; but when full one-third of this number of holdings are each shared among a number of proprietors, the neglect and deterioration that must overtake cultivation can be imagined. Referring to the average extent of each holding, this journal points out that "it is a serious matter for contemplation that these petty holdings average just a quarter of an acre of wet and not much more than 2¾ acres of dry land each, whilst more than 40,000 of them average not much more than three-quarters of an acre each." "The latter are, of course," it is added, "partly of the nature of allotments, and partly small parcels of land not held by the agricultural community ; but when this has been allowed for, as well as the fact that ryots with individual holdings often have shares in other joint holdings and have a certain amount of *inam* land also, the minute *parcellement* of the holding remains as a warning."

In Bombay in the first year of the quinquennium, the average area of each estate was 24·07 acres ; in the last 23·9. This is the average size of the ryotwari holding, but as a fact a very large proportion of these holdings are actually less than ten acres in extent. A contraction of the smaller holdings spells poverty to the cultivator and prospective recruits to famine relief works. In Madras, the size of the average holding is 7 acres ; and the increase in the number of holders between the years compared was far more than the increase in the number of holdings. In Bombay, the state of things seems to be equally bad. There are over one million shareholders owning the same number of estates. But, dividing the number of shareholders or the number of estates amongst a rural population of nearly 15 millions, we come to the conclusion that each estate or shareholder of about 23 acres supports more than twelve persons. But the shareholder in Bombay, probably in many cases, holds his estate jointly with others, although one individual's name might be registered in Government books for the payment of the tax. But 23 acres is only the average ; as we have remarked above, many estates are less than 10 acres in extent. If 10 acres were divided among a number of joint-holders, there might be hundreds of thousands of holdings extremely small, as small as in this Presidency. I entirely agree with the *Times of India* in its opinion that " the improvement of agriculture, as well as of the condition of the agricultural classes, requires that this tendency to divide land into infinitesimal parcels should be checked."

Small Farming.

Whatever may be the difference of opinion among Western economists as regards the respective merits of large and small farming, there can be no doubt that in India small farming is being carried, as is shown above, to a dangerous extreme, and that it already constitutes a serious warning. We have pointed out how the average extent of a single estate held under ryotwari tenure hardly exceeds five acres, and at the bottom of the agricultural order of the population it is much smaller. The Hindu law of equal inheritance, the esteem in which the occupation of agriculture is held by the people, the absence of other occupations, the comparatively stationary state of the wages, the joint family system, and compulsory marriage—all tend towards this deplorable result. While the law of equal inheritance has produced in India the same result as it has produced in France, the counteracting forces that operate in France are absent in this country. As in the Highlands of Scotland and in Ireland, here, too, land has been divided until the plots are too small to support a family. The small farmer in India is a man of no substance; if the season is good, he cultivates the field and pays the tax to Government; if it is adverse, he relinquishes the holding and resorts to daily labour.

The condition of the small farmer is indeed precarious under ordinary circumstances, and, in some places, as in Southerland, where the crofters are fairly well off, the extreme deterioration of the peasants has to be prevented by a strict rule against sub-division of holdings. As a rule, the farmer experiences great difficulty in making an average income over a term of years. As it happens in India, seasons and prices fluctuate, man and beast are exposed to the danger of epidemics, blights and plagues of various kinds occur, and the small cultivator cannot hope, as Professor Nicholson points out, that every year will provide for itself even a necessary minimum of subsistence. As we have already said, the Indian farmer sinks to the condition of the day-labourer, and rarely looks to his land as his chief source of subsistence. This last is the bane of small farming in this country. The well-known saying of Young does not hold good here: "Give a man the secure possession of a bleak rock, and he will turn it into a garden." "The magic of property turns sand into gold." These feats may be accomplished by the peasant in Flanders or Belgium; but the Indian farmer is dead to all such charms of property.

The field he cultivates is practically his property, and until, at all events, the time for the next revision of revenue settlement comes, the improvements he effects will not be taxed by the landlord—in India, by the State. Still, the quality of human nature referred to by Young is not developed here. It is true that the Indian peasant has to contend against unfavourable natural conditions. The greatest need of agriculture is water, and for this he has to depend on the rains from heaven, which are notoriously uncertain. In most places, however, this want can be supplied by artificial irrigation by means of tanks and wells, so that wherever this method of irrigation is practicable, the question is one of capital. But, the Indian peasant is a well-known pauper. Far from being able to invest capital in the improvement of his property, he is in a state of chronic indebtedness, which paralyses all his interest in the improvement of his income. How far the relation of cause and effect can be traced between this want of capital, this state of continued indebtedness, of the peasant on the one hand, and his utter apathy and lack of zeal in the improvement of his property, on the other, it is perhaps ain to attempt to determine. The only capital of the Indian farmer is his labour and the labour of his family, and what skill and knowledge he has inherited; and though he might be expected to turn this to his greatest benefit, he does not do so. "With regard to labour," says Professor Nicholson, "it is plain that the small farmers cannot make an adjustment of work according to capacity so as to fill up the time in the best manner or to the same degree as the large farmers. It is also plain that they are not likely to have the same scientific skill, or what is the next best thing, to have the command of it. Nor are they likely to make experiments or follow a new lead readily. In fact, the one great advantage that the small farmer, as a rule, possesses is inherited and empirical skill, which, however useful under conditions fixed by custom, may, when conditions are changing, prove an obstacle in the way of improvement. The devotion to labour, the ardour in cultivating to the utmost, and the proverbial thrift of peasant proprietors, have also their dark side." In India, these seem to have only one side,—the dark side. In the controversy that has recently gone on regarding the light or heavy incidence of the State's share in the produce of the land, Mr. Dutt and others have contended that the proportionately higher cost of cultivation of the poor soil in comparison with that of the rich soil, is not taken into consideration by Government in estimating the net profit of the peasant. The officials, on the other hand, have maintained that it is the practice in this country to devote less capital and less labour to the cultivation of the inferior land, whereas when the land is fertile and likely to give substantial yield, greater care and expense are bestowed on its cultivation.

The climate and the quality of the soil are the natural conditions of cultivation; while capital and the rate of profit are the social ones. If the former are unfavourable to the Indian farmer, the latter, under present circumstances, are no less unfavourable. Small farming does not, obviously, require the same amount of capital as large farming; but if the small farmers were solvent and accumulate capital, the amalgamation of small estates into large ones would be possible. This seems to be taking place in France, the country, *par excellence*, of peasant proprietors. English writers do not take a favourable view of the results of the system of small holdings in France, and Professor Nicholson has no doubt that, in general, the British agricultural labourer is better off than the French peasant owner. But other accounts present a different picture. According to a well-known writer on agricultural economics,* the greatest increase in the area under wheat cultivation in France is due to those peasant families which themselves cultivate the land they own. Since the end of the eighteenth century, they have nearly doubled the area under wheat as well as the returns from each acre, so as to increase almost fourfold the amount of wheat grown in France. The French peasant is, so far as self-restraint is concerned, a person entirely different from the Indian farmer. While the Indian farmer, whatever his present condition or future prospect, will marry and add to the family, the French peasant is most anxious not to bring into existence more lives than can be fed or started in life decently according to his standard. The population of France has, during the last one hundred years, increased only by 41 per cent., whereas the increase of wheat crop has been nearly 400 per cent. There, too, agriculture has been hampered, within the

* See note p 80.

period mentioned, by various obstacles--taxation, military service, poverty of the peasantry, and, even up to 1884, a severe prohibition of all sorts of association among the peasants. What, then, makes the French peasant so prosperous, whereas the Indian is for ever a child of misery? The chief cause is, indeed, the habit of thrift and self-restraint carefully pursued by the former.

As a fact, however, the Indian agricultural classes do not multiply very fast. Both of Malthus's two sets of causes are in operation in this country, the preventive and positive causes, or causes which diminish the birth-rate and those which increase the death-rate. Low economic condition, such as has prevailed in India during the last decade, and emigration to foreign countries or to distant parts of India itself, such as has almost completely checked the growth of population in the district of Tanjore, diminish the birth-rate. Famine, too, has this preventive effect. In other countries from which famine has been banished, positive checks to the growth of population arise from the laws of nature, as for example, the inclemency of the seasons or the exhaustion of natural resources. Other checks arise from wars, life in over-crowded cities, and excesses. In India, in addition to some of these, there is the great check provided by famine, which, during the last ten years, cut short the growth of the population by so many as 19 millions of souls. As the result of these preventive and positive checks, the growth of population in India is much more moderate than in many other countries in the world.

In India, cultivation does not pay. This is a very important fact. In Western countries, agriculture is to a large extent carried on as a commercial business. In England, amateur farming is said to be increasing. Large farms are cultivated for the sake of the profit on the capital invested. But, in this country, by far the bulk of the occupation of cultivation is prompted by no such commercial spirit. It is pursued almost exclusively as a means of subsistence, and the gratification of certain domestic luxuries is the only profit which the larger class of farmers expect. The smaller farmer, here as well as elsewhere, looks to the employment of his own labour and that of his family. Accordingly, when inferior soils are the only ones available for cultivation, as is the case in India, no profit is expected, but only a reasonable remuneration for labour. When, therefore, wages in other employments are better than in agriculture, it operates as a motive prejudicial to small farming. As a fact, wages in towns are often higher than wages on the village farms, and the former are not subject to the uncertainties of the latter. Employment in towns gives the labourer wages throughout the year, whereas cultivation occupies the farmer only for a few months. It is true that he spends the months, when there is no field work, in working for wages in towns. But, although Indians have an unique liking for the work of farming and for village life, still the old conditions of life both in towns and villages are changing, and when once the farmer acquires a liking for town life, he does not care to devote himself too much to the cultivation of his small holding. Less heavy taxation by the State will make petty farming more paying. It is a questionable form of the exercise of ruling power to tax, as the Government of India tax, the wages of the physical labour of the poorer classes who, in India, while enjoying the least of the good things of the world, pay most to the State in order that a multitude of office-holders, professional men and the rest of the wealth-consuming classes, may sport on the lap of opulence and luxury.

The soil of Belgium supplies with home-grown food no less than 490 *inhabitants per square mile* and there remains something for export—no less than £1,000,000 worth of agricultural produce being exported every year to Great Britain Besides, it must not be forgotten that Belgium is a manufacturing country which exports home-made goods to the value of £9 per head of population (£56,000,000, on the average, in 1886—92), while the total exports from the United Kingdom attain only £6 7*s.* per inhabitant. As to separate parts of the Belgium territory, the small and naturally unfertile province of West Flanders not only grows the food of its 580 inhabitants on the square mile, but exports agricultural produce to the value of 25*s.* per head of its population. And yet no one can read Laveleye's masterly work without coming to the conclusion that Flemish agriculture would have realized still better results were it not hampered in its growth by the steady and heavy increase of rent. In the face of the rent being increased each nine years, many farmers have lately abstained from further improvements * * * While we are so often told that wheat-growing does not pay, and England consequently reduces from year to year the area of its wheat fields, the French peasants steadily increase the area under wheat, and the greatest increase is due to those peasant families which themselves cultivate the land they own. Since the end of the last century they have nearly doubled both the area under wheat as well as the returns from each acre, so as to increase almost fourfold the amount of wheat grown in France. At the same time the population has only increased by 41 per cent., so that the ratio of increase of the wheat crop has been six times greater than the ratio of increase of population, although agriculture has been hampered all the time by a series of serious obstacles—taxation, military service, poverty of the peasantry, and even, up to 1884, a severe prohibition of all sorts of association among the peasants. It must also be remarked that, during the same hundred years and even within the last fifty years, market gardening, fruit culture, and culture for industrial purposes have immensely developed in France, so that there would be no exaggeration in saying that the French obtain now at least six or seven times more than they obtained a hundred years ago. The "means of existence" drawn from the soil have thus grown about fifteen times quicker than the population—*Prince Kropotkin's "Fields, Factories, and Workshops."*—(*The Expansionist.*)

CHAPTER III.

Industrial Pursuits—A Preliminary Survey Necessary.

IN one of our Congress Resolutions, we prayed Government for the appointment of a Commission to inquire into the present industrial condition of the country. We did this in accordance with the recommendation of the Famine Commission of 1878. In their opinion, the root of much of the poverty of the people of India and of the risks to which they are exposed in seasons of scarcity, lies in the unfortunate circumstance that agriculture forms almost the sole occupation of the mass of the population, and no remedy for present evils will be complete which does not include the introduction of a diversity of occupations, through which the surplus population may be drawn from agricultural pursuits, and led to find their means of subsistence in manufactures or some such support.

In 1872, Dr. Forbes Watson, of the India Museum, advocated the undertaking of an industrial survey of India by Government. In a pamphlet he published in that year, he directed attention to the want of a really exhaustive and systematic knowledge of the various products of India in their new and in their manufactured condition

"There are certainly abundant materials for a general superficial knowledge of Indian products, but in order to render such knowledge really useful and applicable to trade and industry, much more precise and comprehensive information is required. Each kind of produce must be accurately described, the different varieties and species distinguished, the places and the methods of production ascertained, the commercial and industrial value investigated, and the question of supply and utilization discussed And when all this is accomplished, provision must be made for rendering the knowledge easily accessible and available for immediate reference, not only by Government authorities, but by agriculturalists, manufacturers and men of business generally."

TWO MAIN COURSES : I. AGRICULTURAL EDUCATION.

At an International Congress on Technical Education, held in London in June 1897, Mr. C. A. Baines, C. S. I., read a paper on Technical Education in India, and there he observed : " In the course of time, there must inevitably be forced on the people the recognition of a fact which is even now apparent in one or two tracts in India, namely, that the pressure of an increasing population has been hitherto thrown entirely on the soil, that in most parts of the country the most fertile lands have been brought under the plough, and that, in India, the limits of remunerative cultivation under the existing conditions have been nearly reached. Further extension becoming impossible, recourse must be had to one of two alternatives.

Either an outlet for the surplus population must be found in some industries other than agriculture, or, by what is known as intensifying the cultivation by the application of the teachings of science, two blades of corn must be made to grow where only one grew before." Since Mr. Baines wrote thus, the severe famines that have devastated the country have brought home to the minds of the people this grim and melancholy truth, and there is now no doubt in the mind of any intelligent person in this country that to continue in the present economic state, means death, disease and destitution to the people, and that the only means of escaping from these is for them to strike and advance along new paths where abundant wealth can be made. I do not know why Mr. Baines says that *either* of the two courses must be adopted. Not either, but both should be adopted, because one is not antagonistic to the other. But in either of the courses and in *both* of them, the key to success is to be found in the steady diffusion of a well-devised and well-organised system of technical education. I have already spoken of the supreme necessity of establishing a central agricultural bureau in Calcutta, with provincial bureaus in different parts of the country. The most important subjects to which the attention of these bureaus will have to be directed are : the nature of the soil ; the best means of irrigation or drainage when necessary ; the enrichment or the renewal of the fertility of the soil by the application of proper manures at the rotation of crops ; the implements best adapted for tillage and for the gathering of the crops with efficiency and economy; and the crops which can be most advantageously produced to answer the special requirements of the ryot's position and with respect to the nature of the soil and climate; the feeding of live-stock, dairy produce, and market facilities for the disposal of his products. The vast improvements which recent discoveries in chemistry and physiology have introduced into agriculture, have lifted it from the position of a merely manual art, and conferred upon it the dignity of a science. It is no longer a pursuit in which the humble villager or ease-loving investor engages for a livelihood or profit. Royalty, the nobility, and men of wealth now take to farming, as well as the professional agriculturist, and take pride in exhibiting the products of their farms. Agriculture is now a scientific occupation, and not merely experimental husbandry. Chemical and geological knowledge are essential to success, and the most ingenious mechanical appliances, as well as steam power, are habitually employed. Side by side with these scientific and highly intensive methods of farming—methods which are improved and modified every day,—we in this country adhere to methods which are centuries old and which neither feed the soil as it ought to be fed, nor extort from it as much wealth as it is possible to make it yield.

II.—Non-Agricultural Education.

But the millennium will not dawn while agriculture, however advanced its development may be, continues almost the sole occupation of the people. It is becoming obvious every day that India's material prosperity is involved in her industrial condition. The great problem is, how India's agricultural produce can be kept within her own limits for the nourishment of her own people, how her raw materials without being exported to foreign countries can be converted into manufactured goods in order that her industry may supply her own comforts and luxuries, and how by these means the ever-growing tide of foreign imports might be stemmed, and how India's economic drain, the drain of her very life-blood, might be arrested. I am in entire accord with Sir M. Bhownaggree, who has done valuable service to this country by his constant agitation of this question in and outside the House of Commons. It is obvious that India's exports of agricultural produce are not exports of her surplus stock. If the wheat and rice that are exported were to remain in India, the poorer classes who now consume less than two pounds of flour per day, might be able to get 2½ pounds. If our oil seeds would remain in our country, cultivation would be made more efficient and our cattle would be better fed. If our cotton, wool, dying materials, hides and skins, bones, and a score of other raw materials, now sent abroad, could be kept in the country, they would furnish openings to our own capital and to our own labour. We deprive ourselves of all these advantages under the present condition of things, and are content to be an under-fed people entirely dependent on aliens for all our articles of comfort and luxury and of daily domestic use. This is a most abnormal state, and obtains in no other country in the world.

I propose, in this place, to quote largely from a remarkably able paper which Sir M. Bhownaggree read at the International Congress on Technical Education, to which I have already referred. Not that his ideas are particularly new or original; I have myself ventilated them on numerous occasions in the press and on the platform. But the reader will certainly be glad to know that one of our countrymen in Sir M. Bhownaggree's position holds on this most important question views which are perfectly sound from a scientific point of view and which are calculated to advance our most vital interests. Sir M. Bhownaggree in his paper analyses the domestic wants of our poorer classes and those above them, and points out how largely these wants are supplied by imports from foreign countries.

WHAT DO THE PEOPLE USE EVERY DAY?

"What do these poorer classes use every day? Take the humblest household first. You will find there metal pots and pans for cooking purposes, kerosine or mineral oil and matches for light, cotton, bone, or metal buttons, pins, hooks and eyes, needles and thread, which enter into the preparation of the family garments of rough native-made fabrics. Then there are tacks and nails, twine and string, a hammer and other tools in many houses. All these articles, every one of them, are of foreign make.

"Peering into another household, a stage or two upraised in the social scale, you find nearly all the articles common to the daily use of a European working man, most of the culinary utensils, lamps, candle, soap, paper, ink, pen, pencil, not a single one of which is made in India. This house is painted with colour or washes of foreign composition, the wood-work of it is varnished with foreign varnish, the occupant's clothes are of European manufacture. One degree higher again, and four-fifths of the articles in the domicile of a peon, a petty schoolmaster or a clerk, and on his own person and his wife's and children's persons, are of foreign make. Then come the household of the middle class, of the successful and comfortable tradesman, the merchant and the professional man. There, and, in a still greater degree, in the mansions of millionaires and the palaces of princes the predominating proportion of articles are all of foreign manufacture. I try hard to recall to my mind what particular article I should find of Indian workmanship in places like these last, and I do not see any of that description, from the kitchen and stable to the drawing-room and the hall. Some critics, who do not fall in with my views, might point to the furniture. That would make a somewhat important exception if I viewed this considerable part of a household as a superficial observer would ; but then he does not remember that, save in the simplest and crudest class of furniture, a good proportion of what is known as local furniture is not native-made at all. The springs of a coach or chair, the lining, the buttons, the threads, the hinges of a cupboard or box, the screws, the nails, the locks, the very tools with which these are put together and formed into shape are all made abroad. So that what remains is the wood and the labour. That even these contribute their due proportion of profit to the Native worker, I doubt. English firms and European employers in very many instances control the production of the raw material and the labor, and very appropriately take the profit of it, the Native's gain being the bare living wages of his daily toil."

A DISMAL TALE OF THE DRAIN.

Sir M. Bhownaggree then briefly enumerates some of the chief varieties of raw material which are produced abundantly in the country and which admit of manipulation in the places of their growth. These are: coffee, coir, cotton, drugs, dyes, fibres, grain and pulse; gums and resins; hemp, hides and skins; horns, ivory, jute, lac, precious stones, seeds, silk, spices, sugarcane, tobacco, tea, timber, and wool. This is by no means a complete list, but it contains a few items which show how far—owing to want of ordinary enterprise and the almost entire absence of skilled labour of the most common sort, both of which would result from technical instruction,—India fails to derive the benefit of the rich stores that nature has bestowed on her with a lavish hand. "The exports and imports, which can be quoted in respect of every article of the raw produce of India which admits of skilled labour, tell the dismal tale of the drain, from preventible causes, of her natural resources to make the wealth of other countries. The wool and skins, the hides and molasses, and nearly all such articles as are packed away from India, year after year,—to be imported again after undergoing manipulation by foreign operatives—would, with the application of a little skilled labour on the spot, offer to millions of her poorest inhabitants the means of subsistence. It would save her, besides, all that large amount of money which is represented by freight, by office and middlemen's charges, and by the difference of exchange, which all goes out of her pocket by the time these articles travel back to her markets and shops in a refined form, or in the shape of articles prepared abroad ready for use by her people. Instead of her keeping as much of this raw material at home as she requires for the manufacture of such articles, and sending out the surplus, either ready manufactured for sale abroad, or at as late a stage of preparation as mere ordinary skilled workmanship would admit of, she chucks it away in bulk and thus furnishes the means of livelihood to millions of foreigners, while her own children are famishing at home.

"Nor is this the case in respect of such articles only as require for their manufacture any particular skill or aptitude which is as yet unknown to them. Tea, coffee and tobacco, for instance, do not require any very intricate operation before they are ready for consumption. Indeed, all the labor they require is exclusively put upon them to-day by the Indian labourer and workman. And yet it is not the Native of India that takes the profit on them. It is the European planter and the tobacco and cigar maker, who is from his boyhood apprenticed in those lines and brings to his work the knowledge and enterprise which are the natural outcome of his training, who pockets the large surplus of gains after the Indian has had his hire. Go through the list of tea and coffee plantations, of tobacco factories, of tanneries, iron and brass foundries, and breweries, oil and flour and bone-crushing factories, woollen and silk mills, and you will find that the proprietor or master or employer who, of course, takes all the remainder of the income after the workmen and establishments are paid, in a large number of them is not the Native of India. This little enumeration engrosses nearly all of what are called large industries ; and alas ! how mean and insignificant, how utterly microscopic are the variety and extent of them compared to the huge population of the country and in relation to the quantity of articles they consume ! The wants of India are numerous and various enough to afford scope for the consumption of all these house-made articles ; all that is required is enterprise and skill. Without skill, there cannot be the necessary impulse for venture ; and for the attainment of skill, the help and guidance of technical education is indispensable.

Efforts made for the first time.

" The workshops of railways and of some of the private factories, and laboratories in a few colleges, used to be the only openings for the Indian youth to obtain a rudimentary knowledge of mechanics and chemistry, until about ten years ago, when for the first time efforts were made in Madras and Bombay to start technical institutions. The scheme of the former has mostly remained on paper, and for some reason Madras has been unable to begin the actual work of instructions. The Bombay project was lucky in having for its guide an educationist of varied experience and Continental reputation in the person of the Governor of the Presidency, Lord Reay, who gave it a sound working committee of business-men, and a secretary who was himself trained in some of the best English industrial centres as a Mechanical Engineer. In this gentleman, the Honorable N. N. Wadia, C.I.E., was combined with great technical knowledge a large acquaintance with the wants of the country and the chracteristics of her people. Those qualities enabled him, with the help of efficient teachers obtained from Europe, to organize a system of instruction in such departments of industry as were most in vogue in Bombay, the result of which has amply proved the utility of the institution even in the few years it has been in existence. Lord Harris, who succeeded Lord Reay, took a lively interest in the growth of the institute; the pupils who studied in and were diplomaed by it obtained lucrative situations in the local mills and factories, and, altogether, from a combination of various favourable causes, the Victoria Technical Institute has been enabled to plant its foot firmly on the soil of Bombay"

VERY LITTLE HAS BEEN DONE.

But, on the whole, in the way of imparting technical instruction, very little has been done. On the other hand, Sir M. Bhownaggree remarks, in terms of indignant eloquence, "the omission of that teaching has already resulted in such an amount of mischief and misery to the land, has so retarded her development, nay, so grievously stunted her resources, so impoverished her people, and so dwarfed all those energies that go to make a country prosperous and powerful, that I thought I would best make out a case for a speedy and vigorous effort in future to repair that serious omission in the past by delineating the evils which it has produced and is ever increasingly producing in the present."

How, then, is this serious omission to be repaired? It can be repaired only by proceeding along the path of other countries which have already acquired pre-eminence among the countries of the world in industry and commerce. Within the last ten years, only one technical institution worth the name has been established throughout India, the Victoria Technical Institute, in Bombay. Sir M. Bhownaggree visited this institution in January 1897, and his impressions of the work done there and of its future capacity for useful work, he has recorded as follows:

A VISIT TO VICTORIA TECHNICAL INSTITUTE.

" I had the privilege of visiting it last January, and I rejoiced to find some of my pet beliefs with regard to the aptitude of the Indian youth to work with as deft a hand and as artistic a faculty as the skilled European artizan—given the same training and the same opportunities—realized, especially when I saw in a newly-created department sign-boards and household utensils in enamelled metal prepared by the students. Hardware and cutlery imports in India in 1895-96 were valued at Rs. 1,422,533, and roughly estimating the price of the description of articles in hardware, which I saw manufactured in the Victoria Technical Institute, at considerably lower than a third of that amount, here is an illustration of how Rs. 400,000 might at once be kept every year in India, which has hitherto gone out of the country on just one common item of import. Many other such results of the efficiency of the teachers and the diligence and capacity of the students were shown to me in this excellent institution, which I cannot attempt to describe in detail. But I came away from it firmer in my conviction that technical instruction was the only means by which India could be saved from her poverty, helplessness and degradation, and sad with the thought that such a feasible mode of securing the country's welfare should have been so long delayed by her Government, and so utterly neglected by her people,—for I am told that there is even now only one establishment of its kind in all the continent, and that, with this exception, the only opening for the coming generation of men to train itself in industrial pursuits, is the narrow door by which occasionally a youth here and there might get by favour into a railway or private workshop to obtain a smattering of mechanical knowledge."

Other Institutes.

Why this should be so in this unfortunate country, while in other countries the State spends crores of money on this object, nobody can say. Private efforts can, no doubt, do much, as is shown by the patriotic benevolence of Mr. J N. Tata, whose name has become a household word throughout India. My enthusiastic friend, Professor Gajjur of Bombay—to whose high scientific knowledge that city owes the redemption of the statue of her late Majesty from hopeless disfigurement by the villanous act of a maniac,—with 40,000 rupees, is able to work a fully-equipped and furnished laboratory, train young men and turn out results which have won public approbation. Another technical school has been established at Ahmedabad with the help of the munificent bequest of the late Rambootlal Chotalal. Here and there, similar efforts on a comparatively small scale are being made. But these are merely ripples in the vast expanse of a stagnant sea, which yields no treasure and in which no life grows It is too much the fashion now-a-days to blame the people for making no efforts of their own. But no statesman who is not a vain deluded dreamer, thinks it possible to lift up a whole nation from a state of industrial prostration and general impoverishment to a state of industrial prosperity, by leaving the task entirely to private efforts.

THE AMBITION OF OTHER COUNTRIES.

At the present moment, the industrial and commercial education of the people, in a more thorough and practical manner than at present, is engaging the most serious attention of many countries. Great Britain herself is extremely anxious about it. Canada does very well in regard to her agriculture; but there are in that country other natural resources, which are lying hidden deep in the bowels of the earth or slumbering on its surface, and which await the application, to quote the words of a recent writer, Otto J. Klotz, of the highest scientific skill and experience in their development. "We have spoken," he writes, "of the value of technical education, more particularly with reference to our artizans and mechanics; but there is another and a higher field, that of *research and discovery,* which needs cultivation. Little or nothing therein has been done in Canada; we have been content, or, for want of funds, have been obliged to be content, with utilising scientific knowledge from outside sources, instead of having laboratories of our own, to disclose some of the secrets of nature and science for the benefit of man. We should be able to produce technologists capable of taking charge of large industrial works, where now foreigners are employed, and capable of directing capital to the creation of new industries."

Such is the ambition of other countries. Why should not India, whose natural resources and whose physical and social conditions are in no way unfavourable to her prosperity, cherish the same ambition and strive after its fulfilment? What did Professor Ramsay say, at Bombay, when he was leaving for England after a protracted tour in India in connection with Mr. Tata's educational enterprise?

WHAT PROFESSOR RAMSAY SAYS.

"One of the most important problems for India," said the Professor, "was to establish in its midst industries by which they could make use of the enormous and bountiful supply of materials in the country. There were two ways of making money from such materials. For example, they could take the iron ore, and export it to other countries. The second and more profitable plan would be to open iron industry in the country and give employment to thousands of Indians. He would press upon every man in India to seriously consider the question as to how the industrial progress of India has to be achieved."

A PROGRAMME.

To make systematic, sustained, and extensive efforts for the imparting of technical instruction in the higher as well as in the more elementary branches, is then the great object to be kept in view. How is this to be done? Have we any ideas on the subject? Have we any suggestions to make? I have tried to make out a programme of what should be done by Government, aided by private efforts, in view to the gradual attainment of this object :—

I. Dr. Forbes Watson's and Sir Louis Mallet's idea —and the suggestion of the Indian National Congress on identical lines—should be carried out, namely, that a survey should be taken of the condition and prospects of industries in India, and a comprehensive treatise, written in a popular style, should be published giving detailed information regarding various agricultural and mineral products, which can be manufactured into articles of utility, the places where they are to be found, the processes of their manufacture, the equipment of the factories, their cost, &c., &c., &c.

II. Five Institutions, like Mr. Tata's Institute of Science, should be established in the five great capitals of the Empire.

III. These should be supplemented by other Institutes like the Bombay Victoria Technical Institute.

IV. In the interior of the country, in various district stations, there should be established Technical Institutions on a smaller scale like the one proposed at Ahmedabad.

V. Mining Schools should be established in connection with the coal mines of Calcutta and the gold mines of Kolar, as well as iron mines, to the development of which Lord Curzon and Sir Edward Law are anxious to give their best attention.

VI. Schools for instruction in weaving, such as the one suggested by the weaving community of Madura, equipped with the latest appliances, should be established in different centres of this industry.

VII. In connection with other select industries, which the result of the proposed industrial survey will be able to suggest, similar schools should be started.

VIII. A large number of scholarships should be instituted to enable Indian youths to proceed to foreign countries where they could receive scientific and industrial training.

IX. The local boards and municipalities should be called upon to devote a portion of their funds to the establishment of schools to afford training in any particular local industry or industries. Two or more of these institutions may be made jointly responsible, where necessary, for the maintenance of these schools.

X. Attached to the Supreme Government and to each of the Provincial Governments, there should be a Bureau of experts, whose sole business should be to direct the industrial and commercial interests of the country—not those of our foreign trade alone, but those of the people in regard to their education and practical activities in this direction.*

WAYS AND MEANS.

This is the programme I have chalked out. Those that have given more attention to the subject will per-

---

* See note at the end of the chapter.

haps be able to modify this, or suggest a different and better programme. It is not, of course, meant that the whole of this should be carried out at once. As it is, the above, no doubt, is a formidable programme; and our official friends will at once try to shut me up, by asking how the funds can be found for carrying out such a programme? My reply is: Such an interrogatory is only the outcome of want of earnestness and thorough conviction. I shall ask them to refer to a single instance, in the whole history of the modern world, of a Government which, convinced of the paramount and most pressing need of a reform, involving the most vital interests, the very life and death, of the nation, has put off that reform because no funds could be provided as easily as funds could be provided for the ordinary needs of the current administration. Great schemes of conquest, offensive as well as defensive wars, the increase of armaments, the emancipation of slaves, construction of public works—all these are undertaken from time to time from borrowed funds, or from increased taxation, if necessary. Have the Government of India reduced their expenditure in any of their departments because of the disastrous period of famine and pestilence that the country has gone through? I have pointed out how there is room for a saving of 5 crores of rupees every year in the expenditure of Government, and if only justice were done to this country by our Imperial rulers, in the matter of military expenditure, the Indian Exchequer would be relieved to the extent of, as Mr. Caine calculated, 7 or 8 millions a year, which would be available for peaceful enterprises in the direction we have in view. In the amount of the civil salaries and pensions, about 2 millions could be saved by the substitution of Indians in the place of Europeans and by paying smaller salaries to the Indian employees.

NOTE.

Within a month after the address containing the suggestion was delivered by me at Cocanada, the Government of India announced a scheme for the formation of a Commercial Bureau at Calcutta. It is proposed that, at the head of the new Bureau in all its branches, there should be a specially selected officer, entitled Director-General of Commercial Intelligence. Under his direct orders there should be placed two assistants; one of whom should be a Director of Statistics, and the other a Director of the Commercial Branch together with the necessary establishment. The primary function of the Director-General, and of the Commercial Branch assistant under his orders, would be to procure, compile and publish all information likely to be of use to the commercial public or to Government in its relations to commerce. This would embrace matters relating to both the import and export trade; to the inland transfrontier trade; to the industrial and mineral resources of the country; to competition of foreign staples with local products in India and Indian staples with foreign products abroad, and to the development of existing markets and the discovery of new ones. The scheme includes a library, an enquiry office and a journal. The headquarters would be at Calcutta.

The Chief of the new Department of the Minister of Commerce is to get a salary, we are told, of five thousand rupees a month, and he is to have two assistants, each with salaries of half that amount. The Department may be splendidly organised in every respect, but unless the man chosen for its head is thoroughly equipped for his work by previous training, he will turn out to be a lamentable failure. In a speech delivered by His Excellency the Viceroy when proposing the toast of the "Bengal Chamber of Commerce" at their recent meeting held at Calcutta (February 1903), he referred to this subject as follows:—

"Finally, there is the proposal about which we have been in consultation with your Chamber, viz., the creation of a Commercial Bureau. I saw somewhere or other that I was expected to make an announcement on the subject to-night. I am sorry to say that that is not in my power, for the case is now with the Secretary of State, who has not yet replied, but whose acceptance of the general principle of the scheme may, I think, be taken for certain. But, Sir, there is one thing to my mind even more important than the scheme itself, and that is the man who is to be its head. You will add very materially to the services that you have already rendered both to the commercial world and to the Government and which have so recently met with a most popular recognition in your title, if you can enable me to put my finger on a man. I want the very best individual in India for the job, and I have no prejudices whatever as to the source from which I take him." On the same occasion, the Viceroy added "We have created a Department of Agriculture with an Inspector-General as its head; and we now propose with aid of the munificient donation that I recently received from a wealthy American gentleman, Mr. Phipps, to unify in one place all the various Departments of scientific investigation in connection with agriculture."

CHAPTER IV.

Protection of Indian Industry.

BESIDES making extensive provision for scientific and industrial education, the Government should directly foster Indian industries by adopting a policy of protection, as is done in other countries. Some thirty years ago, in Germany, the proportion of agricultural classes to the whole population was approximately 60 per cent., whereas it now amounts to only 35 per cent., the rest being absorbed in industrial and commercial classes. The same beneficial change will take place in India, if the statesmen responsible for India's well-being will act as the statesmen of Germany have acted, by granting protection to Indian industries.

Of late, we have noted with the greatest pleasure some eminent Anglo-Indian authorities pleading the cause of India's industrial future in a truly statesmanlike spirit. Speaking at a recent meeting of the Society of Arts in London, at which Mr. Wagle, of Bombay, read an admirable address, Sir Guilford Molesworth, K.C.I.E., said, with an emphasis born of conviction, that "Industries would never be introduced into India until they were protected, not only from foreign countries, but from ourselves also." Sir Lepel Griffin, on the same occasion, pointed out very rightly that the question of free-trade and protection, which differed in every part of the world, must be discussed in India with instant and direct regard to the interest of India itself. Free-trade and protection, he maintained, should not be looked on with English or Manchester eyes, but simply with those of India alone. He advocated the imposition of duties to encourage Indian arts and manufactures, and for revenue purposes, and to raise the dead weight of taxation from the land. For these purposes, he thought protective duties might very justly and beneficently be imposed on India. But, he added, the question should be decided not on English grounds or by English people in England, but by the Government in Calcutta in the interest of India alone.

Besides these two valuable pronouncements, we have beheld a high Indian official in service, with great administrative experience and intimate knowledge of the people, the Hon'ble Mr. Smeaton, courageously advocating the protection of Indian industries before the Council of the Viceroy. "We are in the face of a serious problem," he said, "namely, to attempt to divert a large struggling half-starved population from barren agriculture to fields of possibly more lucrative occupation, and I do not see that the Government of this country should be ever squeamish in taking such steps as it thinks necessary to protect those industries in this country with which the industries of the mother-country may enter into competition." Mr. Smeaton referred to the petroleum industry of Burma, as an instance, and hoped that this new industry "would be left unembarrassed and untrammelled by any foreign systems of monopoly, and that it would be protected against invasion by those huge foreign combinations which kill individual industry, and left to work out its prosperity in freedom."*

UNEQUAL CONTEST.

It is the unequal contest going on between England and India, in the name of free-trade, that divests our whole future of hope. The trade relations between England and India are free only in a most fallacious sense of that expression. There is no freedom in them whatever. On the one side is England armed with abundant resources of every kind and wielding the most arbitrary political power which she can employ to any end or purpose without responsibility to any body but her own conscience; on the other side is India, poor and exhausted, without independence or a voice in her own affairs, without the power to influence her rulers, and without knowledge, training, or experience. Yet these two are said to compete together with perfect freedom, not for the wealth of a third country, but for the wealth of one of themselves, of the weaker of the two competitors. Such a freedom is only a mockery and a farce.

* Lord Curzon, acting in the spirit of Mr. Smeatons' suggestion, has declined to grant the application of the Standard Oil Company of America, for concessions in the working of the oil mines of Burma.

It is protection of the worst kind, in favour of the stronger party. If England could convince the world that there is a shred of logic or fairness in her contention on behalf of free-trade, she would have succeeded in persuading other countries to adopt the policy which has answered so well in her own case. Because free-trade threatens ruin to the country adopting it, countries like America and Germany, not to speak of Britain's own colonies, have persistently declined the invitation of Britain to step into her parlour.

PROTECTION IN OTHER COUNTRIES.

In all countries, where agriculture remains the chief occupation of the people, their policy of international trade is determined by a desire to add to it other industrial occupations. The Finance Minister of Russia, M. de Witte, is said to have stated it as his opinion, that the future regeneration of Russia was dependent to a great extent on her changing from her purely agricultural state of poverty, and very often famine, to an industrial state in which a very large part of the population would be relieved from the fear of famine and from disasters due to climatic causes. It was Prince Bismarck that set his foot down on the faint chances that there were of free-trade taking root in Germany. The warm advocacy of protection by successive American Presidents from Hamilton down to McKinley is well-known. The dream of some British statesmen to effect the consolidation of the Empire on a basis of common commercial interests binding together the mother-country and the distant colonies, still remains a dream; because, while Great Britain will not and dare not accept protection as a part of her international policy, the colonies firmly set their face against any idea of free-trade. Under the policy that the colonies have pursued from the very beginning, during fifty years, they have made rapid progress in wealth, in population, in commerce, and in political importance. Other countries have made similar progress under a policy of protection. The statesmen of these countries are convinced of the fallacy of applying to all the world a policy which has answered well under the exceptional conditions of England.

PROTECTION *vs.* FREE-TRADE.

Great Britain is a small country, endowed with natural facilities in her coal and iron mines, and she had, at a critical time, the wealth of India at her disposal. She is unable to provide herself with sufficient food, and is obliged to import it from other countries in exchange for her manufactures. Raw materials and food-stuffs account for about 75 per cent. of her imports, while her manufactured goods are about 75 per cent. of her total exports. This is the case in no other country in the world.

Nor is the system of protection an invention of modern statesmen. It is a survival of the old belief that, in commerce between nations, the interests are not identical. One nation sought to gain at the expense of another with whom it had commercial relations. In France, Colbert's efforts in the seventeenth century to create a system of State-directed industry and commerce accentuated this belief, and at the close of the eighteenth century restrictions became universal, and England killed the industry of India and Ireland by her high protective duties. The Napoleonic wars at the beginning of the nineteenth century unsettled the old commercial relations of nations and created jealously and hostility. The efforts of Cobden promised to bring about a change for the better, and between 1850 and 1873, France as well as Germany showed a disposition to adopt England's new policy of freedom of trade. But, the hopes thus created were shattered by the Franco-German war. The military spirit was revived; the cost of the war and subsequent military defences caused immense expenditure in both countries. Revenue was required to meet it, and the method of indirect taxation was adopted, it being least offensive and least easily perceived by the tax-payers. The plan of protective duties was resorted to, and being a means of fostering home trade and taxing luxuries instead of food, these duties were popular. Unlike England, these countries are mostly self-supporting as regards necessaries, which accounts for these duties being put up with by the people, while the duties on corn awakened the strongest opposition possible in England. Thus, the countries that import luxuries and are self-dependent in regard to their necessaries, find it not necessary to adopt free-trade; on the other hand, by taxing the imported articles of luxury, they foster home-trade, give larger employment to their capital and labour. The conditions of India resemble those of Russia and America, rather than those of England. "If a country is of vast extent and its climate and products very varied, and if it possesses minerals as well as abundance of land, such a country is most favourably situated for industrial independence; for, it has within itself resources of all kinds, and it will suffer less than others from attempts at being self-sufficing. On the other hand, the smaller the country and the more specialised its products, the greater is the advantage which it gains from contact with others. Relations of mutual interchange with countries differing economically from themselves become essential to small and populous countries, and such in an eminent degree is the case of Great Britain." *

India's conditions favourable to protection.

India is exactly the country whose conditions are favourable to a policy of complete freedom within her own limits, and protection against foreign countries. With its 1,500,000 million square miles of area and 300 millions of population, its infinite variety of climate and production, its rich soil on which every species of agricultural produce can be grown, with its practically unlimited abundance of raw materials, and its vast miner-

* Mr. Armitage-Smith, Lecturer on Economics, London.

al resources, it is a world in itself, and can afford to dispense with every foreign article either in the nature of a luxury or in that of a necessary. Within her own borders, agricultural products and manufactured articles of every description will find the markets needed, the only thing necessary being a complete freedom from restraints on transport from one part of the country to another. The United States place no restrictions on the trade between the several States, and every new territory admitted to the Union is placed on the same footing. The same principle is adopted in the Dominion of Canada, in Russia, and in Germany. Thanks to the wisdom of our British administrators, this essential condition of a flourishing state of internal trade is completely fulfilled in India. The surplus grain of Bengal can be transported to the Carnatic without restraint of any kind, the shawls of Cashmir can be sold in the palace of Mysore, the coal of Raniganj is bought and used by the Madras Railway Company, and, if Lord Curzon's proposed Exhibition at Delhi produces the effect that is desired, the ivory works of Vizagapatam will find a place in the nobleman's mansion of the Punjab. India was industrially completely self-dependent before the establishment of British rule, and so far as we can see, if all foreign imports were stopped to-morrow, India would not starve, as England might possibly starve if another Napolean should succeed in carrying out a plan of commercial blockade against that country Nor would India be deprived of what little luxury her people are now able to enjoy in the shape of foreign imports. For some time, under a system of protective duties, these luxuries will have to be purchased at higher prices—which, however, will be paid by the better classes and will not touch the masses,—and eventually it is quite possible to get most of the luxuries manufactured within the country.

British advocates of free-trade are accustomed to represent the protective policy of other countries as self-inflicted evils; but we cannot easily believe that the statesmen and thinkers of these countries are persistently blind to their own interests and fail to understand what to their British free-trade critics is so obvious. British politicians and journalists invariably predict the worst results from the protective tariffs adopted by America and other countries; but, as a fact, these tariffs have proved most wonderfully successful. McKinley's tariff on tin plates can be quoted as a striking illustration. England looks to India as the chief source of her supply of grain and raw materials. At present, she derives this supply from America, Russia, and from her colonies as well as from India. Russia supplies about 16·3 per cent. of the wheat and flour that England imports, America 55 per cent., and the colonies about 8 per cent.; most part of the rest she obtains from India. Now, as the population of these countries increases, the surplus stuff available for export will diminish, and both America and Russia might be unable to export to England the same quantity of food-stuff that they do now. In times of war, hostile motives might come into play to isolate England. Nor can the colonies be depended upon. The Australian colonies have recently declared their determined adhesion to protection. Their ambition is not to remain a great grain reserve of England. They wish manufacturing industries to develop and their policy is directed towards that end. India, on the other hand, can be handled as her mistress likes, and is, in the name of free-trade, tied to the function of raising food-stuff and raw materials for the benefit of the ruling country, though her own producers and labourers starve.

Export Duty on Corn.

The export of wheat from India to Great Britain, which fell down to a nominal quantity in the last famine, is showing signs of revival. The figures for the last five years are 1,683,543 cwts. in 1897-98, 9,336,707 cwts. in 1898-99, 5,297,767 cwts. in 1899-1900, 7,923 cwts. in 1900-01, and 3,725,040 cwts. in 1901-02 (eleven months). To the British residents of India and to Government, this change is welcome. But is it so to the millions of Indians who consume the wheat and other grains produced in this country? A superficial analysis of the figures will show how in prosperous years large quantities of wheat were exported, while, in years of adversity that followed, there was great deficiency in the food-requirements of the people. If no export had taken place in prosperous years, there would have been plenty of corn stored in different parts of the country and it would have been available to meet the pressure of demand in seasons of scarcity and famine. The prices would not have risen as they did in the recent famine years. It is true that in famine times people die, not from want of food, but from want of money to pay for their food. But in effect there is not much difference between the two. When the local food-stock is insufficient, the insufficiency is supplied by imports from distant countries. But the importation is not done without cost, and the Rangoon rice brought to the markets of Bombay must sell dearer there than in Rangoon. Thus it is that the railways, which Government spends crores every year to extend, instead of levelling down the prices, level them up everywhere in the country, and have virtually the effect of intensifying scarcity into famine. On the face of it, it does not seem to be wise to send away to foreign countries what surplus of food there may be, and, when the surplus is followed by a deficiency, to make good the deficiency by paying prices several fold dearer for imported articles Yet, this is what Government does. More than once has Government considered the question of prohibiting export of food during the prevalence of famine, and more than once has it decided against such a course. But what is wanted is, not merely the interference of Government in private trade during critical times, to stop exports temporarily, but the prevention, in view to the peculiar normal condition of the country, of exports by the imposition of duties in all years, good as well as bad. Mr. Horace Bell, a former Consulting Engineer for Railways to the Government of India, advocated this step for the reasons that I urge here.

England dependent on foreign countries.

England being dependent on foreign countries for more than 70 per cent. of her food, agriculture is not the chief industry of the people there. But, for progress in manufacturing industries, which employ almost the whole labouring population, cheap and abundant food is essential, and can be obtained only by free importation of it from other grain-producing countries. But these considerations do not hold good in the case of India. Her condition is just the reverse of that of England. India produces her own corn; and in her own markets can be sold all the produce of her soil. She has need neither to import nor to export food. On the other hand, as we have already said, she has the utmost need to store every grain of the surplus food which a prosperous year may yield. Agriculture in India is not a new industry requiring to be fostered by Government by import duties. Protection with a view to stimulating the industry is not wanted. The unlimited demand which her teeming population offers is a sufficient stimulus to it. What is needed is the prevention of the depletion of the surplus grain in good years, in view to the needs of years of drought and famine. This protection should be secured by a sufficiently high duty on all exports of corn to other countries. We are aware that

Indian wheat is chiefly exported to Great Britain, and two objections can be raised, from the British point of view against this proposal. Indian wheat will become dearer to the consumer in Britain, and depending, as she does, for the most part of her food-supply, on foreign countries including India, she cannot allow her own dependency to stop its contribution towards the wants of the ruling country. In reply, it may be observed that, though India supplies a portion of the-food stock of England, yet this portion is very small when compared with the supply received from other countries; and therefore the price of wheat will depend, among other causes, on the harvests in the countries which export to Great Britain by far the greater portion of her requirements :

Wheat imported into Great Britain in 1893-95.

From	Per cent.
Russia	16·6
Other European countries	4·7
The United States	50·3
Canada	5·2
Argentina	11·0
India	6·8
Other countries	5·4

HOW INDIA WILL PAY FOR HER IMPORTS.

Thus, India contributes only 6·8 per cent. of the whole quantity of wheat consumed by Great Britain, and amidst the larger quantities of wheat from other countries, the exported wheat of India is practically a drop and will have no influence on the wheat prices of London. Nor does the other objection hold good, viz., that in a time of war, when hostile nations may choose to stop all commerce with England, and when possibly the whole population may have to face starvation, India should be free to send to England as much food-stuff as she may be capable of sending. This, however, relates to an exceptional state of things, and there is nothing to prevent India from adopting exceptional measures to suit it. It may also be objected, how, if India does not export corn to Great Britain, will she pay for the cloth and numerous other articles she now imports from England? In the first place, the contention is not to impose duties on all exports, but only on food resources which India, facing, as she has to do, frequent bad seasons, has the utmost need to husband. What imports are necessary from Great Britain can be paid for by other articles of export. In the second place, India's imports are all more or less luxuries, while her exports are necessaries of life and raw materials of manufacture. No serious harm would happen to India if no cloth were imported from Manchester, or if the better classes of people pay more for it.

ANOTHER ARGUMENT.

There is another argument in favour of preventing the export of Indian corn to foreign countries. The export duty on coal in England has not roused the indignant protest of Free-Traders, because the coal of that country, like the copper of Spain, is limited in quantity. Each ton of English coal sent abroad leaves a diminished quantity available for use in England. Although this fact may not render necessary a policy of general protection of the trade, still a restriction of the export is demanded in the name of the common good of the nation. No exception can be taken to the desirability of the husbanding of important natural agents which cannot be manipulated to give unlimited produce whenever required. There can be no doubt that in India the growing export trade in grain, by an excessive stimulation of its cultivation, is leading to the exhaustion of superior soil and to the tillage of tracts of inferior quality. The American farmer raised successive crops of wheat without regard to the drain on the natural fertility of the land that he cultivated. The export of wheat was in fact an export of the fertility of the country. Not only was the exhaustion of the soil caused, but the export carried away from the country the manure which should return to the soil.

THE POLICY OF ENGLAND.

Now, the British Government of India would do exactly as the Government of the United States did. In all the great measures that it undertakes and in all the important policies it follows, Government has two considerations in view. It no doubt considers how its measures and policies will affect the interests of India; but to the consideration how they will affect Great Britain, more importance is attached. In the matter of controlling the trade between the two countries, the same double object underlies the policy. To give to India the benefit—as our rulers understand it—of British capital in the development of her industries, and, also, to make India the chief exporter of grain, tea, coffee, indigo and raw materials to England, constitute the chief aim of this policy. "For some forty years past," writes the author of an elementary treatise on Free-Trade, "the policy of developing the resources of India by British capital has been powerfully advocated, both in the interests of the natives and also as a means of increasing our commerce. It was maintained that India would thus become a producer of corn, tea, and other valuable crop, and would yield a profitable return on the capital sunk in her development, while she would also become a purchaser of British manufactures. This has now been partially achieved; British capital flowed to India for both private and public undertakings. Roads, railways, irrigation, planting, and cultivation have followed. By these means, and under a strong and capable government, India has enjoyed peace and prosperity. The anticipated results have only been partially realized as yet."

This is the policy of British Government in India in regard to her material development and her trade. Great Britain is the greatest manufacturing country in the world; and as she goes on extending her manufacturing industry, old markets should be improved and fresh markets found for the products of her industry. India with her 300 millions of people is a market, the like of which cannot be found in any other part of the world. Therefore, England makes the best use of it. To carry away all the grain stuff and all the raw materials that can possibly be carried away, to thrust her own articles of use and luxury on the Indian people, and to provide every possible facility for this at their expense, is the policy.

CHAPTER V.

Exploitation by Foreign Capital

Lord Curzon, in a speech which he recently made before the Bengal Chamber of Commerce, dwelt on the importance of British capital being attracted towards Indian investments. He regretted that, in spite of all that the Government of India had done towards this end, it shows no disposition to flow into this country, and added that in the near future the Government would be called upon to take steps to strengthen its hands by securing the service of experts in science and commerce. He ridiculed those that differed from him, more especially the Indian politicians who regarded as a cause of drain on India's wealth the systematic and State-aided exploitation of it by foreign capitalists. Forgetting that, not Indian politicians alone, but many persons in other parts of the world—in Great Britain as well as elsewhere,—who are no less competent than Lord Curzon himself to express an opinion on the question, take the same view and deplore the steady impoverishment of this great dependency under the economic policy that has underlain British rule in India from its first establishment, he spoke harshly of them all, and summarily dismissed the great problem of rearing the industry of India on a basis of national independence, by remarking that if Indian people would not apply to their own industries the 825 crores of rupees that lay locked up in underground cellars and in other dead investments, they deserved no better fate than the one that stared them in the face at present. There can be no more authoritative pronouncement on the side of the vested interests of British investors than this speech made by Lord Curzon towards the end of his Viceroyalty; and we propose, therefore, to examine it in some detail.

What is the purport of his speech?

The purport is, Government are doing and will do everything necessary or desirable to attract British capital to India, but if Indian capital is to be stimulated and applied to the industries of the country, the people should look out for themselves. Capital is the limit of industry, and, according to Lord Curzon, it is the British capital alone that is available and can save India. Yet British capital is singularly cantankerous. In spite of all the bribing that Indian Government resort to, it shuns Indian investments. This phenomenon has perplexed Lord Curzon and made him often sad. "I have often set myself," he told the commercial magnates that listened to him, "to ponder over the causes that have hitherto retarded our development, that make it to some eyes appear so low." What is the result of this pondering? Lord Curzon foresees that fields of investment in other parts of the world will come sooner or latter to be occupied by Britain's rivals, narrowing to an increasing extent the scope for British investment, when, by virtue of the law of gravitation, British capital will be driven to India. India will be, of course, always open; she is at the disposal of her alien rulers, and if the resources with which nature has so abundantly endowed her were not available to Britain, India might as well be a sandy desert or howling wilderness. Towards the British and the Indian capitalists he showed a difference in his attitude, truly regrettable. We shall quote the remarks of one of the most respected and sober Indian journalists, the editor of the *Indian Nation*, of Calcutta. He writes, "The fact is, European capitalists are really invited in endearing tones, and native capitalists are roundly scolded not so much for not laying out their capital on exploitation as for their impudence in throwing out expressions of jealousy at the foreign exploiter."

The Indian people have the colossal amount of nearly 825 crores—this might be for Lord Curzon's purpose, 1,000 crores—buried underground; and if a foolish people choose to dispose of their wealth in that way instead of mobilising the whole of it and applying it to the development of the industries of their country, they deserve no better fate. In order that British capital may pour into India, the benign rulers have changed the currency of the country, taking the money from the pocket of the Indian producer and putting it into that of the British merchant. In order that these merchants and the army of British officials with which India is burdened may make more money at the expense of the Indians, these latter have been taxed additionally, in consequence of the currency policy, to the extent of many crores differently computed. Towards the Chambers of Commerce, Lord Curzon's Government have been in a constant attitude of deference, apology and flattery. To the planters he has been a most ready and servicable friend; and to the non-official European residents, the fountain of his sympathy has overflown on all sides along abundant streams. In spite of such solicitude, the British capital refuses to turn India-ward. Both the Government of India and the wise men of Sir Henry Fowler's Committee expected that the currency had only to be changed, and British capital would regain confidence in Indian investments, and India's millenium would dawn. Prosperity would smile on the land, and British trade would multiply tenfold. Alas! nothing of the kind has taken place. British capital is as shy as ever, and the trade between the two countries has not increased in proportion to the growth of population.

The only true cause of this shyness of the British capital, Lord Curzon did not choose to understand. The true cause is the conviction that is growing on the minds of the British investing public of the intense and growing poverty of the country. The Indian people are in fact becoming less paying as British customers. They cannot buy good costly articles. They can buy only cheap trumpery things, which it does not pay to manufacture. The enormous cheapness of the Indian labour is no doubt an attraction. But British capitalists are now beginning to see that the Indian cheap labour is not in the long run so cheap as is imagined. Thanks to the impoverishing effect of the British rule, the Indian labourer is undergoing rapid physical deterioration. He cannot work long, and can work only in that sluggish and inefficient way in which starving people work. Government is doing its utmost to enable the British employer to exploit to his heart's content the Indian labourer. It has made stringent laws so that the British planter and the miner may extort from him the most work for the least wages. Yet Lord Curzon regrets that Government cannot do more for British capital! He regrets that the Government of India is not up to date; it "does not know everything about agriculture, commerce, emigration, labour, shipping, customs, the application of science to every form of production, the secrets of coal, iron, salt, oil, tea, cotton, indigo, jute." New posts will have to be created and new experts introduced into the administration, and they will both be done at an early date. Then British capital, driven by competition from other parts of the world, would pour into this country, and India's exploitation would be complete. The process that has begun long since, of reducing the Indian people to the lot of a race of coolies under white masters, would then reach its culmination.

Lord Curzon's criticism of the Indian view of the economic condition of the country is as unsound as it is uncharitable. For, what is his criticism? "The whole industrial and commercial world," he says, "is one great field for the tiller to till, and if the man who lives on the spot will not cultivate with his own spade, then he has no right to blame the outsider who enters it with his plough." Has he not? We deny the soundness of this policy. If a British nobleman's rich estate was neglected by his heirs, would Lord Curzon justify the neighbour or some strong man in the street entering the estate, exploiting it, and carrying away the profits, leaving the owner to his fate? And just as an occupied estate is the property of the individual owner, so does this huge estate of a large continent belong to its people. They are the ward for the time being of the British nation, who are under a solemn obligation to preserve the minor's estate intact and, training him in all possible ways to enable him to manage his estate, to hand it over to him when he attains majority and is able to manage it himself. We are aware that the unsound and unrighteous policy enunciated by Lord Curzon for the enlightenment of the Indian people is the policy which the powerful white nations are pursuing in their heartless exploitation of the coloured races throughout the world. The policy has no support whatever in righteousness or humanity. It is truly international robbery made possible and justified by brute force. But India is under

British rule, and is, therefore, not like other countries inhabited by primitive races.

Nor are Lord Curzon's analogies correct. Is he sure that England does not bewail the inroad of American capital and the seizure of her paying businesses by her dear cousins over the other side of the Atlantic ? If the flooding of England with American capital was so welcome to the Britishers, why did Lord Curzon disallow the American Oil Company from working the oil mines of Burma ? Why do the British ship-owners, and locomotive manufacturers raise a row when Americans or Germans snatch the trade from them ? Labour is capital in a sense ; and if capital can be as free as air, blow where it listeth, why do the British colonials take up an attitude of barbarous antipathy against Indian immigration ? It is true that, but for British capital, Calcutta and Bombay would be non-existent. But if these were not now existent, other cities built on entirely Indian industry and capital would be. We suppose Lord Curzon has heard of the Indian city called Delhi, and that it was once, long before the British people acquired a footing in India, at least as flourishing and wealthy as Calcutta or Bombay is now. He must have similarly heard of old Indian cities like Surat, Goa, Calicut, other ports and inland cities, that astonished foreign visitors and attracted the cupidity of foreign plunderers, by their very opulence and magnificence. No, Lord Curzon, it is to be much regretted, talked without thought in this matter. By emphasising a policy so opposed to humanity and justice, and by coolly calling those that differ from him foolish and dangerous, he has not improved his position.

It is British rule that has drained, during the long period of a century and-a-half, the wealth of India, and has made growth of capital exceedingly difficult and slow. To kill India's manufactures and to build her own industry on their ruins has been the deliberate policy of England in India. To convert India into a vast field for the cultivation of raw products and convert her people into customers for British trade and into wage-receiving labourers for British employers, has been the steady end of the philanthropic mission that England has spontaneously undertaken in India under the dispensation of an all-merciful Providence. The same policy is now pursued more effectually than ever. India is a great storehouse of cheap labour for the whole Anglo-Saxon race. That is the destiny considered most appropriate to her; and so far as England can help it, she, for her part, will refrain from leading this country away from the path to that destiny. She will teach the Indians how to cultivate their fields with cotton, jute and wheat; she will teach them how to use European tools; she will by law and executive orders make them docile to their white masters. In short, to enable them to produce raw stuff in the cheapest manner possible and to muster them in numbers before British employers as skilled and unskilled workmen on minimum wages, British rule will leave no stone unturned. But it is not its business to train Indians to manufacture their own raw materials, to enable them to grow their own capital, or to organise their own enterprise. They may be too helpless to withstand the crushing competition of British capitalists; but to discover a remedy is the Indians' look out. If they want to gain a footing, let them bring out their hidden treasure of 825 crores and make the best of it. This is the sum and substance of Lord Curzon's gracious message to the people of India, to which he has a place in his heart next only to his mother-land! Yes, next to his mother-land. How true to his word! His mother-land is the first heir to India's latent and undeveloped wealth; and Indians are at liberty to take what crumbs and pieces may be dropped by her enterprising sons!

Lord Curzon's economic fallacy.

Lord Curzon laid down as a rudimentary doctrine of economic science that, if the Indian were too ignorant or too lazy to exploit for his good and for the good of his people the rescources of his own country, a foreigner had a perfect right to seize those resources and exploit them for his individual benefit. Though this doctrine is inconsistent with his admission that "the country whose capital is self-generated and self-employed is in the strongest position," still he sees nothing wrong in individuals belonging to other countries establishing themselves in India and, with the cheap indigenous labour, raising remunerative crops on her soil, working her coal and iron mines, and digging out the gold and other valuable contents of underground deposits of wealth to carry them away bodily to their native land. He knows as well as we do, that the gold mines of Kolar, for instance, will be within the next 20 years thoroughly exhausted, that all the gold contained there will have left the shores of India, and that to the people and State of Mysore nothing will remain in these mines but the wrecks of a broken establishment of a foreign enterprise. Lord Curzon is apparently of opinion that the gold of Mysore in the pockets of rich men in London is the same as that gold remaining in the country and fructifying by investment in productive industries. It is true that for the moment Indians are unable to exploit these mines; but is it impossible that they will become fit to do so in the course of a generation or two? Considering that a generation or two are but as a minute in the life of a nation, is it not the duty of the State to keep the future of the nation in mind in the direction of its economic policy Similarly, foreign intruders working our coal and iron mines sell for their own profit the products they obtain at the expense of the ill-paid and half-starving native labourer, and carry the profits away to their native country. The profits of industry, the wealth of mines, and the savings of officials and merchants once carried away, often return to this country and are employed in further exploitation of fresh resources. It is wrong to suppose that the British capital flowing into this country is entirely the capital of the Britisher, that is to say, capital accumulated by him out of the resources of his own country or of countries other than India. It is to a large extent India's own money, accumulated and multiplied at India's own expense. England receives an annual tribute of nearly 40 millions from India, and most of these forty millions comes back and is profitably invested. Is there a more melancholy and pitiable phenomenon, presented in the history of any country in the world, than this unique process of ceaseless and self-expanding drain to which under British rule India is subject? Yet Lord Curzon contends that this heartless bleeding is not only legitimate and sanctioned by economic science, but is actually beneficial to the millions of the Indian population. India is not like Africa or other unoccupied or sparsely occupied regions in remote corners of the world, inhabited by savage primitive people, who do not multiply, who want little, who have reared no indigenous system of industry or art, who are ignorant of their own interest, and who are incapable of advance in civilization. It is possible in such regions that the intrusion of foreigners to carry away their wealth, which is not and will never be wanted by the native inhabitants, may do no harm, and may do good by placing at the service of civilization resources which must otherwise lie useless in the womb of the earth. But in India which is inhabited by hundreds of millions of people, who have in the past built up an elaborate and highly effective system of industry and art, who are growing in numbers and intelligence every year, who want, very badly want, for their own consumption, every article in the nature of a luxury or a necessary which is produced now or may be produced in future, the policy upheld by Lord Curzon must, it is obvious on the face of it, end in the most disastrous consequences. The Indian community is not a young nation settled in a large fertile country where there is a superabundance of latent wealth, but is a nation which, in consequence of climatic and political conditions, is poor, and is subject to a perennial drain of its wealth. Much of this drain is inevitable, but it is the obvious duty of the State—as an institution representing and responsible for the collective interests of the nation, its present and future interests, not only material, but moral and spiritual—to reduce this drain to a minimum and use all possible endeavours to prevent any addition to it. It is not this negative service alone that the State is called upon to render to its people, but it is also its most solemn and imperative duty to protect those interests against foreign competition and to advance them for the benefit of future generations. How Lord Curzon can believe that the present policy of British rule in India towards its industries is calculated to accomplish this end, we find it difficult to make out or believe.

Economic science as taught by English writers, by Adam Smith and his successors, is one-sided and imperfect. Their teachings were, no doubt, suited to the conditions of England; but applied to any other country in the world, they are calculated to work injurious results. Adam Smith reflected, in his "Wealth of Nations" ideas on economic reform prevalent in his time; and devoted himself to the demolition of what he believed to be erroneous doctrines which guided European Governments. From the Physiocrats of France, he inherited his prejudice against the interference of Government, and also his excessive faith in unrestricted competition, in the natural equality of all individuals, and in the right which each individual possessed to seek such enjoyments as he could acquire by his labour and skill, and, therefore, in the freedom of exchange. His conception of the social economy is essentially individualistic, the individual being treated as a purely egoistic force, working uniformly in the direction of private gain without regard to the good of others or of the community at large. Nor did Adam Smith pay due regard to the ethical side of human nature, to the fact that man should be not only rich, but also moral, that is to say, should cultivate sympathy with his neighbours, with his nation, and with humanity at large. Smith's conception has not led to unexceptionable results when applied to the inter-individual or inter-class interests of a community, and a too rigid enforcement of his principles has led to socialism and other troubles that agitate and vex so many rulers and statesmen of the Western countries. But the British rulers of India have mostly applied those principles to India in her relation to Great Britain, and to-day we see Lord Curzon gravely defending a system which pauperises one nation for the enrichment of another, as it has hitherto tended in the country of its origin to make the rich richer and the poor poorer. Lord Curzon seems to believe that the prosperity of the individual is synonymous with the prosperity of the nation, nay, that the prosperity of the foreign exploiter leads to that of the native community. He forgets that the immediate private interest of the separate members of the community will not lead to the highest good of the whole, and is frequently opposed to it. Between the individual and humanity is the nation, formed into a unity by various cementing factors. On the maintenance of the unity and progress of the nation depend the security, well-being and civilization of the individual, and private economic interests, like all others, must be subordinated to the completion and strengthening of the nationality. The true wealth of the nation consists not in the quantity of the exchange values which it possesses, but in the full and many-sided development of its productive powers. These principles have been applied by the statesmen of the continental countries and of America, and have led to marvellous results in the growth of the industrial life of those nations. If they are true in the case of these independent and self-governing countries, much more should they be true in regard to a country like India, on which is forced an order of national and international economy entirely different from the latest stage of its indigenous system, and which is menaced and injured by the dominance of the interests of the foreign nation that rules it.

No amount of foreign exploitation can permanently lift the industrial condition of India. In England, it was not the selfish efforts of the man of wealth, of "the economic man," bent on advancing his private interests at the sacrifice of his poorer neighbours, that produced her industrial revolution. It was the work of massive popular tendencies which are dominant wherever mankind is possessed of vigour and freedom. If India were to realise the future that Lord Curzon so hopefully anticipates, it could be possible only by the masses becoming imbued with this vigour and with this freedom. But under a condition which makes foreign capitalists masters of industry, and the masses drudging labourers under them, the latter being imbued with these qualities is evidently impossible. Theoretically, of course, the people of India enjoy freedom; but we deny that the relation between them and their European exploiters is one of real freedom. It is one of unfair and unequal competition. The British exploiters with their unlimited resources, with their great powers of organization, and with their political prestige, can in no sense be said to be equal competitors with the poor, backward and neglected Indians. The conditions of this so-called freedom of competition are such that they have made the latter practically helpless before their Western rivals. A full and many-sided development of the nation's productive powers cannot take place under a condition under which the profits of all great industries are swept out of the country, and the bulk of the nation either are a mass of ignorant coolies incapable of self-effort or organisation, or remain occupied in agriculture as the sole means of their livelihood. A great moral and mental stimulus is necessary to lift the nation above its present low standard. A desire for higher standards of life, for greater comforts and for a richer life, should be created. Says Sir John Herschill: "To produce a state of things in which the physical advantages of civilised life can exist in a high degree, the stimulus of increasing comforts and constantly elevated desires must have been felt by millions; since it is not in the power of a few individuals to create that wide demand for useful and ingenious applications, which alone can lead to great and rapid improvements, unless backed by that arising from the speedy diffusion of the same advantages among the mass of mankind." We ask Lord Curzon whether such a state of things can be produced under the present industrial condition of India or under its developments in the immediate future; and whether to such a state of things India has no right to aspire under the rule of Great Britain.

CHAPTER VI.

The Hoarded Wealth of India.

In the last Chapter we referred to Lord Curzon's observations on the hoarded wealth of India. He said he had seen calculations to the effect that this amounted to over 825 crores of rupees. "Whether these figures are correct or not," he added, "they represent an approximation to the truth." The data on which the calculations are based, are not made known in the speech. The *Times of India*, however, has come to the rescue of the reader. Adopting the figures of Mr. Fred. J. Atkinson and those of Mr. Clarmount Daniell's estimate of 100 crores of rupees worth of gold (including jewellery) at the beginning of the nineteenth century, and adding them to the 125 crores of silver and gold (excluding jewellery) since the commencement of that century, this journal points out, we get a total of 225 crores, which is 600 crores less than the estimate accepted by the Viceroy as approximately correct. "If, on the principle adopted above, we deduct one-half of the total value of gold in the country at the beginning of the century for ornaments, the amount is reduced to 175 crores, to which has to be added the amount of silver in the country at the beginning of the last century. As we have said above, we have no means of even roughly conjecturing what this might have been, but everything considered, and having regard to Mr. Atkinson's warning against popular exaggeration on the subject, we think it would be a safe estimate to take the gold and silver hoarded in India at the present time at about 500 crores of rupees."

Thus, according to official calculations, the value of hoarded precious metals including those in the shape of jewellery, is only about 60 per cent. of Lord Curzon's estimate. But in this estimate are included hoardings that were ever made in the country during the whole course of its long history embracing many centuries. How anybody was able to calculate the value of India's hoarded wealth for centuries,—and Mr. Clarmount Daniell's calculations extend over 25 centuries,—passes our understanding. The wealth of India in any movable shape was on numerous occasions carried away by foreign invaders from time to time. There is no record of the amounts thus carried away out of the country. Again, precious metals used to be hoared by rulers, who entrusted their secrets to one or two confidants. The ruler and his confidants often were either suddenly killed in a revolution, or driven away as exiles, with the result that all knowledge of the hoards and the clue as to where they were hidden were lost for ever. So far as the object with which Lord Curzon lamented the locking up of so much wealth is concerned, or any practical object whatever, such hoards are as useless as any of the contents of undiscovered mines in the country. There is another fact that detracts from the value of these calculations. All jewellery is liable to rapid deterioration in value on account of its wear and tear. The amount of jewellery as estimated at the beginning of the 19th century, cannot be the same after one hundred years. It would hardly be worth half its value. If due weight were given to these considerations, the accuracy of even the less extravagant figure adopted by the Bombay journal would be open to doubt.

In his evidence before the Herschell Commission of 1887, Sir David Barbour, a former Finance Minister of India, gave it as his opinion that the hoarding of gold and silver in India, since the year 1835, approached £300,000,000 ; that is, this was the total during a period of about 50 years. The average annual hoarding, therefore, is 6 millions or 6 crores of rupees. The classes of the Indian population that are too poor to use ornaments of any value are calculated to be about one-third of the total population of India. The number, therefore, among whom the hoarding has amounted to 6 crores every year, does not exceed 200,000,000 or 20 crores roughly. If then 20 crores of people convert silver and gold into ornaments, that would give about 5 annas a year per individual for ornamental purposes. But, considering that the average of 6 crores includes gold as well as silver withdrawn from circulation, the average of 5 annas is more than the actual hoarding of every individual throughout the country! Sir David Barbour made the interesting statement that, besides large quantities of silver brought to the mints for coinage during periods of famine, in the years of the great famine in Madras and Bombay, a large amount of gold was sent to England and was evidently ornaments melted down. In his evidence before the Currency Committee of 1898, Mr. J. G. O'Conor said that there was comparatively little gold hoarded in India, and that what hoards of that metal there might be were those of the ruling chiefs. So far as jewellery went, he pointed out, nearly 30 per cent. of the population were too poor to afford it ; and taking the total population who could do so to be two hundred millions, and the imported silver to be 40 ounces a year in recent decades, they did not give a large average for ornamental purposes.

The jewellery of the middle class is partly of gold, whereas that of the poorer classes, which is all their savings, is entirely of silver. Sir David Barbour was of opinion that the amount of silver hoarded in all forms was decidedly greater than the amount of gold similarly hoarded, and that the silver hoards consisted of coins as well as of bullion. This last opinion was not shared by Mr. O'Conor. For, he said before the Currency Committee that it was ascertained that most of the silver imported into India immediately after the closing of the mints, and absorbed among the population, was converted into jewellery. "Before the closing of the mints, practically all the silver imported, with the exception of about 4 per cent., passed into the mints and was coined. Then the assumption used to be that at least half of that remained in the currency as coined silver, and the other half was melted down. But it looks now, judging from these figures, as if that inference was not quite correct, and that a very much larger portion of the rupees that were coined must have been melted down into ornaments. I do not believe that any of these imports of silver have been got into hoard."

Mr. F. C. Harrison's figures are different from those of Sir David Barbour. They are, as he gave them before the Herschell Committee of 1893, 510 crores, being the amount of silver in every form in India; of which 66½ crores (in 1893) were in active circulation, 50 crores hoarded in the form of rupees, and 300 crores, roughly speaking, held in the form of bullion, obsolete coin and ornaments. Mr. Harrison also calculated that the quantity of gold in India was about 180 millions sterling, which, added to 300 crores of silver hoards, yields a total much smaller than Lord Curzon's figure. If then, as a fact, the hoarded silver wealth of India amounted to 300 crores, it is very hard that such a vast possession of the bulk of the population should be arbitrarily depreciated in value on account of the currency policy of the Government. Lord Curzon who scolded the people for hoarding their "talents" did not think it necessary to justify the policy that reduced the value of these hoards by more than 33 per cent.

The depreciation of the value of these savings is not only a loss to the people, but is a serious disadvantage to the trade of the country which largely depends on the currency. A short memorandum was placed before the Herschell Committee of 1893 by Mr. F. C. Harrison on this subject. Therein he said:

It is often urged that a successful attempt to raise the value of the rupee by making it scarce will seriously injure the peasant, in that his bullion will be depreciated. I have not the time to write at length upon this aspect of the question, but I may point out some facts which are of some importance in this connection.

(a) The Coinage at the Calcutta and Bombay mints during the last 20 years does not fall much short of 130 crores, whereas the receipts into the same mints of country silver and ornaments are less than 5 crores of rupees. In other words, such receipts do not form 4 per cent. of the total.

Too much stress must not be laid upon the smallness of this percentage. The amount of country silver and ornaments tendered varies from year to year, and the percentage to the receipts, is considerably greater in time of famine, *e.g.*, in Bombay in three years, 1877-78 to 1879-80, about 3-30 crores were tendered; in Calcutta, for the last 30 years, the largest amount tendered in one year was 6½ lakhs.

(b) In my first memorandum I have estimated the silver in India to be about 510 crores. Of this about 166½ crores is in active circulation; 343½ crores remain to be accounted for. Of this considerably less than 50 crores is hoarded in the form of rupees. Roughly speaking, it may be said that 300 crores may be held in India in the form of bullion, obsolete coin, and ornaments.

In Madras 1822-23 was a famine year, and the country bullion (silver) brought to the mint was 92½ lakhs.

The intimate connection between the currency and trade in India and the effect of the depriving of bullion of its convertibility into coin, were well pointed out by Mr. David Yule in his evidence before the Fowler Currency Committee. Alluding to the cry of lack of loanable capital, he pointed out that so long as silver bars or ornaments were convertible into rupees, those reserves supplied and invited funds into the interior; and he described how this ready convertibility gave confidence to the thrifty portion of the population, also facilities for the money-lenders. But since these funds in the shape of rupees were made by the Act of the State into "dead metal difficult of sale," there had been, as Mr. Yule computed, "a loss of loanable capital to the extent of 501 crores of rupees." Whatever might be the opinion as to this amount, he went on to point out that the effect of depriving them of the use of their savings had been to drive them (the people) into the clutches of the money-lenders. In turn, these retail bankers had "become anxious about their outstandings," and were "refusing to make advances to pay for seed and cattle." The first effect of this was to drive the village banker's spare funds into the presiding towns—not for trade purposes, but to be invested for safety, in gold or silver bullion, the trade use being thus lost to the country. And Mr. Yule considered that this lack of convertible currency was driving trade in the interim into a state of barter, which "is a menace to the export as well as the import trade of India."

Lord Curzon scolded the educated classes of Indians for their perversity in regard to the industrial exploitation of India. He was most astonished that "those who own this (hoarded) wealth, who tie up their talents in a napkin and bury them underground, are never so vocal as when they are denouncing the introduction of British capital into India to fill up the gap which their own timidity or indifference has let open." What a mistake for a Viceroy to make! It is not the class that are most vocal that hoard wealth or "tie up their talents in a napkin and bury them underground." Those that do this are entirely different. The chief sinners are the Maharajas and Rajas, but not the educated classes. These latter, no doubt, are guilty to some extent in converting a portion of their income into jewellery. But this all classes of Indians, except the very lowest, do. It is intended, in the case of the poorer classes more especially, as an investment to be turned to use in times of difficulty. During famine times the poorer classes sell off their silver ornaments, and even the more well-to-do classes dispose of their gold jewels. The Indian people may be said to be more fond of ornaments and display than other civilized nations are; but there can be no doubt that, in the minds of foreign observers, this weakness on the part of our people appears in exaggerated magnitude.

All nations indulge in luxuries which are of an unproductive nature, and we do not believe that a careful observation will establish that, in this manner, Indians waste practically more of their wealth than other nations. It is unreasonable to expect the people of this country to discard to a greater extent than other human communities do, personal show, a desire for which seems to be ingrained in nature. In the case of the better classes, investment in jewellery is chiefly of gold, and is prompted not only by a fondness for show, but by a sense of one of the evils of the Hindu joint family system. The earnings of a member of an undivided family are considered to be a part of its common stock, in which the co-parceners have a claim for equal shares; and in order to obviate this claim, the earning member, instead of converting his savings into tangible property or into other productive investments, is content to turn them into jewellery, which is the personal property of the wearer and on which the other members can advance no claim. Jewels also serve as ready securities for small amounts borrowed.

In illustration of the exaggerated notions in the popular mind regarding the value of the hoarded wealth in certain places, the *Times of India* quotes Mr. Atkinson as follows : "It is, however, certain that the popular idea is a very exaggerated form of the truth, and the enormous hoards that are said to exist are very frequently, as has often been proved, mere efforts of the imagination." He instanced the case of the late Maharajah Scindia, who had been reported to have hoarded an almost incredible-amount ; but when he died in 1889, his hoard was found to amount to four crores only. Some years back, a man represented to be the wealthiest individual in the North-Western Provinces, was said to have hoarded at least ten crores of rupees. On his death, under half a crore was found. These are two instances out of many. "The fact is, after a certain point, the popular imagination is apt to multiply lakhs to crores and thousands to lakhs." Nor does the official mind seem to be free from this tendency. We have seen that Lord Curzon himself has shown it. Mr. Atkinson and Mr. Daniell, with all their care to avoid exaggeration, seem to us liable to it.

The habit of hoarding had its origin in the misgovernment of former times. But as the people now get accustomed to a settled and constitutional form of government, they would see the folly of hoarding their savings and would be more willing to seek a safe and profitable investment for them. That the old habits of the people are changing, there are proofs to show. Investments in the post office savings banks are increasing, and Indian capitalists are coming forward to an increasing extent to invest their savings in remunerative industries. It is assumed that the habits of the people of India do not change. In spite of the tendency for the habit of hoarding to diminish among the upper and more intelligent classes, Sir David Barbour was of opinion that among the great mass of the people that tendency was absent. I do not know that it is so. As I have said, there is very little hoarding of silver among them, all the savings being turned into ornaments.

This they do because they do not know how else they can dispose of them to their best advantage. The pittance that they are able to save at a time cannot be remunera-tively invested. I believe an extensive system of village banks will arrest this tendency. The post office savings banks do not offer sufficient inducement to these people to invest their small savings in them. Rural banks offering somewhat higher rates of interest will prove successful. That the masses are not reluctant to put by their small savings in view to future use, is evident from the growing popularity of mutual benefit societies in Southern India. The most remarkable feature of Indian enterprise during the last half of 1902, as disclosed by the returns of Joint Stock Companies registered during that period, is the number of these societies started in Madras. These number nearly 40, with a nominal capital of over Rs. 20 lakhs. The *nidhis*, as they are called, are not, properly speaking, Joint Stock Companies at all. This is a primitive method of co-operative credit when compared with the Raiffeisen and other European systems, and has been found to be liable to abuse. But its popularity shows that the people of India are quite ready to adopt co-operative methods when they see they are to their advantage, and the *nidhis* might well be used as a step to a more enlightened form of credit. Another lesson which might be drawn from the statistical statement is the need for some law under which such Associations could be registered, for the Companies Act is plainly unsuited for the purpose.

CHAPTER VII.

Organization of Credit.

THERE is abundance of natural materials all over the country, on the surface of the earth as well as underneath in its bosom, from which wealth might be made. Still, such materials, though by all laws of nature and by the traditions of human history they belong to the people and ought to be utilised by them for their own benefit, are turned into wealth by foreign capitalists, and the most part of it is carried away from the country. Of such a lamentable inversion of nature, there are no doubt political causes, and to a large extent we have no alternative but to submit to the results of their operation. But, making due allowance for these, it is necessary to inquire whether there are not other causes, not of a political nature which at present we are unable to control, but of a nature for which we as a people are alone answerable. It is usual amongst our writers and speakers to regret the absence of large accumulated capital which, in the hands of a limited section of society, might sustain industries, and to satisfy themselves that, having expressed this regret, they have accounted fully for the industrial prostration of the country.

The orthodox idea is that the three factors of wealth are Land, Capital, and Labour. But, as the late Duke of Argyll well pointed out, land, in this sense, means not merely the surface or the interior of the earth, but the whole earth, air and sea, and also all the manifest and latent powers of nature, including heat, light and electricity. Similarly, labour includes not merely the active exercise of the muscular power of man, but his whole internal nature, such as intelligence, skill, power of co-operation, enterprise, ambition, and so forth. Capital itself is not a separate entity in nature. It is the storage of wealth, already acquired, often intangible and usually lying scattered in atoms and small units. Looked at in this sense, there is in our country plenty of capital which has only to be gathered and organized into a certain state when it will be capable of being utilised to supply man with articles of pleasure and utility. The utilisation of another factor of wealth—land—is no more subject to restrictions from political or other causes against our people than it is against the politically dominant class, and we have seen that, in its undeveloped form, wealth exists in abundance. In order, therefore, that India might acquire more productive wealth than it possesses at present, she has to cultivate and make proper use of the third factor, her capacity for labour.

It will not be denied that this capacity for labour exists in sufficient plenty to enable us to start on a career of wealth-making, which will grow and expand at each step taken in advance. So far as muscular labour goes, it is cheap and abundant and is freely exploited by European adventurers. But, taking the word in its wider sense—to mean intelligence, skill, providence, and certain other moral and mental qualities,—we are aware that our people are by no means poor. It is only necessary to get these qualities, this full capacity for labour, infused and vivified with certain other qualities in which the Indian people are deficient. An able writer writing on economic topics in the columns of *Capital* (of Calcutta), observes: "Considering that the natives are not lacking in labour, skill and intelligence, how is it that they so seldom produce a *combination* of these qualities, such as to raise the possessor to a position of authority or opulence? We can only conclude that it is want of individualism, a want which is more marked in the East than in the West of India."

Mr. Murray, a writer in the same journal, in a pamphlet recently issued by him, dwells at some length on the practical absence of co-operative credit in India and traces it to the social and racial peculiarities of the people. The productive employment of money, in his view, represents an advanced stage of national sentiment where the individual feels that his interests are bound up with the interests of the community, and that whatever advances the latter is calculated to advance the former. "The natives of India," he writes, "are still behind the greater part of the civilized world in respect of banking, chiefly because they have not yet evolved the sentiment above-mentioned. The idea of community in anything outside the sphere of their several sects is still in some measure repugnant to them. This offspring of insensate religious bigotry is less evident in money than in social matters, but even the cosmopolitanism of commerce has not yet eliminated the sectional spirit which has hitherto retarded among them the growth of the banking system which has done so much to increase the wealth of Western nations." From this sweeping indictment Mr. Murray excludes the Parsees, "some liberal-minded Mahomedans and a few enfranchised Hindus," and, in a broader view, the West as compared with the East of India. Commenting on this, the *Times of India* objects to Mr. Murray attributing to religious feeling what is essentially an economic sentiment, and observes that, as a matter of fact, some of the keenest of the commercial classes in India retain to this day religious prejudices which, from a Western point of view, must be regarded as narrow and exclusive.

Whether the sentiment is of a moral or economic nature, its existence is lamentable, and is the cause of large amounts of wealth that can be made to grow and fructify by productive investments, lying idle. The Hindus are by no means averse to the pleasures of wealth. In spite of the passionate appeals of their religion to them to be absorbed in spiritual culture, but not in the delusive and degrading pleasures of the world, they have as much weakness for these as any race in the world. But as the result of the general degradation of the nation by centuries of foreign rule and by the tyranny of priestcraft, they have become ignorant, superstitious and wanting in enterprise. Their belief in alchemy and astrology and their readiness to discover hidden treasures anywhere as if they were the products of underground mines, and to bring them out by magic, and animal—alas! sometimes, human—sacrifices also show that they would have all the enjoyments of wealth without deserving them by hard work and enterprise.

Individualism, self-confidence, or force of character, is the element which is wanting to leaven and invigorate social life and to bring into organized activity the labouring capacity that is in latent abundance. In the conditions of her by-gone times India was prosperous and happy. While other nations were poor and in a backward industrial state, India attracted the world by her opulence due to flourishing industries. But Western nations evolved fresh conditions which they met with a spirit of enterprise and progress, whereas India remained stationary and easily succumbed to the ambition and greed of foreigners. Still, modern Indians are not altogether wanting in some of the essential qualities of wealth-making. Desire for wealth and thrift can be seen in the savings of the people deposited in banks, and in investments in small industries, and in petty trades. As individuals, working for themselves on a humble scale, interested in their own well-being or in the well-being of their own caste or relatives, our wealth-making propensities are active enough. But this selfish and sectional nature of our sympathies partly contributes to our failure to turn to full account the natural facilities that face us all round and invite us in vain to organized exertions on a large scale. Individual well-being and national well-being are interdependent, and in proportion as the latter is neglected, the prospect of individual well-being is restricted. Similarly, the prosperity of an individual nation depends on the ability it shows to realise the conditions under which the whole community of the progressive nations of the world pursue their career and accumulate wealth. Nations are no longer isolated and self-contained units as they were in former times. And as the writer in *Capital* observes, "the world, linked up as it is now by rapid communications of steam and telegraph, cannot exist in sections. We must join the universal throng or perish in solitude."

Realising the full effect of this great principle of co-operative exertion, we should try to bring into a working union the different elements of labouring capacity in different individuals. In other words, an extensive system of mutual confidence should be brought about. It is this system of mutual confidence that is called *Credit*, which is the principal accumulator of wealth in every country. Credit is self-reliance and mutual trust,—qualities which our social institutions unfortunately do not encourage. Left to themselves and their natural instincts, our people will, as a rule, prefer a life of retirement and pious *Karma.* Instances are well known of Hindus of high culture and worldly sympathies, preferring in their later years worship and contemplation to a participation in the activities around them. We do not say a word against this tendency—generally so elevating and inspiring. But let us not forget that we owe a duty to our fellow-creatures, and to discharge this duty honestly and with devotion is as acceptable a service to God as any other meritorious way of spending time. Millions of God's creatures starve and are disease-stricken before our eyes; nowhere has the condition of man ever called more loudly or more piteously for prompt help. It behoves us to do our best to assuage the suffering, if we cannot enehance the happiness, of these poor creatures.

Other conditions of our economic progress being what they are, our first duty and effort should be to study and develop this system of credit, which will bring the small, scattered and lifeless atoms of wealth into organized and living capital capable of infinite expansion, and stimulating, training and enlarging our wealth-making capacity. In modern times, credit has largely replaced money as the circulating medium, and is availed of to a marvellous extent by means of joint stock banks in Western countries. By means of such banks, credit has become in those countries the most effective and economical of all circulating media, and the countries where this system largely prevails are now the wealthiest and most progressive in the world. It cannot be denied that the full importance of this system is beginning to be understood in this country; and, among the people of Western India, it is bearing striking fruit. But even there, the system has to be studied and developed further.

A certain system of banking is not unknown to the people of India. From time immemorial, there has been a large and influential class of usurers. They served as bankers as well as money-lenders, and though, as is their lot everywhere in the world, in India also they were looked upon with jealousy and dislike by the people and sometimes were oppressed by the rulers, still to these latter they were often extremely servicable, and to the people they rendered themselves indispensable. Indeed, the practice of individuals receiving deposits as well as giving loans is very ancient in this country. The great Hindu law-giver, Manu, ordains : "A wise man should make a deposit with a person of good family, of good conduct, acquainted with law, a speaker of truth, possessing numerous relations, wealthy and honourable." That the receiver of deposits answered, as a rule, to this description, we cannot say. But though it is only too probable that the savings of many wise as well as foolish men were never returned, the system seems to have suited the comparatively primitive conditions. The system still exists, and in many places large savings are deposited with money-lenders who have a reputation for solvency and honesty, and who pay smaller rates of interest to the depositors than those they receive from their debtors.

No better system could have been perhaps evolved in those days. The social as well as the industrial conditions of the country did not require the modern system of co-operative credit or joint stock companies. In the days when personal wants were few and simple, when industry was mainly domestic and trade extremely localised, the need for large capitals was not apparent. The very use of coined money was limited, as is evident from Manu prescribing the rates of interest in the case of deposits consisting of grain or cattle. The artizan and the trader pursued their business on their own account, and though in ancient and mediæval India there was a large trade with foreign countries, the system of joint stock companies seems to have been unknown. Latterly, it may be believed, that the restrictions of caste, the immobility of the people generally, either within the limits of their country or abroad, the narrowness of feeling and interest fostered by a decaying state of society, rendered impossible the growth of a spirit of mutual confidence and co-operation.

In the principal towns, more especially in the capitals of Native States, rich bankers live. They have sometimes a number of branches in other towns, and carry on business on a large scale. They lend money to people on personal or more substantial securities, and form an important factor in supplying the trade with the necessary capital. But they curtail their own usefulness as bankers by the high rates of interest they demand. They do not keep sufficient money in reserve for the accommodation of their customers in times of need. They are also less reliable than a corporate bank, because the customers have to deal with an individual who is subject to greater vicissitudes and risks than a body. Moreover, the Bannia banker is useless, so far as the object of collecting together the exceedingly small sums kept in a large number of hands, goes. And it is in that shape that the major portion of the capital exists in this country. It would be a very desirable departure if the individual Hindu bankers could be persuaded to amalgamate their capitals and establish a bank as a Joint Stock Company. The existence of a large number of banks in all parts of the country is essential for the growth of capital, and considering how the industrial regeneration of India mainly depends on this necessary condition being satisfied, there is reason to hope that such institutions will sooner or later spring into existence. A large portion of the capital and the deposits of the existing Anglo-Indian banks which finance the foreign trade of the country is the money of the Indian people. They have also nearly 2 crores of rupees in the Post Office Savings Banks. There are besides indigenous institutions, of the nature of Mutual Benefit Societies, that work with large paid up capitals. These should be enough to constitute the initial capital of banks established in the interior of the country entirely for the purpose of helping and encouraging internal trade and indigenous industries.

There is no reason wh y the State should not liberally subsidise these institutions. We shall see further on how the Anglo-Indian banks in the Presidency towns are helped by the Government who deposit a portion of their cash balances, to the amount of about 2 or 3 crores, in these banks, and how these public deposits, that is the deposits of the taxpayers' money, form the chief portion of their funds. If to do so is necessary in the interest of India's foreign trade, to help enterprises such as we refer to, is equally necessary in the interest of the internal trade and industry of the country. It would be too obstinate an adherence of the Government to an economic creed which has never taken root in any country except England and which even there is rapidly losing ground, tc feel squeamish in the transgression of the orthodox limits to Government interference, in the face of a serious national want. The last Famine Commission, presided over by Sir Antony Macdonnel, recommends a loan of moderate amount by the State to the banks that are to come into existence when the scheme of agricultural banks is put into operation. In India, most of the loanable capital is in the chests of the village money-lenders. They have always been an essential feature of our village system. Of all people in a country, the agricultural classes are least able to command cash whenever they want it. More especially it is the case in India. Agriculture is not a commercial occupation. It is not rich Dukes and Earls or capitalists that cultivate lands as a means of investment. The crops are raised, not for sale, but for consumption. The portion which is sold is chiefly sold for the sake of the cash required to meet the demands of the State. In many villages this continues almost the only money transaction of the people. The wages are yet, in the rural parts, mostly paid in kind. Barter, but not money, is the medium of bargain. As a rule, therefore, the cultivator is not much in need of money. When he wants it, he either raises a loan from the village money-lender, or sells away his silver ornaments. Anyhow, the money-lender is as necessary a part of the village system as the headman or the accountant. Until he is replaced by a simple system of credit on behalf of the tax-payer, his business will flourish.

Any means by which the cultivator can be made less dependent on the professional money-lender will tend to the diversion of the loanable capital from the village to the town. It is understood that the establishment of agricultural banks will not have the effect of driving away the village usurer altogether. If the Government of India adopt the suggestion of the last Famine Commission to limit the objects for which these banks are to make loans to those of a strictly agricultural and reproductive character, there will still remain a tolerably wide scope for the business of the money-lender, in the demands for accommodation to meet domestic wants such as marriage, &c.,

or even for maintenance. But, in that case, the security that the borrowing peasant can offer will be much diminished in amount and value ; and higher rates of interest will have to be paid. This may possibly lead to the practice of greater thrift on the part of the villager, and to a curtailment of demands for loans. Or it may make him reckless and pay much higher rates of interest than he does at present to make up for the insufficient security he is able to give. Anyhow, it is extremely probable that the establishment of village banks will break the backbone of the Sowcar. If he is wise, he will come forward to finance the banks that are to be established. The Famine Commission suggest that central banks should be established in the districts to finance the village banks. In those European countries where the system of agricultural banking has taken root, such an arrangement prevails. But in India, the Commission observe, "there is no hope, in the beginning at all events, that these central banks or Joint Stock Companies will come into existence." They suggest, therefore, the creation of such local agencies. If the first efforts to create them, they add, be not successful, as they may not be, there should be no objection to the State lending its aid to finance experimental village banks. But, in all likelihood, in many places it will be found possible to establish central banks, or such of them as are already in existence may be utilised for the purpose in view.

"In the tract of country to be served by village banks," say Sir Henry Macdonnel's Famine Commission, "there doubtless will be found influential landlords, merchants and others who, apart even from their desire to take part in a movement for the public good, will find it to their interest to lend their aid. It will be possible to organise these gentlemen into a society for the purpose not only of providing funds for financing the village banks, but also for the purpose of stimulating their formation and guiding their action. The money may be subscribed in shares, each of small amount, and bearing interest, say, at 4 per cent. per annum. Such a Society should be called the Organization Society; and should there be any difficulty in subscribing the requisite capital, there is no reason why, to begin with, the Society should not borrow the amount from Government." The village Sowcar will not be unwilling to join such an organization. He is not always the heartless harpy that he is represented to be. Recently, in the Central Provinces, through the intervention of Government and patriotic private citizens, the Sowcars willingly remitted large portions of their loans to the peasants.

In the Presidency of Madras, there will not be the same need as in other provinces to start these Organization Societies. The system of "Nidhis" or Mutual Benefit Funds is well-understood and is popular. In many places they are already in existence and are under the direction of the most intelligent and influential classes of the local residents. Their funds are constituted partly by deposits, but mostly by the paid up subscriptions of the shareholders; and from these funds are loans made at a moderate rate of interest, as a rule between 6 and 9 per cent., only to the shareholders. If the paid up subscriptions of the borrowing shareholder are sufficiently large in amount, that is regarded as security for the loan made; if not, the borrower is required to offer substantial security in the shape of immovable property or of jewels. But if a shareholder, merely because he is such, is given loans on substantial securities, there is no reason why outsiders, who are not shareholders, should not be accommodated on the same condition. The rules of these Societies can be slightly modified so as to make this departure possible, when these Benefit Societies, which are already doing considerable good by stimulating thrift and providence among the people, will finance the village banks. The directors of these Societies are generally men in touch with the borrowing classes. They will be so, especially when their Societies are established in the smaller towns amidst a cluster of villages. There is of course need for banks in aid of rural industries as well as in aid of agriculture. This double purpose is served within a limited sphere by the Mutual Benefit Societies already referred to. But their sphere should be enlarged and public confidence in them strengthened, by special legislation granting them privileges and guaranteeing periodical official audit and a limited official control.

CHAPTER VIII.

How India's Foreign Trade is Financed

PERHAPS it is not generally known that the foreign trade of India, which is almost entirely in the hands of Europeans, is financed mainly by the people and tax-payers of India. The various banks established in the capital cities and in some district stations and directed by Europeans, are the sources from which the merchants draw their money. There are the three Presidency Banks (Bengal, Bombay and Madras) and the Joint Stock Banks whose offices are located in India, namely, the Allahabad Bank, the Alliance Bank of Simla, the Bank of Calcutta, the Bank of Upper India, the Commercial Bank of India, the Oudh Commercial Bank of India, and the Punjab Banking Company. There are then the other class of Joint Stock Banks, known as Exchange Banks, whose head offices are located outside India, *e.g.*, the Chartered Bank of India, Australia and China ; the Comptoir National d' Escompte de Paris ; the Delhi and London Bank ; the Dentsche Asiatische Bank ; the Hong-Kong and Shanghai Banking Corporation ; and the National Bank of India.

This list, though almost exhaustive, omits one or two banks very recently established or abolished some time ago. The total capital of all these banks amounts roughly to 14 millions sterling. The foreign trade of India amounts roughly to 145 millions sterling, so that the total banking capital is under 10 per cent. of the value of the imports and exports. Of the joint Stock Banks of the United Kingdom; the total subscribed capital in 1897 was 267 millions sterling, and the total foreign trade about 814 millions sterling, so that the banking capital was about 32 per cent. of the foreign trade, thus presenting a striking disparity with the low figure of 10 per cent. in India. Not only is the total banking capital small relatively to the foreign trade which has to be financed, but compared with the banking capital of the United Kingdom, it is also of slow growth. The internal trade as well as the foreign trade of India, more especially the former, has rapidly grown of late, but in proportion to this growth the banking capital of the country has not increased. Besides their capitals, the banks take deposits which form an important element in their finance. The total amount of these deposits has within the last thirty years increased rapidly. In the year 1899 it was nearly 21 crores; that is to say, as much as the total amount of the capital of the banks.

These deposits are received from two sources, from Government and from private persons. The amount deposited by Government is, for obvious reasons, more or less fixed, being between 2½ and 3 crores; but the total amount deposited by private persons in the various banks is no less than 18 crores, of which 36 per cent. is in the non-Presidency banks. Besides these deposits, there is the additional facility placed at the disposal of the import and export merchants of India by the peculiar system in which the Government of India pay up their sterling obligations in London,—obligations which amount to 18 millions a year. The system consists in remittances to London being effected by exports from India, for the requirements of the Home Treasury, in excess of those needed for the settlement of the rest of the account between India and the external world. The Secretary of State for India receives what amount he wants from London merchants by drawing bills on the Indian Treasury for the same amount. These bills are paid on presentation by the Government of India to the agents sending exports to London. So that, to the extent of these 18 millions a year, the Government of India are the bankers of the export merchants. If the Government were at liberty to speculate on the exchanges, the merchants in India would have to keep more money in their banks, instead of which, under the existing system, they are in a position to utilise the cash balances of the Government of India in their various Reserve Treasuries in Calcutta, Bombay and Madras, in their District Treasuries, and in the Presidency Banks and their branches. The total Government balances in India vary from year to year, and have within the past 10 years ranged between 15 and 25 crores. The amount in 1900-01 was 15,89,841,715. Of this amount, about 2½ to 3½ crores are deposited in the Banks, the remainder being kept in the Government's own Treasuries. What service the balances of the revenues of the Government render to the foreign trade of the country is seen from the constant cry raised by the merchants to deposit more of these balances in the banks than 2½ or 3½ crores, as is the case at present. Of course, the balances of the Government are the proceeds of the taxes paid by the people, and a considerable proportion of the private deposits is similarly the money of the inhabitants of this country, European as well as Indian.

We have said that within recent years private deposits have increased by leaps and bounds. This increase is the result of the increasing amount deposited in the banks not merely by individuals,—by those that have money to deposit after their current expenditure is met—, but also by business associations who keep their money there for safe custody. What proportion is contributed by European residents and what by Indian depositors, we have no means of knowing; but to suppose that one-fourth of the total private deposits is the money of the Indians would not be wrong. In other words, in the various banks established mainly in European interests and directed by persons belonging to that community, the Indian people have no less than 5 crores of rupees deposited. Now, the question arises, whether all these five crores should necessarily be deposited in these banks, and if there were banks working mainly in the interests of he Indian people and directed by Indian gentlemen, this amount could not be deposited there. Could not the Government themselves deposit a portion of their balances in these Indian banks, were they in existence, as well as in the Presidency Banks, and their branches? We do not forget that it is the interest of the Government of India to do everything possible to stimulate export trade, so that the demand in London for remittances to India or for bills on the Government here, might increase. If the demand increases, the Secretary of State will be able to obtain better rates for his bills. That is to say, he will get more sterling money from London merchants as the equivalent of his silver money he may offer for sale. But there is no reason why out of the total deposits, Government and private, of about 21 crores, the portion of the former should not be 2 crores instead of 3, and the Indian banks should not get the benefit of the remainder of the amount which the Government of India find it convenient to spare for the purpose of helping the trade of the country. Adverting to the proposal recently pressed on the Government of India for the establishment of an amalgamated Central Bank in India, a proposal which has since been abandoned on the ground of its being impracticable in the present circumstances of this country, Sir James Westland said in a minute he placed before the Currency Committee in 1899: "The truth is that in India where it is too much the habit to look to Government for every thing, it seems not unnatural to expect the Government to finance not only the administration of the country, but its trade and commerce also. Accordingly when commerce finds a deficiency of available funds, the cause of the deficiency is sought for, not in the scarcity of the banking capital, but in some action of the Government, which is expected, with resources that are often barely sufficient to meet the financial requirements of its own administration, to supply also all that is wanted for the movements of two hundred crores of imports and exports."

With the help of the Government money, the banks are able to lend, and merchants to borrow, at cheaper rates of interest. If the Government were to withdraw their deposits, there would be less money to lend, and the rate of interest would rise. On the other hand, if the Government were to adopt the suggestion of the banks and place at their disposal all the 25 crores of the public balances, there would be more loanable capital, and the rate of interest would decrease. Cheap money is an advantage to merchants, and the British exporter in India is thus placed at an advantage in his competition with his rivals of other countries in the markets of London. In the judgment of those that do not look upon the merciless foreign commercialism of India as the Divine dispensation for her salvation, the State thus financing the foreign trade appears objectionable. It is very much like a bounty on foreign exports, which take away almost the whole raw materials and much of the food-stuff produced in the country.

There is another aspect in which the question can be looked at. According to a Parliamentary return of 1892, the salaries, pensions, and allowances paid to Europeans employed in India amounted to £10,274,246. This does not include salaries below £ 1,000 a year, nor allowances to Europeans who have retired from Indian service, nor the pay of soldiers, policemen, railway employees drawing less than £100 a year. Nor does this amount of 10 millions and odd represent the money drawn by Englishmen from India as profits on their various commercial and industrial enterprises. Calculating these latter to be another 10 millions—the amount is very likely more,—the total amount of money taken away from this country and added to the capital of the industrial classes of the United Kingdom, is not less than 20 millions a year. What becomes of this money ? A large proportion of it finds investment in one or another of the industries and trades carried on in India by Englishmen. Thus, the system of the East India Company which invested the revenues derived from the taxes of the country in the purchase of exports on its own account, is reproduced in the present day ; only the investment includes wider resources and is manipulated by a company consisting of a much larger number of men and imbued with less responsibility than the East India Company was.

CHAPTER IX.

Artizans, &c.

BETWEEN the large section of the population who derive their subsistence from agriculture and the people who live on their daily wages, there are large classes engaged in non-agricultural occupations. Some are mere professional people, such as barbers, fishermen, &c., who get remuneration for the services they render to the community. These are on the same footing as lawyers, medical men and public servants who render certain service to society and receive remuneration. These do not contribute to the material wants of the people. But a much larger section is constituted by artizans and mechanics, who supply material substances to the public and who are reckoned to constitute 18½ per cent. of the total population of this Presidency. Of this percentage, about 6 per cent. of the total population are those that prepare vegetable and animal food. drink, condiments, narcotics, &c., &c. The next numerous class is that engaged in the manufacture of textile fabrics and dress, and constitutes about 5 per cent. of the total population. Then there are the people that are firewood sellers and tax gatherers and cowdung-fuel preparers and sellers. It is chiefly females that are engaged in these occupations. In this class are also included oil-pressers and sellers and oil-seed and oil-cake dealers. These constitute together about 1¼ per cent. of the total population. Those that are engaged in buildings, metals and precious stones, "wood, cane and leaves," "leather, horn and bones," constitute each class a little over one per cent. of the whole population. I have given these figures to show that these classes who are engaged in the preparation and supply of material substances ought to be more numerous than they are, and, as a rule, they are in an exceedingly depressed condition. Their condition depends on the general prosperity of the community. If more luxurious food were taken, if more clothes were purchased, if more indigenous oil were used, if more houses were built, if more articles of artistic merit were patronised, these classes would be more numerous and in a more flourishing condition. They receive no such thing as education, there is no organization among them, and they adhere to the same crude methods that were followed by their ancestors centuries ago. In regard to the class of suppliers of food and drink, I need not say that there is a deal of room for improvement. The art of dietary might be taught in schools, especially in girls' schools, with great advantage; and the whole system of Indian dietary placed on a more rational and health and strength giving basis than it is at present. Then in regard to the class of weavers, I need not say how depressed and wrecked these are, and how they are fallen into a condition of destitution and misery from the prosperous condition they once occupied. The class of mechanics and artizans that work in metals, precious stones, pottery, stoneware, wood, cane, leather, horns, bones, &c., are equally badly-off as can be observed by anybody in practical experience. These classes require to be raised from their present miserable state.

The Indian artizan is skilful, patient and talented. But, he is lazy and would not take the trouble to think how his occupation can be improved and made more paying. He is not a progressive man, is careless of small things, generally of unsystematic and of slovenly habits, and is incapable of making present sacrifice for future gain. He has few wants and is content with small wages, and is generally an inefficient labourer. Mr. Wallace, who once came out to India and has published a book on Indian agriculture, says of our artizan classes; 'Strangers from more advanced countries, who visit India, are generally impressed by the backward state of the crafts of this country. They observe that the Indian artizan does less work with a given amount of labour than the European. The amount of labour that an Indian artificer wastes is a proof of a deplorable want of method and technique. It shows that he has not been properly instructed, and, if you examine his tools, you will generally find them blunt and out of order. He is also careless with regard to measurements and has consequently to perform many operations several times over; and so, although the Indian can live for a month on a day's pay of an English artificer, the latter can produce goods which undersell those of the former in his own market. When we reflect upon the vast resources in natural wealth, mineral and vegetable, of India which, up to the present time, are to a great extent undeveloped, when we know that of all countries raising agricultural produce for export, India gives the least per acre, and that other countries import enormous quantities of her products only to manufacture and return them, we realise how much the working population has yet to learn in order that the wealth of India may be properly utilised". The Indian is far behind the Japanese artificer in technical skill. In Calcutta, almost the whole of the carpentry work is done by Chinamen. To educate these classes, and bring them under a feeling of self-consciousness and common interest, is one of the most important conditions of the industrial regeneration of India.

About the beginning of last year (1901), the Government of India desired to encourage a revival of our indigenous manual industries. To this end, they said they were willing to provide funds to the extent of four or five lakhs of rupees, and entrust the expenditure and control of this money to a specially selected committee in "whom absolute confidence will be placed, so that the experiment will be conducted with discreet enterprise and in the way best calculated to afford the prospect of a successful issue. It was thought that, properly organised and skilfully directed, the cheap labour of the millions of India might find profitable employment in the manufactures of articles of commerce which, for various reasons, are still produced by manual labour, and that, as such forms of industrial enterprise offer little attraction to the ordinary capitalist,

Government intervention is desirable in the interests of workers themselves." This was in the beginning of the year 1901. More than two years have elapsed, and nothing has been heard of the Government's desire to come to the rescue of these industries. The proposal of Mr. Alfred Chatterton, Superintendent of the Madras School of Arts, to re-organise that School by opening classes to represent (1) art; (2) metal work; (3) wood work; (4) textile fabrics, still remains a proposal. There are scores of articles now imported from foreign countries, which, with a little help and encouragement, our own artizans, with their manual labour, are competent to supply. And there is absolutely no need for our articles seeking markets outside India. There is room enough in this vast country with millions of population to consume all the products that may issue from the industry of Indian artizans.

In regard to the department dealing with art, no commercial considerations will in any way enter into the management. All the industrial pupils and apprentices will attend suitable courses of instruction in drawing, and special provision will be made for such of them as show marked artistic talent. At present, Mr. Chatterton proposes to try the experiment of placing this department under the Assistant Superintendent of the School of Arts, who is an Indian, an artizan by caste "of great originality and talent." In regard to metal work, Mr. Chatterton thinks that natives show skill in modelling, which can be improved by suitable instruction, and that articles of utility can be turned out to replace those that are now imported from Europe. "Cocks and valves and water supply fittings are largely used out here and are almost all imported," and Mr. Chatterton is sanguine that, with suitable machinery, he will be able to train men to do equally good work in this country and at prices which will pay. "In this and other similar directions, an enormous impetus would be given to local industries if the Government of India could see their way to issuing orders that the public works in this country are to be carried out with locally manufactured stores whenever it is possible to do so." In this department, Mr. Chatterton adds, "the most important matter for future consideration is the resuscitation of the native iron industry." The industry in wood work is now in a decadent state, not so much because the artizans have deteriorated in skill as that there has been no one competent to furnish good designs. "If these can be procured or the services of a competent English art furniture designer engaged, it is not improbable that a very large foreign business could be gradually built up." In this connection, Mr. Chatterton suggests that there should be in some important centre a commercial showroom containing a collection of specimens of the best Indian art, and these specimens should be offered for sale to the class of people who patronize such articles—a suggestion which might receive the attention of the Madras Victoria Technical Institute. As regards the textile industries, no attention has been paid to them in the Madras School of Arts beyond the setting up of a few carpet looms. Weaving is the most important of all the indigenous industries, and though it has suffered severely from the competition of imported piece-goods and the production of Indian mills, yet, Mr. Chatterton thinks, it is by no means in a very bad state. " The fine fabrics must all be made on hand-looms, and the depraved condition of the weavers is due to the fact that wealthy classes no longer use or buy so many fine cloths as they did formerly," and Mr. Chatterton thinks that European hand-loom might with advantage be used for much finer counts than are customary in this country. He has lately started some experiments in this direction and attempted to produce piece-goods of the type now imported in such large quantities. This will necessitate dyeing and printing and he hopes that " the earlier experiments will prove sufficiently successful to justify an application to Government for the service of an expert from " home." "If in other parts of the world, there is any demand for cotton fabric of higher quality, there would not be any difficulty in meeting it, as the Indian weavers retain all their old skill, and only complain of the few opportunities they now get for exhibiting it."

The great difficulty that is experienced in dealing with the number of industrial schools that are being established by Missionary bodies and municipal and local institutions here and there, is in providing them with suitable teachers, especially in connection with such industries as carpentering and blacksmith's work. Sometime ago, in the Engineering College of Madras, a class for imparting instruction in these and kindred subjects was opened. The workshops there were fairly well equipped with tools and machinery, and the instructors, who were employed in teaching the engineering students, were fairly skilled artizans. These took up some of the best students who had undergone a long training in the industrial schools and trained them in carpentry and black smiths' work. These students were kept under training for three years, and they were paid six, seven and eight rupees a month in each successive year ; and during that time they received a training in the higher branches of carpentry, in fitter's work, in blacksmith's work, and so forth, and at the end of that time it was hoped that they could be sent out as teachers. I hear with regret that this apparently good arrangement has been abolished.

CHAPTER X.

Our Labouring Classes.—The Day Labourer.

IT is natural though not reasonable or just, that while the grievances of the upper classes of society receive attention from the State, those of the silent poor remain unnoticed and unknown. In the twelve topics of the Viceregal Hercules, the poor labourers' condition is not one; nor in the programme of our Congress and Conferences does it find a place. Still it must be remembered, the wealth of the nation is founded on its labour; and that this labour should be efficient in every way, must be strong, healthy and intelligent, is the first condition of the nation's prosperity. I, therefore, propose to devote a few pages to point out certain serious change that is coming over the condition of our labouring classes, and the poverty and misery that characterise their lot. Our labouring population may be divided into two classes, the agricultural labourers and day labourers, those that work on farms in villages and those that work in towns or in their vicinity on receipt of daily or weekly wages. This latter class is increasing in numbers as industrial enterprises and large pnblic works carried on by the State and private individuals spring up. And even in the condition of the agricultural labourers, considerable change is taking place on account of the general collapse of the Village system due to the disturbing causes introduced by British rule.

"In the changed industrial and economic conditions of to-day. the great concentration of capital and the massing of thousands of the employed have brought about new problems.In the old times, master and men lived and worked together—there was a daily point of contact, a continuous personal touch. To-day all is changed. The employer, in many cases, is as much of an absentee as were the nobles in France in the latter part of the eighteenth century and the landlords of some of the worst tenements in slumdoms. With the growing intelligence on the part of the workers, evidencing itself in a dissatisfaction with their social and economic surroundings, they are slowly learning how to crystallise their incoherent wants and their smothered discontents into definite propositions for an improvement of their conditions."

"The personal touch between employer and employed has largely been lost, and it is not desirable, even if it were possible, to return to the earlier days. But for the successful conduct of the business of the twentieth century, a point of contact must be sought for and established, though in a different way. This need has created a new profession, that of the "social engineer," a man who can tell the employer how he may establish a desired point of contact between himself, his immediate staff, and the rank and file of his industrial army."

These observations, made by a writer in an American magazine, in view of the existing conditions of Western countries, are not without their importance as applied to the modern conditions of India. In Western countries the modern conditions are a spontaneous development of the past, but in India they are the result of foreign influences, and mark a state of transition which is in its initial stage. As the industrial system of India shifts from the old indigenous foundation and rests more and more on the modern basis, the labour problem of the West gradually emerges into sight. In former times, most of our industries were carried on in villages, and the labouring classes lived there rather than in towns. Agriculture absorbed most of them, and the artizans and mechanics, being their own capitalists, peacefully pursued their vocations independently and with an income more or less assured. The agricultural labourer was attached to his landlord and was virtually part and parcel of his family. His income did not consist of daily wages paid by grasping employers, but was received annually and was supplemented by his accounts with the village banker. Similarly, the artizan and the mechanic did not work for the profit of other persons. the capitalists, who exploit labour for their own profit. They knew their customers and their market and were content to work with what tools, materials and capital they were able to command. In like manner, in towns, persons who lived on their manual labour were mostly personal attendants and domestic servants, who, by their devotion and fidelity to their masters, made themselves indispensable to them. Thus, the problem of the day-labourer, with a precarious means of livelihood and depending on the mercy of large capitalists, did not arise.

But this old system is now changing. The numerous and large public works carried on by the State and by private enterprise, and the large factories established in towns, the European plantations in remote hill-tracts, mining operations in various parts of the country, and the facilities for foreign emigration, have all shaken the old immobility of labour, with the result that numbers of labouring classes move on to distant and strange places, preferring higher daily wages to the old steady, though moderate, income. It is these people who contribute most to the difficulty of relief in times of famine ; and at other times the ascendant interest of the employer and the helplessness and ignorance of the working men, often bring about a situation suggestive of the approach of the socio-economic evil which is baffling European statesmanship and philanthropy at the present moment. The frequent strikes of these men in Calcutta, Bombay, and Madras fairly illustrate the direction in which glimpses of the future labour broblem are visible in this country.

When the detailed Reports of the last census are published, we shall be able to know the exact number of labourers working under modern conditions in factories, in large plantations and in Government public works. Meanwhile, it may be noted that in the factories subject to Government inspection, which numbered 79 in all British India in 1899, there were 452,796 persons employed daily on the average. The tea-gardens of India employed 654,600 labourers in all. In coffee estates 27,634 persons were permanently and 82,656 were temporarily, or a total of 110,290 were, employed. In the coal-mining industry, there were 72,000 people employed; in the Kolar gold mines about 40,000 coolies. If, to these figures, those relating to other industrial enterprises such as Jute and Indigo factories, Railway workshops and Government public works, be added, the total will reach about two millions of people—a number large enough to deserve the sympathetic protection of the State.

In a consideration of what we have called the Labour Problem in India, we cannot lose sight of that large class of labourers, who, under a statutory contract, are drafted to distant countries to work in European plantations for Eurapean employers. Those that have read the recent debate in the Supreme Legislative Council on the Assam Emigration and Labour Act and in the Madras Council on a similar measure, cannot resist the conclusion that ere long the whole system which regulates the relation between the employers and employees on these estates, will have to be revised, with increased regard for justice and humanity. Apart from the particular issues raised in that debate, it is evident from the facts and figures placed before the Council by Sir Henry. J. S. Cotton, that the lot of the contract labourer is by no means enviable and that the law is more in favour of the planter than of the labourer. The object of the Legislature seems to be to enhance the facilities for the growth of certain industries;

and towards this end it is considered expedient to subject the coolies to various restraints and disabilities incompatible with their freedom. The law, as it stands, in the words of Sir Henry Cotton, imposes on the labourers serving under contract thereunder in the tea-districts, penal provisions of extreme stringency to such a point that they cease legally and practically to be free men. "When we speak of the interest of the tea industry, we are accustomed," he said, " to mean the interest of the proprietors of tea gardens, of the shareholders of companies, of the agents in Calcutta and London and of the employers of labour, and this customary use of the expression is a true indication of the fact that we are too apt, not only in our language, but also in our thoughts and actions, to contemplate the interest of the industry exclusively from the capitalist's point of view." This is the only explanation of the extraordinary decision of the Supreme Legislative Council to postpone by two years the operation of the new provision in the law to increase the coolie's wage from Rs. 5 to Rs. 5-8 a month—a wage which was smaller than the wage earned by the unskilled labourer in Assam itself.

A friend of the Assam tea-planters recently wrote long articles in the *London Times* criticising Sir Henry Cotton's views on the condition of the Assam coolie. He therein extols the humanity of the planters and paints in bright colours the prosperity of the coolie. The conclusion of a writer with a bias of this kind may be easily foretold, and it is that, under the existing laws, the Assam tea estate is the very paradise of the labouring classes. His average wage is between Rs 3-8 and Rs. 5. Such a wage in his own country would be considered low. Yet in Assam it is considered a prosperity wage. It is open to the coolie to work harder than he does and earn enhanced wages ; still he will not work harder and earn more. This is attributed to his laziness. The same criticism is made of the labourer in the Bengal coal mines. There too, he does just the quantity of work required for earning his bare necessaries. Now, I attribute this fact, not to the coolie's laziness or his want of care for the future, but to the hard and irksome conditions under which he has to work. He is too weak or has too little inducement to work under conditions imposed on him and under the supervision of the unsympathetic manager of the garden.

If the coolie is too lazy to work, why does he prefer an independent farmer's life to that of a labourer on the tea estate? When the newly imported coolie has settled down on the garden, become acclimatized, and mastered his work, his "curious tendency," as the writer in the *Times* terms it, comes into play, to break away from garden labour and assimilate himself to the indigenous industry of the soil. All his superfluous energy is put, not into extra work upon the garden, but into the gradual establishment of a life altogether apart from and independent of tea. His petty savings are spent on vegetable gardens, on fowls and goats, pigs and ducks. He invests them in cattle and carts also. As in the Bengal coal mines, so in the Assam tea-gardens, the managers allow the labourers to be coolies and peasants by turn, because they know that it is the only way of securing a contented labour force. Now, is it not obvious from the above that the coolie is *not* a lazy person contented with little and careless of the future? He is as glad to save money and improve his lot as others are.

If only the labour in the garden were moderate, the wages high and other conditions attractive, why should the coolie be so impatient as to give up the garden work? "It is indeed only to be expected", says the writer in the *Times*, "that, as more and more cattle accumulate in the hands of coolies and more and more cultivation is permitted by employers and sanctioned by dustoor, there will be a reduction of the average effort on a garden and consequently of the average wage . . . . Far from deploring any general fall in wages, I am not sure that there does not exist a distinct presumption that, with a fall, the coolie's real prosperity, as measured by his own ideal, will increase." If this is the fact, it completely proves the coolie's aversion to the garden work which is made a stepping stone to the position of an independent farmer. It follows that this aversion is due to no innate instinct of the coolie, but to the fact that, as his nature goes, neither the garden work nor the mine work is agreeable to him. In order that the Indian labourer can reconcile himself to work under European conditions, he wants adequate compensation in liberal wages and in general sympathetic treatment.

I have referred above to the Planters' Labour Act, recently passed by the Government of Madras. The conditions of Southern India are such that no system of forced labour is necessary, and the interference of Government in the spontaneous relation of labour and capital, on behalf of the latter, is entirely uncalled for and unjust. Though the labourer is supposed to accept service under the planter by a voluntary contract, still every one knows that the contract is a farce, and he no more knows about his contract than the man in the moon. The maistry goes about the country with a bag of money; he goes into villages, and pries into the secret quarrels and differences of families, and, by plenty of false promises, allures the discontented male or female member of the family away from the village. He does not tell his victim whither he is taking him or her, whether the place of destination is near or far off, or beyond the seas. The would-be labourer on the planter's estate has no idea of the nature of his work, of the wages he will receive, of his treatment from the planter from the manager or the magistrate. Of the terms of his contract which is in a language he does not know, he is thoroughly innocent. These serious omissions in the Bill the representative members of the Council fought hard to have supplied. But they fought in vain. The reformed Legislative Council, so far as the influence of public opinion on Government is concerned, is worse than a failure. Indian members, under the old rêgime, were able to exercise some real and effective influence on Government. Then there was a sincere desire on the part of Government to know Indian opinion and give effect to it as far as possible. There was a time when Bills, before they were introduced into the Legislative Councils, used to be sent to public bodies and select individuals for their opinions. But, now, the only public bodies consulted are Chambers of Commerce, and the individuals are their leading representatives. The present Bill was several times revised by the planters, until every desire and freak of theirs were met in its provisions. But how it affected the interest of the labourers, the Government did not care to know. No individual Indians nor Indian public bodies were consulted. The tender mercies of the planter were enough for the coolie.

The independent members of the Council fought courageously. But every time an amendment was proposed by any of them, the whole compact band of official and English members opposed him as one man. The Indian members that opposed the Bill had bestowed much time and thought on it. They are as intelligent as other members of the Council, and they are as solicitous of the security of public interest as others. Still, to be outvoted by a compact majority in a high-handed manner, even when some of them at any rate are apparently convinced of their error, must be most disheartening. And, it is honourable and creditable to these gentlemen that they thought that to do their duty honestly was as important as to win their points. If their sole object was to obtain better terms for their down-trodden countrymen, they might as well have submitted their amendments beforehand and taken the decision of the Government as it chose to give it. But they had the equally important object in their mind to show to the public that their cause was right and that the Government was using arbitrarily, in the interest of a powerful class, the power vested in it by law. Official members are bound to vote on the side of Government whether they vote according to or against their conscience. Never was a system of legislation a more solemn farce than the Indian system is at present ; and never did the Legislative Council of Madras show less fairness or dignity than it did in carrying through this hateful measure in March 1903.

That the condition of the two millions of the coolie population working in workshops, manufactories and in European plantations is deplorable, is proved by ample evidence. Notwithstanding the special pleading in the *Times*, facts and figures are definite enough to show that Sir Henry Cotton was right when he said that the labourers in Assam earn " a miserable average pittance, inadequate to maintain them in health and comfort." The Indian coolie works willingly for Municipalities and Railways, where the work he has to do is by no means less disagreeable than work elsewhere. Neither the Municipalities nor Railways complain of scarcity of labour. On the other hand, the agents of the Assam planters are not now able to recruit so largely as they could do in former years. Moreover, in 1900, as Sir Henry Cotton pointed out, in the Assam tea-gardens the mortality was 43·5 per thousand among Act coolies, and 23·2 among non-Act coolies. Sir Henry Cotton reports that cases have come to his notice where rice was not provided at the statutory rate, or where subsistence allowance was not paid to sick coolies.

Labourers in Mines.

In the year 1900, there were 271 collieries working in India, producing more than 6,000,000 tons of coal, valued at over 20,000,000 rupees. Indian labour is universally employed. In 1900, nearly 90,000 people were employed in coal mining, the average pay for underground work being about 1¼ rupees a week. Modern machinery for haulage is being gradually introduced into the Bengal mines, and the "gin" and bucket worked by women are less commonly seen. The mines are owned partly by joint stock companies and private individuals, and partly by the State through the railway companies. The Indian coal at the pit's mouth is much cheaper than imported coal. The wholesale selling price of the Bengal coal was, in 1900, 4s. 5d., whereas the average wholesale price of imported coal was 32s. 1d. Considering the comparative novelty of the labour, the deteriorated physique of our labouring classes, and the poor wages paid, it is not surprising to hear coal companies complaining that the "labour is always causing trouble." There are far too few miners The average miner never attempts to earn more than a day's wage, although he might work himself up to a position of comparative comfort if he would try to. The working hours are from 6 A.M. to 6 P.M., and perhaps later when extra work is required. Only four days a week real work is done, and the consequence is that the collieries must have a far greater number of working places than the same output in England would warrant. All the miner's family work with him, carrying or training his coal. Picks of English pattern and make are now universal, the crow-bar and single pick having been ousted. In some coal fields the payments are weekly, on Sunday mornings, the miners resorting to the East Indian Bazaar which was established to attract local labour and which has done so. The labourers consist of low caste Mahomedans and Hindus. The miners live in small villages, aggregations of mud walls, of bricks set in mud, with thatched or tiled roof. The hut consists of one room, sometimes two, of from 6 ft. × 6 ft to 10 ft. × 10 ft. in size. Those better-off have cow-sheds and granaries; these two latter with the dwelling forming three sides of a quadrangle. The larger proportion of the labourers cultivate during the rainy season, say, from October to June. Some of the labourers have settled down to coal-cutting as a calling, and these work constantly, always excepting Monday, which is invariably a holiday.

The coolies at the coal mines will not give up their caste pursuits, and any discontent makes them bolt bag and baggage. Labourers have been attracted to settle in the immediate vicinity of the mines, we are told, by allotment of land at nominal rents, on the understanding that, when cultivation is over, they shall work in the mines. From the beginning of July to November, the cultivation, and then the religious festivals, keep the coolies away, and the output at the mines is low. Naturally, in prosperous years when food is cheap, labour at the mines is scarce, whereas in years of adversity it is abundant. Still, we are told, the general state is "want of labour." A few, however, have settled down as permanent miners, and they work steadily.

Women and children work underground, and are principally employed in carrying the small coal and dust. The women often take their babies, two and three months old, down the mine, taking with them also a small cot on which the child sleeps or plays while its parents are at work.

The coolie's power of endurance enables him to work for hours at the bottom of a sinking shaft with water pouring over his naked body, or to work all day long and day after day in driving a "rise" gallery, perhaps hundreds of feet from any current, in an atmosphere which is fœtid and laden with steam. The ventilation of the underground workings receives very little attention, and in most collieries none at all. The ignorant labourer has not yet recognised that his health and longevity are in question, and he has besides helped much to prevent ventilation from becoming a necessity by the wonderful power of endurance he has shown. This is a hard lot, indeed, for the coolies, and it is a wonder why this blot on the system has not been noticed and removed by the authorities concerned. I have already referred to the fact of the coal miner being imperfectly protected and given low wages, and to his ignorance of which the employers take advantage.

The Mines Act, recently passed by the Indian Legislature, regulates the conditions of labour. One of its provisions is to require that all mine managers should hold certificates that they possess certain qualifications. This is an excellent stipulation, which no one who has the interests of coal-mining in India at heart, could possibly object to on general grounds. It is, however, alleged that no facilities are provided in India, by means of a properly-established mining school or otherwise, to enable men to acquire the necessary qualifications, and the result is that a new burden will be imposed on the industry by reason of men having to be brought from abroad to act as managers at higher wages than would be paid to properly qualified local men. "I do not feel confident" says Dr. Dunstan " to say how far these objections may hold, but I am confident that great good will result from the establishment in India of a Government School of Mines and Metallurgy, in which those who intend to engage in mining and metallurgical industries could receive a thoroughly practical and efficient training, in modern and scientific methods, not only in engineering and mining, but also in physics and chemistry in their applications to metallurgy." This necessity exists in regard to other mines also.

CHAPTER XI.

The Agricultural Labourer.

I have already pointed out that the lot of the agricultural labourer is, on the whole, better than that of the day-labourer. His income is less precarious and his life in the village less costly. Still, as the old village system gets more and more loosened, the old attachments and predilections give away, and new ambitions present themselves. The village labourer is getting discontented with his lot. And the recent famines and droughts have aggravated this sentiment. One direction in which this discontent is manifesting itself, is the labourer's increasing tendency to run away from the village and seek his fortune in distant countries beyond the sea.

In Southern India or in the Presidency of Madras, the class of field labourers constitute a substantial proportion of the total population, being about seven millions or 20 per cent. of the whole. They consist of a number of castes of great antiquity and ethnological interest. Some of these castes are : (1) The Pariah numbering about two millions and inhabiting the Tamil Country ; (2) the Palli, more numerous than the first, numbering over two millions also found in the Tamil country ; (3) the Pallans found chiefly in the Districts of Tanjore, Trichinopoly, Madura and Tinnevelly, about 800,000 in number; (4) the Malas who number about 1,400,000 and who are the Pariahs of the Telugu Country ; and (5) other Castes of less numerical importance living in certain limited areas of the Presidency. Of these the Pariahs and Pallis are the most important, not only in regard to their numbers, but also in regard to their qualities as agricultural labourers, as sepoys, and as domestic and menial servants under alien residents of India. They are intelligent, enterprising and honest. They possess a good physique, and are capable of much endurance. These mostly profess Hinduism as their religion. Many have become converts to Christianity, especially in the more Southern Districts of the Tamil Country.

Whatever the social position and the general influence of Pariahs and other low classes centuries ago, their position at present is one of the utmost degradation. They are exceedingly poor ; they live on the scantiest and least wholesome meal and are treated with contempt and neglect by the higher classes. They live in "locations" at some distance from the village proper where the landlords and their caste dependants live. Their huts are of the humblest description and contain nothing like furniture. They are not allowed to enter or pass through the village, and when they talk to a person belonging to a higher caste, they must stand at a distance, lest their approach should communicate pollution. A more abject condition is hardly possible to conceive than that of these long-suffering, but most useful, classes of peoples. Still, it must be acknowledged that the caste landowners of the village treat these people not without consideration or sympathy. In most cases, the caste landlord and the Pariah labourer have lived in a relation of mutual attachment for generations together. The attachment of the Pariah is, as a rule, faithful and sincere, and often he willingly sacrifices his person and even risks his life in the service of his master. The master, on the other hand, takes a paternal interest in his Pariah tenants, considering them as a part of his own property. Besides the wages, or part of the produce of the field to which they are entitled under the custom of the village, they generally receive advances from time to time from their master, not merely for agricultural purposes such as the purchase of cattle, seeds, implements &c., but for their domestic needs also, such as marriage, worship, funerals &c. They are given occasional presents of clothes and small sums of money. Altogether, the ignorance and the good character of the Pariah, on the one hand, and the landlord's sense of his self-interest, on the other, have rendered the relation between the two one of smoothness and contentment. The Pariahs indeed are absolutely without education, and nothing takes place in their life to rouse new hopes or new standards of comfort. The same is the case more or less with regard to the great bulk of the rural population in India at present.

Causes are already at work to disturb this time-honoured and cordial relation between the landlord and his Pariah tenant. The village population of India is no longer altogether immobile. People of all classes have learnt the need and the advantage of moving about. New avenues of employment are being opened in all parts of the country. Neither to the owner of the land nor to its cultivator is there, therefore, the same inducement to be fixed for ever in the same spot or attached for ever to the same person or family as there was under the old order of things. To the villager his village is no longer his world, and he is often attracted to places where more remunerative employments are available than in his village. The petty landlord often sells his estate and takes to trade, or his son has become a public servant or a member of some learned profession, and he finds that the convenience of his family requires his landed property to be sold away. In the same way the field labourer finds his ancestral occupation not sufficiently paying, or is moved by the example of a fellow-labourer who has left the village and has found employment in some public work carried on by Government or in the mines or coffee estates in the adjacent district where better wages are offered. These fresh influences necessarily bring about a relaxation of the old attachment between the employer and the employed in the villages.

There is another important change that is taking place in the Indian rural economy and is causing a dislocation of our system of labour. The Hindu law of equal partition of an estate among the heirs and the natural expansion of cultivation due to the growth of the population and the decay of non-agricultural industries, are rapidly increasing the number of petty land-holders who own a small number of acres, often less than five, and who cannot afford to employ hired labourers. Their capital is their labour, and their profit does not exceed the wages of their labour. In some districts, especially in inland districts, there is taking place a constant migration of labourers from towns to villages, and this necessarily aggravates the competition of labourers for employment and impairs the old hereditary personal relationship between the proprietors and the labourers. These causes are ceaslessly at work, and although the village community, like other strongholds of conservatism, continues to preserve many of its old characteristics, still the causes we have referred to are leading to a considerable unsettlement.

The Pariahs of the Tamil country constitute the bulk of the emigrants from the eastern coast of the Madras Presidency to some of the British Colonies. From the districts of Tinnevelly, Tanjore, North Arcot and South Arcot, there is a regular stream of emigrants pouring into Ceylon, the Straits Settlements, Mauritius, Natal, etc. During the recent years of agricultural depression, this stream was flowing in broader and more rapid currents. Where the failure of monsoons causes a shrinkage of cultivation, there is a proportionate diminution of labour in the village. When scarcity curtails the means of the more well-to-do classes, they spend less on luxuries and comforts, and therefore on payment of wages to labourers. By far the larger proportion of paupers during times of famine are content to obtain what relief they can from the charity of Government and private agencies. But the more enterprising individuals seek a better lot in foreign countries where they are sure of steady and remunerative employment. The agents of these foreign Colonies are particularly busy during such hard times, and during the years 1900-1901, it is said that there was not a group of villages in the districts mentioned above where these agents had not reaped a rich harvest in capitation fees for men and women, whom they every week handed over to the emigration depôts in Madras and Negapatam.

The Christian Missionary puts his own construction on the exodus of the Pariahs to strange lands beyond the seas in search of a new life. In the fulness of his sympathy with this down-trodden and degraded class, he attributes their self-imposed banishment from their native place to the intolerable tyranny of the higher castes that employ them. There is reason to think that this view is shared by some Anglo-Indian officials also. But, on the face of it, it is unreasonable to hold that either the tyranny of the employers or the caste disabilities of the Pariahs drive the latter away from their villages. Because, these are not new features of the village system, but have characterised it ever since its first establishment. There is indeed a good deal that is most lamentable in the normal lot of the Hindu low caste people, but thanks to their ignorance and to their peaceful and gentle nature, they have on the whole remained content with their lot and nothing has recently taken place to rouse them to an attitute of resentment against the treatment they receive from their masters. The more true explanation of the increasing emigration of the labourers is the natural enterprising nature of the Pariahs, stimulated by a keener struggle for life in recent years.

A writer in the *Madras Mail,* who is apparently a Christian Missionary gentleman, furnishes the following explanation :

"The Pariahs have found it impossible to live under the old conditions, and, after years of mute endurance, are shaking the dust of their native land from their feet, and going out to discover what a new world will offer them. The exodus seems to afford proof positive that the pressure of hunger on the lives of the lowest and landless classes has been and is far greater than has ever been admitted by the authorities who are responsible for the condition of the people in times of scarcity. We are asked to believe that the people will not travel five miles to obtain Government employment on famine test works, while we have before our eyes proof that many of them are only too willing to cross the black water and pledge themselves to hired service for long years in strange lands. We are told that they will not accept famine labour at famine rates ; but here they are waiting for ships to carry them across the sea willing to dare its dangers, rather than endure hunger at home."

The writer, however, admits that this is neither the chief nor the sole cause of this phenomenon, and recognises causes more deep-rooted in the permanent transformation of the economic and social system of India on account of Western influences. The old order such as we have briefly described above, is giving place to a new one. The Pariah no longer belongs to the soil, and no longer can he claim a share, however small, of its produce. He is now sinking to the lot of " a day labourer employed to plough and to plant, and left idle till harvest when he is called in for a brief spell of work and turned adrift again. Under these conditions, even in the best of seasons, there are times when life is barely possible for the working classes, while, in a year of scarcity, life rapidly becomes an intolerable burden." Moreover, the frequent recurrence of famine and Government undertaking the sole responsibility of feeding the whole pauper population have demoralised the land-owners who are ceasing to recognise their old responsibility for the protection of their tenants.

The activity of Christian Missionaries in the field of proselytism is another cause which drags away numbers of these poorer classes from their old occupation in the Hindu villages into fresh occupations, mostly non-agricultural. There is no part of India where the population of Native Christians has recently increased more rapidly than in Southern India, and unlike those in most of Northern India, the converts to Christianity in this Presidency are recruited almost entirely from the classes of Hindus which are lowest in the social scale. These classes being exceedingly poor, it is no wonder that they are easily tempted to quit the fold where their ancestors have lived for centuries and to enter that of the Christian faith in times of difficulty. And such occasions having recurred several times within the last quarter of a century, the Native Christian population has increased with striking rapidity. In the year 1891, the native Christians numbered 879,437 in this Presidency, and this has increased since then to 1,038,854 in 1901, which is an increase of 18·1 per cent. In the decade between 1881 and 1891, the increase among them was even more striking, being 48·8 per cent., and, during the last thirty years, it has amounted to 99 per cent against an increase in the population as a whole of 22·1 per cent. In other words, as the last Census Report puts it, the Native Christians have multiplied four and five times as fast as the population generally.

In consonance with the theory that the poverty of these classes is the chief inducement to their deserting their ancestral faith, it is observed that the increases are most marked in districts particularly liable to droughts and scarcities. During the last twenty years, more recruits have joined the Christian religion in the districts of Godavery, Cuddapah, Kurnool and North Arcot than in other districts. The number has been least in Madras and in Tanjore.

It is important for our purpose to consider how the poor Indians belonging to the labouring classes are brought up under the care of their Missionary patrons.

So long as they remain in the village of their ancestors, little change takes place in their condition. They receive no education, and nothing takes place to disturb the monotony of their humble and simple village life. But once a Pariah becomes a Christian, his whole life changes. He is to some extent educated by the Missionaries who also help him in learning a trade or in obtaining a place in the public service. Some plucky converts even manage to enter one or another of the learned professions. The patronage and sympathy of the Christian Missionaries, who belong to the ruling race, give the Native Christian a new status which he is not slow to appreciate. Above all, in due time, he can choose from among the number of neatly-dressed and somewhat educated girls of the Mission, a wife who will come up nearer than any village girl can, to his ideal, as he has newly understood it, of a housewife. These circumstances lift the Native Christian to a new ideal of life, and his dislike for the hereditary occupation of his class is not less strong than that of the ordinary Indian who has passed through a course of teaching in a modern English school. The depletion, therefore, in the strength of the labouring classes available for the carrying on of the agricultural and other industries in the country, caused by these conversions, must lead to its own economic results.

Of late, however, efforts have been made to establish agricultural settlements for the benefit of the Pariah and other low caste converts. Some Missionaries have been able to obtain from the Madras Government large areas of land on favourable terms for the purpose. As only a nominal tax is demanded by Government, in the initial stage of the settlement, they have generally proved paying. A report recently published in this connection says: "The great object is to raise the Pariahs, Pullas, Irulas, etc., from their state of practical slavery, degradation and poverty and to train them up as self-respecting Christians. Every District Missionary knows how closely the Missionary problem is wrapt up in the agricultural one. No Mission can flourish under a condition of practical starvation. We have found work and food for thousands of poor people during the past two years. They have gladly come to us because we treat them well. There is no forcing of religion upon them, but when they wish to remain with us and become Christians, when they work well and abstain from theft, we take them on as regular settlers and train them for holy Baptism. The children we teach in schools and the adults we instruct to rally during the evenings. We have now 43 adult settlers and 41 children, and of these 43 are now being prepared as *catechumens*." It should be remarked here that these convert settlers will remain only as the tenants of the Missionaries, and they will not share in the produce of the soil any more than their brethren under Hindu landowners. The Missionaries are the proprietors of the land, responsible to the Government for the payment of the tax, and will appropriate such profits as may be derived from the cultivation of the settlements. Nor will the Pariah settlers have the benefit of those customs and traditions which secure to the Pariah tenants of the Hindu village certain privileges and rights. Nor is it reasonable to expect from the Missionary proprietors that familiarity, and that sympathy extending even to minute domestic matters, which characterise the relation between the landowners and their tenants in the villages. In so far as these converts are not settled entirely as agricultural tenants and are trained for non-agricultural occupations, they will constitute a loss to the facilities of agricultural operations in the country. Nor will the Pariah convert, once planted in the settlement, but instructed in modern schools, choose to stick to the occupation of agriculture any more than the non-Christian lad similarly instructed does. Moroever, the Christian Missionaries do not manage the settlement personally. They have to employ a well-paid manager, on whom will depend to a great extent the prosperity and contentment of the labourers. It is calculated that one of these Colonies will yield not less than Rs. 7,000 a year, and after all the expenses have been met, there will be a balance of not less than Rs. 2,000 a year. The whole of the balance will be added to the funds of the Missionaries and will be utilised in founding other settlements in other places and in adding to the Christian recruits from the followers of non-Christian religion.

That these Colonies should be looked upon with jealousy by the Hindu peasants goes without saying. Christian Missionaries are nowhere popular in India, and however philanthropic their effort may be from an abstract point of view, they produce strong dislikes in the

Hindu minds, first because, they are prompted by hostility to their own religion, and, secondly, they interfere in the old time-honoured village economy under which rural life has gone on smoothly for centuries. Neither the Christian Missionaries nor the converts care always to conceal their dislike and disregard for their "heathen" neighbours. The Pariah who was until recently almost a slave—a willing and obedient slave of the high caste Hindu—has become an important man and, with the Missionary sympathy to back him, puts on airs and defies his former master. The Hindus are conscious of their inability to resist the Missionary's encroachment on what they regard as the communal rights of the village from time immemorial. As a member of the ruling race, he is a friend of the district officers, and the Hindu landowner often believes, rightly or wrongly, that the Missionary is able to make use of his friendship with them to obtain possession of lands and important concessions, which the Hindu applicants fail, as a rule, to obtain from the same authority. Thus a Missionary agricultural settlement amidst a group of Hindu villages is a constant source of mutual irritation and often leads to unprofitable litigation.

The attitude of Government towards these philanthropic, though sectarian, efforts of the Missionaries is, as may be expected, one of ready sympathy. Any endeavour calculated to reduce the congestion in the agricultural occupation of the country and raise the status of the working classes, is welcome from an official point of view. The Christian Missionary is undoubtedly far more intelligent and enterprising than the average Indian landowner, and there is more probability of the former employing rational and scientific methods and perhaps of investing more capital, than there is in the case of the latter. Large areas of inferior soil which, under the ownership of Hindus, will hardly yield any produce worth speaking of, may be expected to produce more and go to feed a larger number of mouths. But there is a political aspect of the question, which the Hindus are not slow to press on Government. Government being pledged to a policy of strict religious neutrality, the Hindus question the propriety of rendering active help, at their direct cost, in the advancement of objects openly hostile to the interests of their own religious faith. To enable ministers of a foreign religion to acquire property in the country and from the income of that property to extend the work of proselytism, aiming at the undermining of the indigenous faith, does not look altogether like a rigid observance of a policy of neutrality. Whatever the avowed policy of the Government may be, and, so far as official declarations go, its desire to abstain strictly from partiality to one religion or another, still the *personnel* of Government and the numerous officials employed in carrying on the administration, cannot possibly override their own consciousness of the faith they profess. They often yield to the insidious influence of their religious bias and give rise to occasions when there is an apparent and unjustifiable departure from one of the fundamental and most cherished principles of British rule in India.

There is yet another change taking place in the conditions of labour in Southern India, which is causing apprehension in the minds of the landowners. Government takes special interest in the stimulation of the cultivation of such agricultural crops as are intended for export to foreign countries. Of such crops, ground nut, a valuable oil seed, is a most important one. The quantity of this nut annually exported from this Presidency is estimated at nearly one and a half millions sterling. The chief ground nut producing districts in this Presidency are North Arcot, South Arcot, Chingleput, Tanjore, and Trichinopoly, the largest extent under this crop being in South Arcot and the adjoining French settlement of Pondicherry. There is a coast trade in this article which is exported from the ports of this Presidency to other ports in India, besides a large export trade to Europe, especially to France. During the last few years, this industry has undergone vicissitudes of fortune. Among the reasons for a gradual decline in this industry some years ago, was regarded a deterioration in the quality of the local seed as one. Accordingly, the French Government at Pondicherry and the Madras Government introduced new varieties of seeds from foreign countries. These varieties are said to have proved remarkably successful, one great advantage of the new seeds being that the crops can be harvested within four months instead of six, and can be put in the ground at any time of the year provided the crop can be irrigated. This last fact has stimulated cultivation to such an extent that the crops are gathered not at any particular period of the year as was formerly the case, but almost throughout the year. The picking of seeds, accordingly, attracts a large number of coolies from the neighbouring villages to the detriment of the ordinary operations of agriculture and even other kinds of labour service in towns. The coolies employed on the ground nut soil are paid higher wages, much higher than the coolies get on the paddy field or from manual service in towns. The result is the whole neighbourhood suffers from scarcity of labour.

An Indian gentleman, writing recently in the *Madras Mail* and described as a well-known and recently retired native official and landowner, says : "Things used to be bad enough to the ordinary employer of labour when the old variety of the seed was in vogue which was grown but once in a twelve months ; but with what has now taken its place under the name of the *Moris Kottai* or the Mauritius nut, and which can be sown three times in a year and cropped as often, the demand for unskilled labour has been so chronic that the work is coming pretty near to a dead lock in several departments of every-day life. The ordinary cultivator of paddy is the first to suffer from this state of things. During the harvest time he needs all the labour that he can procure, but he is greatly disconcerted to find that exactly at that time the coolies have disappeared, and have gone to pick ground nuts, and unless he raises his own rates to double the usual ones, he fails to get the needed supply of labour." According to this writer, not only is the employer of coolies on a large scale affected, but every ordinary employer of labour, including the house holder, suffers to an inconvenient extent. The dealers in rice cannot get coolies to pound the paddy, neither women nor men coolies. Even the domestic servants desert their old homes and resort to the ground nut fields, being attracted by higher wages.

These and other inconveniences are pointed out by this writer, and it is not necessary for me here to dwell on them at length. My object in drawing attention to this phenomenon in the usual labour economy of the country is to point out how various causes are combining to produce an economic change which is not unlikely to reach the dimension of a revolution in the condition of the labouring classes in the near future. The Indian employer is not, as a rule, an employer of labour on a large scale. Competition hardly enters into the relation between the employer and the employed ; the wages are determined more by custom than by competition. In the rural parts of the country, labour is still paid in kind. By the side of such a state of things, the effects of a system of production on a large organised scale, such as European enterprise is introducing into the country, may be imagined. All or nearly all export products are coming under European capital. Not only the ground nut, but sugarcane, cotton, coffee and tea are no longer cultivated by the ryots entirely on their own account. They are getting indebted to the British capitalist who advances them money in the cultivation season and buys the products at the harvest season at prices fixed under a previous agreement. Unless his operations are organised on a large scale, they do not pay. His enterprise which is, at present, largely encroaching on the agricultural as well as the manufacturing industry of the country, is a new factor which is bringing the relation between the employed and the employer under competition instead of *mamul*, and is beginning to cause a serious disturbance of the old arrangement. Nowhere will the effect of this change be more felt than in the villages, where by far the great majority of the labouring classes are employed. The landowners are already showing signs of discontent. Recently the landowners of the district of Tanjore memorialised the Government of Madras against the unchecked emigration of labourers from South India. They pointed out that the agricultural operations have been much impeded and at times endangered by the constant and sudden desertion of agricultural labourers, who, after entering into contract to cultivate the lands on certain conditions, emigrate to foreign parts without the slightest notice to their employers. They pray that facilities for emigration of agricultural labourers to foreign places might be restricted.

There can be no doubt that, in other districts than Tanjore, agricultural operations are similarly hampered. Paucity of labourers would mean rise in wages, and rise in wages would necessarily enhance the cost of cultivation, in which case the landowner will have a right to demand a remission of the rates of taxation assessed on his lands. Under the present system, the State levies a tax from the land which is equivalent to half its net profit after deducting the cost of cultivation and certain other items of expenditure from the gross produce. If the wages show a permanent tendency to rise, it would be but fair to the landowners that a careful investigation of the new economic change that I have dwelt upon, should be made by Government, and such relief as the landowner may be found to be entitled to should be given to him. It is, of course, impossible that the labourer can be sacrificed for the well-being of the landowner, although it is only too likely that the latter would bring every pressure possible on the Government to interfere in his behalf. It would be a good day for India when, owing to the increased cost of labour, the land-owner tries to make good his diminishing profit by a more rational and productive system of cultivation than the simple primitive one that he and his ancestors have followed from time immemorial.

CHAPTER XII.

Wages.

IT is a well-known fact that, within the last 20 years, the prices of provisions have increased from 25 to 50 per cent, while the rates of wages have remained more or less stationary. The consequence is what Mr. W. C. Bonnerjee related to an interviewer in London, that the lower middle classes and the labouring classes have to pay for their articles of food nearly twice as much as was paid some years ago. The wages are not uniform everywhere. Within the same area, the wages vary for the same kind of work; and for different kinds of work, according to their nature, different rates of wages are paid. In some places where machinery instead of manual labor is employed, higher rates of wages are paid on account of special skill or knowledge. In the cotton mills of Cawnpore, for instance, the *maistry* gets between 1½ to 3 rupees a day according to the department he serves in; but the spare unskilled hands get only 2 as. and 9 pies a day. In the coal mines of Bengal, the miner gets only 1¼ rupees a week; that is, about 3¼ annas for 6 days, the seventh day being a holiday.

In Government public works and in works carried on on railways, the contractors that employ labourers do not pay them more than the market rates. The old indigenous industries having died out, there is very little scope for the employment of skilled labour. Factories and workshops established in modern times, chiefly under European management, employ, however, some amount of it, and with the exception of this infinitesimal section, it may be said that the great bulk of the labouring population have to eke out their livelihood on the pittance of an anna or two received as wages for a whole day's work of between 9 and 12 hours. Those that maintain that the average income of the people has increased recently, fail to make due allowance for this fact. The agricultural and the day labourer, in the face of an advance of 50 per cent. in the prices of articles of food without a proportionate increase in the wages, must have the hardship of their lot greatly aggravated even in ordinary times.

We have seen no official document in which the question as to the causes of this stationary condition of wages is discussed. The rulers of the country are satisfied that its material wealth is increasing, that there is now more capital, the prices have risen, the standard of life has improved—all, ordinarily, according to European political economists, causes which bring about a rise in wages. But European politica economists write solely with European conditions in their minds, and the principles they lay down have to be considerably modified in their application to the conditions of India. Adam Smith's celebrated opening sentence in his chapter on wages is that "the produce of labour constitutes the natural recompense of wages of the labourer," but he modifies this in his conclusion wherein he says "the demand for those who live by wages, it is evident, cannot increase but in proportion to the increase of the *funds* which are *destined* to the payment of wages."

(1) "The wages fund" is a general term used to express the aggregate of all wages at any given time in possession of the labouring population; (2) the average wage depends on the proportion of this fund to the strength of that population; (3) the amount of the fund is determined by the amount of general wealth applied to the direct purchase of labour.

Thus, population, capital, and competition are the three causes according to this theory, that determine the general rate of wages. Tracing the operation of these causes in the history of wages in India during the last 20 years, we see that the first cause, the labouring population, having kept pace with the growth of the general population, or, perhaps, having multiplied rather more rapidly, it has, in the face of causes that would naturally raise them, neutralised those causes and has kept the wages stationary. Other conditions being the same, it is obvious that an increase of the labouring population will cause a fall in the general wages, and *vice versa*. The most striking example of a great improvement in the condition of the labouring classes in English economic history is found immediately after the occurrence of the Black Death in the middle of the 14th century. The sudden and extensive thinning of the ranks of labour was manifestly the principal cause of the great improvement in the condition of the survivors. Has a similar result followed the equally large reduction in the labouring population during the three great famines of 1877, 1897 and 1899? Turning to the Government publication of the "Statistical Abstract of British India," we find no figures indicating any such result. On the other hand, during years of famine and scarcity, when living is dear, the labour market invariably shrinks, the competition of the labouring classes for work increases, and wages necessarily go down. Nor do the wages rise after the famine is over. Large numbers of the labouring classes die, and it may be expected that the survivors will obtain increased wages in the labour market. But no. The fact is, the bulk of the classes that employ labour also suffer and their employment of labour dwindles.

In other words, the available capital competing for labour, which is the second cause determining the rate of wages, is reduced during hard times—the capital competing for day-labourer in towns as well as the capital competing for agricultural labourer in villages. It is erroneously contended that it is not the classes of landowners, but of labourers, that are affected by famine, although, as a fact, the Government of India were obliged to write off two crores of arrears due from the landowners, and, at the present moment, various charitable measures of relief are in operation to put the prostrate landowners on their legs again. Thus, the landowners, themselves in a condition of destitution immediately after the famine, are not in a position to compete for labour. Similarly, the day-labourer in towns is affected by other demands on the capital or wages fund caused by dearness of provisions, and competition for labour is less strong than in normal times. In illustration of the principle that the wages depend on supply and demand in the labour market, it may be stated that the wages of certain domestic servants, of cooks more especially, have risen within recent years, because fewer men now compete for that species of service; whereas the wages of school masters have considerably gone down, because the competition for their places by the graduates and under-graduates of our Universities has greatly increased. It should also be remembered that, in this country, a large portion of the labourers' competition is for service not intended to bring a direct profit. Here and there European capitalists have made investments in view to profit, and in their service a fraction of the labouring population is absorbed. The inducement, therefore, which is so powerful in the industrial countries of the West, the inducement to grow money from money, is absent in India. A good deal of the indigenous capital is invested in unproductive objects such as jewellery, is locked up in hoards, or is spent on perishable enjoyments. The amount actively competing for labour is small, and it competes for it in order that articles of necessaries may be supplied ; and not that profits may accrue. There is, therefore, no inducement for the offering of liberal wages to the labourers. High profits, it is obvious, depend on high prices, and these both being found in India, foreign capitalists rush into the country and establish industries, which thrive well on the whole. From this cause, foreign capital invested in the country increases, although it has had no appreciable effect on wages in general "If we turn to the great class of employments", says an English writer, "in which the labour is embodied in a material product, we find, on examination, that wages vary with prices in a real, and not merely in an illusory, sense. Suppose, for example, that, owing to a great increase in the foreign demand for our produce, a rise in prices takes place, there will be a corresponding rise in nominal wages. and in all probability a rise in real wages. Such was undoubtedly the case in Great Britain on the conclusion of the Franco-German War." But a similar rise in prices and a similar rise in profits have failed to produce this effect in this country.

There can be no doubt that, in India, the increase in the labouring population, the scarcity of capital and the inefficient competition of labour, account for the low rates of wages that prevail. The first and last may be taken as one cause. There are several causes disturbing the natural operation of the principle of labour competition in the determination of the rate of wages.

THE LAW OF SUPPLY AND DEMAND DISTURBED IN THEIR OPERATION.

In India, as well as in other countries, the great majority of the labouring class are in such a state that they must work independently of the rate of wages. But, as a fact, all that usually eke out their livelihood by manual labour, do not always labour. When the wages are too low, a large number easily sink into pauperism and live by crime or beggary. The former is not so common as the latter. In this country, the restriction on beggary resorted to as a profession, laid by social feeling or legislative authority, is exceedingly weak. From time immemorial, Indian society has looked upon beggary rather as a meritorious mode of living than as one deserving of social odium. Beggary did not originate in India as the profession of the pauper. It began as the most eligible means of the religious order of society obtaining their required sustenance of life. Princes and priests took to begging for their food from door to door in proof of their indifference to the pleasures of the flesh. For about ten centuries, the system of monasteries and asceticism flourished in this country, and a large proportion of the population, including women to some extent, lived a life of renunciation and self-mortification. To take up the life of an ascetic and to beg one's meal from house to house, became in a sense fashionable, and gradually even the lower classes put on the yellow or copper robe and adopted this means of living. So far, begging incurred no social odium, because it was not associated with idleness and pauperism, but with a life of spiritual self-abnegation. But from this last to the profession of idle paupers, is but a step ; and, eventually, an occupation which is condemned and despised in other countries, has come to be largely regarded with a feeling akin to approbation. No Indian, Mahomedan or Hindu, would speak harshly to a beggar, and in his mind the giving of alms to the poor, or to the spiritual devotee, is an act pleasing to God. It, therefore, happens that, in India, there is a far larger proportion of the population living by beggary than in other countries And in hard times it absorbs considerable numbers, who in better times would work for their means of livelihood. An aimless wandering of the people their movement from village to town, and the increasing number of beggars infesting thorough-fares, are considered indications of the advent of famine by our administrators.

Another cause, peculiar to this country, disturbing the ordinary operation of supply and demand in regard to labour, is the social system under which the various industrial occupations are constituted into separate castes, and which discourages the exchange of occupations according as one or another makes a larger demand for labour. Except under the most intolerable pressure, no indigent weaver, or mason, or petty hawker will resort to another occupation. He dislikes manual labour and daily wages, and will stick to his inherited profession until actual starvation drives him to the labour market or the Government relief camp. When this latter takes place, it has the result of enhancing the supply of labour and of lowering the rates of wages below the point of sustenance. On the classes a step higher than these, the result of the caste system is to accentuate the feeling of self-respect engendered by the prestige of caste and to keep at home, frequently in a miserably destitute condition, people who would be the better for going abroad and earning their livelihood by manual labour.

The immobility of labour in this country is another cause that disturbs a free competition between labour and capital. In other countries, labour, as well as capital, migrates to foreign places where there is a better prospect of employment. In India, too, within recent years under special inducements offered by private enterprise and by Government, labour has shown considerable tendency to move from one place to another. Sometimes it moves voluntarily as is shown by the emigration of Indian labourers to British Colonies. But the usual ten dency of Indian labour is to be moving about in the vicinity of its native place, content with what return can be had under existing conditions of competition for employment. This necessarily brings about a plethora of labour in the most populous parts of the country, while other parts, where population is sparse and the field for employment of labour practically unlimited, suffer from want of a sufficient supply of it.

In countries like America and British Colonies, every increase in the number of labourers is accompanied by a more than proportionate increase in the produce and, thus, in the wages of labour. This is not the case in India, except in undeveloped outlying tracts like Assam and Burma. The chief produce being agricultural, already the pressure on the soil on account of the bulk of the natural increase in the population having to be fed from the same source, is so great that the soil is becoming over-cultivated and exhausted, and the fresh tracts brought under cultivation are of increasing grades of sterility. There is, accordingly, no room in agriculture for the absorption of fresh increase in labour. Nor are there manufacturing industries to furnish employment to the excess labour population to which agriculture is unable to afford living rates of wages.

In India there is no organization among the labouring classes. So long as the village system prevailed in its ancient vitality and constitution, the labourer had his status assured to some extent. But since the disruption of this system, and the growth of towns with their population of day-labourers, and the introduction of machinery and the factory system, the necessity for organization among the various labouring classes, to protect themselves against the encroachment of employers not more than against the ignorance of their own members, has become apparent. As we are dealing with the subject in its outlines, we have no space to enter into details. But we may point out that, at the present moment, there are occupations in which the wage-earners might very profitably organize themselves into unions, and resist what they consider to be an infringement of their rights on the part of the employers. Whether there is any infringement in any particular instance, the labourers alone can judge. That such infringements do take place is evident from the frequent strikes to which the labourers resort in the assertion of what they believe to be their rights. There are over 650,000 labourers employed in the tea gardens of India; in coffee estates about 100,000; in the coal-mining industry about 100,000; in the Bombay factories about 25,000; in the gold mines of Kolar about 40,000. Surely, the interests of these people are large enough to be protected against the cupidity of the employers, who are mostly foreigners ignorant of the ways of the Indian labourers, and apt to assert their rights arbitrarily and with harshness. There is no social opinion to denounce any unfair acts of the employers; on the other hand, the society of planters and managers of mines will be disposed to take no particular notice of them. Every help should, therefore, be given to these labourers to form themselves into societies for the protection of their interests.

Take the class of printers. Large numbers of them are employed in almost every town in India and they are increasing from year to year as the result of expanding civilization. They are, necessarily, a class with some education, and are susceptible of organization more or less efficient. More than this or any other class of artizans does the class of weavers stand in great need of some organization. Mr. Alfred Chatterton, who has given great attention to the interests of this class, is of opinion that "it is very desirable that there should be instituted some kind of association of weavers and that funds should be subscribed to be devoted to commercial enquiries, to diffusing useful trade information, to opening new markets, and generally supplying the ignorant hand weavers with all the information relating to their trade which will enable them to keep abreast of the times. In the first instance, there is no doubt that Government would have to initiate the organization and supply the necessary funds, but if it proved of real assistance to the trade, it would soon become self-supporting."

Mr. Chatterton refers here to traders. But we are now concerned with wage earners. Soon, the factory system would be necessary even in regard to hand weaving; and then the trade would be divided into employers and employed, or profit-earners and wage-earners. The former would be much more intelligent than the latter, and better able to take care of their interests. But it is the labourers, whose extreme poverty renders any efficient competition out of the question, that require every protection and encouragement that friends of the poor can give them. We do not here suggest anything like the labour organizations of England or of European countries. The time is yet remote when such union and solidarity among the poorer classes of India can be possible. There is no reason, however, why a beginning should not be made. It is a prefectly legitimate thing for the labourers, as it is for any other section of the industrial classes, for the artisans, for the traders and for the merchants, to combine for the purpose of self-protection. For a long time, British legislators were jealous of workmen's power and prohibited their combining against their employers. But in the year 1824 combination was legalised, and that marked a fresh start, and ushered a new epoch, in the career of the labouring classes. It is organized labour that has made the labouring classes such a powerful factor in the Western civilization. There, in the words of John Burns, "originating in England, developed in the Colonies, followed the wide world over, the growth of organized labour has made social freedom broaden slowly down from precedent to precedent" We need not say that we entertain no extravagant notions regarding the immediate future of the Indian labouring classes; we have no millenium to promise for them; no political freedom, no social emancipation. But, as the most useful and indispensable members of society, members whose ignorance, poverty, and suffering are no faults of theirs, and who are oppressed and starved by the higher classes of society taking advantage of their ignorance and helplessness, they have a claim, a rightful and paramount claim, on the active sympathies of the more favored classes, in order that they may be raised to the position of human beings, like all sentient creatures of God, who can enjoy the comforts of plenty and health, and who are endowed with aptitudes, like the higher classes, for an indefinite measure of progress in their material condition and in their moral purposes

In the case of all day-labourers, and in that of a large section of agricultural labourers too, the rates of wages are determined by competition, and wherever this is so, the wages are paid in cash. But in many places in the interior, the rates are determined by custom and paid in kind. There are also places where the wages paid consist partly of the customary quantity of grain and partly of a small addition in cash. It is obvious that, wherever the wages are paid in grain, the labourer's nominal wages reckoned in their cash eqnivalents rise. But in fact the real wages remain unaffected. Because, the grain paid in lieu of wages is not converted into cash by the labourer or exchanged for other articles whose prices are reckoned in cash. The grain is merely consumed by the labourer, and, with what he or his women or children earn in the shape of cash wages, he purchases other provisions. In the rural parts of the country, competition among employees for labour is very inefficient, while, owing to the absence of industrial occupations in adjacent towns and the generally immobile character of Indian labour, the competition of wage-earners for labour is no better. The rural rates of wages depend on the prosperity of landowners. If the landowners make profits from their lands, they embark their savings in the improvement of their property or in building better houses, or in other enterprises involving a demand for labour. But if their condition is not prosperous and is one of depression, the demand for labour shrinks, and the landowners' condition reflects on that of the agricultural labourer. Whether the demand for labour is low or the demand for employment excessive, the result on the wages is the same, and we think that though both the causes have been in operation, for some years past, to produce depression in the wages, still, the result is more due to increased pressure of the labouring classes for employment than to the decreased competition for labour on the part of the landowners.

The prices of articles of consumption have, during the past twenty years, risen by over 20 per cent, and though theoretically the rise should have gone to benefit the producers, still, that they have not been so benefited is apparent from the fact that agricultural wages have not only been stationary, but in several places have gone down. It is remarkable that labourers who obtain employment in the new and foreign industries established in towns within recent years, would not give up their lien on the agricultural occupation. If the season is bad, they work in factories and mines, and earn higher wages. But if the season is favourable, they prefer their old hereditary occupation to that of the new alien one in spite of the higher wages that can be got from it.

Sometimes the employers and the labourers enter into an understanding that the latter are to work only during the months of the year when no cultivation takes place. The spirit of the Western 'economic man,' who works for wages and has one sentiment associated with his occupation is different from that of the indigenous Indian farm labourer who looks upon work on the fields where his ancestors worked as more honourable than that in factories and mines amidst a miscellaneous multitude in receipt of wages paid from day to day or from week to week.

Taking different stations at random, we make out the following statement showing the monthly wages of the able-bodied agricultural labourer :—

Monthly Wages in Rupees, of Able-bodied Agricultural Labourer.

	Patna.	Cawnpore.	Rawal-pindi.	Ahmeda-bad.	Raipur.	Salem.
1891	4 to 5	5	6	7·5	4	3·33
1892	4 ,, 5	3	6	6	6 to 7	3·75
1893	4 ,, 5	4 and 5	7	6	5·62	3·75
1894	4 ,, 5	4 ,, 5	7·5	7	4 to 6	3·75
1895	4 ,, 5	5 ,, 5	6·09	7	4	3·83
1896	4 ,, 5	3·28 ,, 3·75	6·56	7	5	3·83
1897	4 ,, 5	4 ,, 5	6·56	7	4	3·83
1898	4 ,, 5	3·44 ,, 5	7	7·5	4	4·19
1899	4 ,, 5	3·45 ,, 5	7	5·62	3	4·37
1900	4 ,, 5	3·56 ,, 5	7	5	4	3·44

Thus, in many parts of the country, agricultura wages have fallen in spite of the pronounced advance in prices, which militates against the contention that increased prices have brought increased profits into the pockets of the producers. The fact is, the profits arising from increased prices are intercepted by middlemen. In most cases, the ryots are unable to choose their own time or conditions in the disposal of their produce. The great majority are so poor that the produce of the land hardly suffices to feed the family for more than some months in the year; the deficiency being made good by wages earned in the village or in the neighbouring town. The ryot cannot, therefore, meet from his produce the requirements of himself and his family as well as the demands of the Government and of the money-lender. For one or the other, often for both purposes, the ryot borrows at a usurious rate of interest; what produce he makes up his mind to sell off, he sells off when the pressure from the Government or the Sowcar is most tight, at prices which are considerably lower than the prices prevailing at certain seasons in the year or in adjacent towns or at the sea-ports. To the question, who intercepts the profits of the producer from increased prices, the reply is, partly the Sowcar, and partly the middleman who buys the grain from the villager and sells it at a time when the market is dear.

The daily labourer has not fared better during recent years. The following table shows the rates of wages for certain classes of labourers in the same stations as in the above statement:—

Monthly Wages, in Rupees, of a Common Mason, Carpenter or Blacksmith.

	Patna.	Cawnpore.	Rawal-pindi.	Ahmeda-bad.	Raipur.	Salem.
1891	7 to 8	8 to 10	22·5	18·75	10 to 15	11·5
1892	7 ,, 8	7·5 & 9·37	22·5	18·75	8 to 15	11·67 to 12·67
1893	6 ,, 7	7·5 ,, 9·37	22·5	18·75	11 ,, 22	11·67 ,, 12·67
1894	6 ,, 7	7·5 ,, 9·37	22·5	18·75	15 ,, 25	11·67 ,, 12·67
1895	6 ,, 7	7·5 ,, 9·37	23·9	18·75	10	11·67 ,, 12·67
1896	6 ,, 7	7·5 ,, 9·37	21·87	22·5	12 to 15	11·67 ,, 12·67
1897	6 ,, 7	7·5 ,, 9·37	23·12	22·5	15	12 ,, 12·69
1898	6 ,, 7	7·5 ,, 9·37	24·33	22·5	10	12 ,, 13·69
1899	6 ,, 7	7·6 ,, 9·37	22·5	18 to 22·5	7·5	12 ,, 14
1900	6 ,, 7	7·5 ,, 9·37	21·5	15 ,, 25	8 to 10	13·5 ,, 15·94

It is clear from the above that a rise in prices has not uniformly led to a corresponding rise of wages; on the other hand, a fall in wages has not been incompatible with a rise in prices. The fact is, in regard to daily labour, in our present social condition, the chief factor determining the wages is the principle of unrestricted competition, or of demand and supply. The competition of the labourers is most inefficient and unintelligent. Incapable of either co-operation or organization, each working man caring for himself and not considering the interest of his neighbour or of the whole class, without a desire or motive to improve his lot, the Indian labourer is doing injury to himself by his thoughtless competition.

Is the law of competition, of demand and supply, the right principle in cases of this kind? The competition is most unequal, the labourer, though nominally free, being the slave of the imperative requirements of his daily life. Starvation or the sale of his labour at any price, is the only alternative. In such a case, the economic law of competition should be ruled out, and a principle more rational, just, and regardful of social interests as a whole, should be enforced. This can be done by a spontaneous development of a feeling of generosity or charity on the part of the employers towards the helpless poor, or by the action of the State. We do not assert that the former is impossible; but the development of such a feeling in uncertain and indefinite, and its practical operation must be spasmodical and capricious.

The State is, therefore, the only agency that could and should take up the responsibility of protecting the weaker side in this unlimited and really unequal competition, erroneously called free. The British political thought has not quite risen to the level of the German thought in regard to the duties of the State as the organized and collective custodian of the totality of social interests and of social well-being. Modern German economists have rightly condemned the British conception of society, from this point of view. "That conception is mechanical, automistic and purely material; it reduces to nullity all moral forces and ignores the necessity of a moral order. It is at bottom no more than a theory of private property and private interests, and takes no account of the life of a people as a whole in its national solidarity and historical continuity." The evils arising from unrestricted competition have been brought to the surface by German writers, and the necessity of the State to act in accordance with the wider interests of large communities has been emphasised. It is urged that the State ought to protect the weaker members of society, especially women, the aged, and the destitute. It ought to secure the labourer against the cupidity of the sweater and the profit earner, and against the consequences of the labourer's own ignorance. It ought to help, through legal recognition and supervision, the efforts of the working classes for joint, no less than individual, self-help. If this conception of the State were to prevail in this country, the necessity for its interference would become apparent. That the Indian labourer is unable to protect himself against the consequences of his helplessness is clear. The low wages he is content to receive are steadily bringing about a dangerous deterioration in his physique, health and morality, and calls for prompt and effectual remedies.

What are low wages? We have become so accustomed to the poverty, squalor, and degradation of these unfortunate clases that we have become callous, and our rulers, as well as ourselves, have no qualms of conscience at their condition, which is truly the result of the neglect and oppression of the higher classes of the community and of the State, during centuries. Indians want but little, and that little not long—seems to be the postulate with which certain critics of India's economic condition start. Such a postulate is serious enough when society is left to itself in the adjustment of its dealings with the labourers dependent on it; but when the State, which is a large employer of labour and which ought to protect the ignorant and helpless, more especially the manual labourer, against the oppression of the higher classes, starts with that assumption and is satisfied it has done its duty when the labourer manages somehow to keep his life within his body, the consequence to these down-trodden creatures can be hardly less serious.

The only reasonable standard of wages is that they should be enough to enable the labourer, not only to procure sufficient nourishment and moderate comforts in ordinary times, but to save a small portion of his earnings to serve him in bad times. He should gradually rise to a higher standard of living, when he would clothe himself more fully and less dirtily ; live in decent cottages ; and surround himself by sanitary conditions. He should be gradually taught to value education, and his children should be able to receive at least the rudiments of knowledge. When the adequacy of the labourer's wages for his daily wants is considered, it is often forgotten that the labourer is as subject to illness as others, which disables him from earning his wages; or that the illness of others in his family keeps him away from work. He is subject to accidents, which have the same effect. He reaches old age without having made any previous provision for his maintenance, and becomes a dependant on others or resorts to begging. Besides these, the labourer has to meet extra demands on his slender income, like marriages, caste feasts, religious worship, and so forth, and it is unnatural to expect the Indian labourer to relinquish these innocent and often edifying duties. Does any intelligent observer of the condition of our labouring classes, more especially manual labourers, believe that the pittance of a penny a day will enable them to meet these various wants? Any rate of wages that will fail to do this is certainly a low rate, which must gradually work the deterioration of the large classes who live on the strength of their muscle and sinews.

The relentless law of competition, or supply and demand, by which the rich become richer and the poor poorer, has reduced our labourers to this pass. They are ignorant and do not understand the importance of self-restraint. The poorer classes in no part of the world have fully realised this. The poorer the individual, the more reckless is he in enlarging his family. One of the greatest curses of India, from the economic point of view, is the system of compulsory marriage. As a fact, it is the hopeless poverty of the lower classes that encourages their recklessness. If so, a rise in their standard of life may—and we have no doubt, will—bring about an improvement. It may be said that the better classes of Indians do not show a better appreciation of the importance of self-restraint. But in the case of these latter classes, marriage is considered more or less a religious duty. Every man and woman,—woman more especially,—must marry before a certain age, and failure to do so incurs social odium. But the working classes do not regard marriage in this light. Neither the man nor the woman is compelled to marry, though, as a rule, this discretion is more rarely availed of by the woman. But she can marry at a comparatively advanced age; and a widow is permitted to marry again without social disabilities following her doing so. The labouring man can remain unmarried all his life, and his society takes no notice of it. It is, therefore, by no means an unwarranted inference that we make, the inference, namely, that a substantial improvement in the material condition of the labouring classes will make them more provident and self-respectful than they are in their present abject condition.

The exceedingly low wages that the labourers receive have the tendency, in consequence of unrestricted and inefficient competition, to pull them down deeper in the slough of poverty. A labourer content with 2 as 6 pies a day will not hesitate, under pressure, to take 2 as. He already gets hardly one meal a day, and we are told by competent official authorities that millions of Indian labourers hardly know what it is to have their hunger fully satisfied. In this state, the labourer feels that a few pies gone out of his usual wages is of no consequence. If he gives up the job, another labourer is only too ready to take it up at the reduced rate. There being no combination among these people, the labourer that undersells his fellow labourer is subjected to no penalty of any kind by his community. In a country where the labouring classes are accustomed to decent living and are self-reliant, their misery below a certain point becomes intolerable, and is soon ended by the labourers striking work or refusing to accept wages below a certain rate. But in India the labourer has reached the lowest depth of degradation, and does not mind sinking one step deeper. The employer, solely mindful of his interest, pays only the wage that the labourer can be induced to accept. Here and there a solitary employer of labour may chance to be actuated by a sense of charity or generosity, and pay to the workman a reasonable wage ; but the conscience of the general community of employers has not been roused, by any effort till now made or by public opinion or by religious sentiment, to a sense of its duty to its poorer members in this respect. When labourers are employed in a spirit of charity or philanthropy, as they are employed by Government and private individuals in times of famine or severe scarcity, the rates of wages, if below the usual scale, connot be made subjects of legitimate complaint. But in normal times when the labour is purchased to meet the employer's need, the employer strains his right and takes advantage of the labourer's ignorance and want, and pays him what will not suffice to satisfy his craving, not to speak of maintaining his physical efficiency.

A sympathetic observer of the poor labourers in the roads of Madras will be struck by the abject distress to which they are patient victims day after day and which degrades them to the condition of brutes whose place they take in dragging heavy laden carts—laden with piles of rice bags, of rough skin, of deal wood boxes, and of firewood. Two or more of them join together,—often a woman among them—and plod along, under the pouring rain as well as under the scorching sun, with a piece of rag to cover their nakedness and another to protect their head against the sun or to make less hard the impact of the heavy vehicle which they push with their head from behind, and with perspiration running in streams down their frame from the top of the head to the very sole of the feet. The brute itself will refuse to work so heavily. But these helpless creatures willingly degrade themselves to brutes, for the pittance of four annas, which hardly leaves a balance for fuel for warm water to soothe their aching frame in the evening. Excessive work often makes them ill, and they fail, too, to get a job. Sometimes they meet with accidents confining them to their homes. Most of these unfortunate people do not own their own house, but live in hired rooms, miserable dens, nurseries of disease and epidemics. Even these dens are rare luxuries to the class filling a lower stratum, to the class of Pariahs who live all the day with the whole family—with wife and children—on the gutters or in the nooks and turns of the road, and. in the night, sleep somewhere convenient. It is unreasonable to expect these persons to insist on any minimum wage for their work. Under the pinch of hunger any trifle is welcome, and, thus, clad in dirty rags, badly and insufficiently nourished, amidst the most abominable insanitary conditions, the sands of their hour glass run out. They are ignorant and helpless and cannot take care of themselves. Is there anybody whose duty it is to enquire how these people get on, and whether anything can be done to make their lot less abject and less brutal? So long as they are in this state of hopeless degradation, they will be constantly subject to the temptation of sinking deeper. If they are once enabled to have a taste of comfort and decency, they will develop a sense of self-respect and will raise labour to its dignity as the foundation of the prosperity of the nation. On the whole, the lot of our labouring population is such a slur on British rule that, earlier or later, its amelioration will claim the earnest attention of Government. In the opinion of the writer in the American magazine we have already referred to, one of the first steps towards improving the condition of the employed is the provision of clean and comfortable rooms where men or women may eat their mid-day meal, away from the noise, dirt and routine of the work-bench or machine. The most far-sighted employers have been quick to see that taking care of their employês was good business, and have fitted up kitchens where a warm meal of plain substantial food may be served at cost. The captains of Industry will slowly learn a lesson from the captains of War, who set great store by the physical equipment of their army, fully recognizing that the best-fed and the best-nourished soldier is the most efficient.

"In advising an employer what form of industrial betterment he will find the most important, I place a provision for a home, which, after all, is the true social centre. In the work-shop, the worker is under discipline; his course of action is thought out for him, and he thus becomes a part of the system, a cognisant, an intelligent machine, so to speak. In his home he is absolutely free; if the surroundings are such as to keep him in good health, to enable him to enjoy the charms of family life, he becomes a better man and a better citizen."

Thus, the first and the greatest want of the labouring classes is good health secured by decent dwellings as well as by sufficient nourishing food. The second want is intelligence. The Indian labourer is neither healthy nor intelligent. The poverty and privation to which the agricultural labourer is subject are well-known. He cannot possibly be healthy when his average income is less than one anna a day, and when in times of distress he can get no more nourishment than one full meal in two days. The day-labourer in towns under employers of large capital is hardly better.

Though his wages are slightly better than those of his brother of the village,still theyare not good enough to meet the requirements of the more costly living in towns. It is not always borne in mind that, more than on the property of the people, on their health and vitality do famines produce disastrous effects. Looking at these diasters entirely from the point of view of public revenues, Government declare that the famine is over the moment that rains fall, and congratulate themselves on the increase in revenues and detect a marvellous recuperative power in the tax-paying classes. But, as a fact, the famine does more harm by its after effects than by its ravages during its actual career. As Mr. Vaughan Nash observes : "Famine is not over and done with, when the rains are falling and crops are being gathered. The effect of months of starvation cannot be summed up in the death rate of the current year or the year that follows the famine. Fever sweeps away millions whose stregth has been undermined, and the full effect of the birth rate is not felt, until the time comes when in the ordinary course of things, the children, who have died of hunger, would have married and become parents." Of the true magnitude of this evil we do not see much public consciousness ; yet, as Mr. Mulhall says, "it is certain than an unhealthy nation has never yet been a prosperous one." In the weak, sickly and deteriorated condition of the labourer, the State and the nation are undergoing a very serious material loss. If, in regard to their health, our labouring classes are in an abject state, they are no better in regard to their intelligence Very few know how to read or write, and though in general intelligence they are not worse than the labourers of European countries, still, in their knowledge of the world and of human nature, they are at the lowest stage possible, which makes them helpless whenever their interests get into conflict with those of their powerful emloyers.

The interests of a humble and neglected class cannot easily be made a subject of interest to statesmen. Still, human evils do not for ever remain without rousing indignation in some virtuous souls, and even the Indian labourer may have a Lord Shaftsbury or a Mr. Robert Owen, rising to denounce his hard and neglected lot and press for adequate reform. In England, where, at the beginning of the Victorian era, the labouring classes were in a much worse condition than they are at present in this country, the day of awakening did at last come. The legalising of combination in 1824, the extension of political power in 1832, the growth of Chartism, the earnest activity of philanthropists,—these, with the extension of railways, steam industry and education, taught the workmen that other times meant other ways. The English labourer is an altogether different person now to what he was 70 years ago. He has access to more plenty and more comforts ; he knows his rights and his power ; he can combine with his fellow-labourers and defeat the employer ; his freedom and his intelligence have made him an honourable citizen with aspiration and hopes ; he is in fact no longer a negligible factor in society. There is no reason why the poor Indian coolie should remain for ever what he is now, and should not realise an honourable and happy future.

CHAPTER XIII.

Free Trade and Labour.

NUMEROUS writers have come forward in England just now to instruct the electors on the respective benefits of free trade and of protection with reference to the tariff proposals of Mr. Chamberlain. To the people of the United Kingdom the issues raised are of the most serious importance. To us in India they are not less so. In the inquiry that is now being made by the Ministers, India is said to be also included, though from the debate in the House of Lords* it does not appear that any important departure from the present policy will happen. It is unfortunate that the enquiry is not conducted publicly, and that no opportunity is to be afforded for Indian opinion being represented. It is very desirable—it is necessary—that the policy under which the economic growth of India has been directed ever since the connection between England and India began, should be reconsidered, in view to what results it has produced in the past as well as to the results it is calculated to produce in the immediate future if it be not modified with exclusive regard for the happiness and contentment of the Indian people. We need not say that, not the exclusive interests of this country, but chiefly

* July 10, 1903.

those of the ruling country have determined that policy. It is no wonder, therefore, that, during a century and a half of British rule, the millions of this country have steadily deteriorated instead of prospering in their material condition. That the British statesmen should express satisfaction with the results of the system of free trade adopted in India is not new. We are accustomed to hear even our best well- ishers among British statesmen eulogise the so-called beneficial results that have followed it. Lord Northbrooke and the other ex-Viceroys that spoke at the debate, all expressed themselves in favour of free trade and against protection in regard to this country It is extremely unfortunate that experienced and sagacious statesmen who know India and who sincerely sympathise with her people should think so ; because, far from having prospered under free trade, India has been ruined, and would be further ruined in the future if the same policy were pursued. Free trade has been a blessing to the people of the United Kingdom, more especially to the poorer classes. It has furnished an enormous stimulus to her manufactures and trade ; it has given to the poorer classes cheap food and higher wages, and it has brought untold wealth to the capitalists. But in India, in regard to every one of these respects, the reverse has taken place. Free trade has destroyed our old valuable industries ; it has made articles of food dearer, has prevented the rise of wages. It has drained India of her capital ; it has brought into the country thousands of foreign exploiters who have monopolised every source of wealth. Even agriculture is no longer secure against these foreign intruders.

That this is the deplorable result of British rule, is not the opinion of the Indian people alone. Educated persons in other countries, are of this opinion. The recent famines during which the British Government of India, unable to protect the people from its exhausted resources, appealed for and obtained pecuniary help from every country in the world, have revealed the hollowness of its cry about the prosperity of India. In America and Germany, there are intelligent men and women who know that India is sinking into the slough of poverty and despair. "Step by step," to quote one of the many American papers that have recently written about India, "almost insensibly, the people of India are sinking deeper and deeper into poverty. Lord George Hamilton recently, in presenting the Indian budget to the British Parliament, described the prosperity of that great dependency, and based his statements on the fact that there was a surplus in the revenue. He failed, however, to say how it was created and at what cost to the people of India. He did not describe the seizures from famine and plague-stricken people for long arrears of rent, and how, to meet the inexorable demands of their alien rulers, the unfortunate *rayats* had had to part with their brass cooking utensils which found their way to the brass foundries of Bombay by cart loads from the interior; and women had to sell their silver ornaments (depreciated in their value by the British currency policy), which were in many cases cherished heir-looms and represented the poor savings of years and generations. How little the science of Government is understood by the class that is ruling India will be understood from the fact that the present financial adviser of the Government of India is neither an economist nor a financier, but simply an ex-Major of British artillery, the instrument of the necromantic influence alluded to." "The people of England, who are theoretically responsible for India through the British Parliament, are both indifferent and ignorant alike to their duties and responsibilities, and, so, the affairs of India, as Lord Salisbury once described, "drift" on to the day of reckoning."

Is there a day of reckoning ? Will that be averted or accelerated ? Which of the two will happen entirely depends on the wisdom and honesty of the rulers. That India, once so prosperous, should have been reduced to this miserable plight, in spite of every condition that makes for prosperity is only to be expected. Between India and England there is no similarity of conditions ; on the other hand they are as poles asunder in their economic state, and instead of a distinct policy suited to India being pursued, the same policy of free-trade suited to England, and to England alone among all countries in the world, is being pursued. In the earlier years of British rule, when the industries of India were in a more efficient condition than those of England and when free trade might have benefited India, a most heart-rending and oppressive system of restrictions and prohibitions was appli ed to the manufactured exports of India, and through many channels her wealth flowed to London. While the import and consumption in England of the manufactured articles of India were prohibited, her treasure was carried away by British adventurers and it created a class of capitalists with large accumulations of Indian money. This money stimulated the credit of this class, imparted mobility to their energy and enterprise, and within fifty years, England was able to rise to a level of prosperity not only unprecedented in her own history, but unmatched by any country on the Continent.

By the beginning of the 19th century, the foundation of British prosperity had been well laid on the spoliation of India and Ireland. A class of merchant princes had risen to prominence ; and the landlords had been stirred to emulation to amass wealth from the profits of their estates. From England did almost every country in the world borrow ; from her came the capital for every great commercial or industrial enterprise abroad ; and a craze for railway-building seized the monied classes. The industry of agriculture was neglected, and manufactures were pushed by every legitimate and illegitimate means, so that her own factories might supply the wants of the world and her own ships might absorb the carrying trade. She exchanged her manufactures for the food and raw materials she imported and for the large amounts of interest due to her on account of her foreign investments. Thus was created the condition which rendered a perfect freedom of import necessary, and with freedom of import came naturally the freedom of export. It only wanted the genius of Cobden to give practical fulfilment to this condition. England created her industry, as the Russian Finance Minister truly observes, "by rigorous protection, and when by this means she had become industrially and commercially stronger than any other nation, and, therefore, feared no competition, she adopted a policy of free trade."

Nor can exception be taken to M. de Witte's *dictum*, that "the State, in the province of consumption, should furnish the population with cheap and suitable produce ; and in the province of production, develop the productive powers of the country." In the experience of every country in the world, it has been seen, at a certain stage, that it is more important to develop its productive powers than to supply its people with cheap produce. England herself did this throughout the eighteenth and the first half of the nineteenth century. For, if the productive powers were developed, making full use of the home markets, a number of national industries would spring into existence, and cheap food and high wages would be eventually enjoyed by the population. When England imposed heavy duties on the Indian silk and cotton manufactures, and prohibited their consumption by her own people, she adopted this policy. She would not allow the cheap and nice articles from India to be used by the English people, but was content with the home-made dear and coarse fabrics. She even re exported to the Continental countries, at considerable loss, the imports from her factories in India. Thus, at the cost of her own consumers, England developed the " productive powers" of the people ; and in the wake of the developed productive powers, came flourishing manufactures and skilled mental and bodily labour. America, like other countries, has resisted the fascination of the British free-trader's siren songs and has reached an economic state which, as M. de Witte says, emboldens some of her citizens to call for a system of free-trade. Germany and Russia have yet to reach such a state, and they stick to a protective system in the hope of attaining it earlier or later. But, under the system of free trade in India, the State has neither furnished the people with cheap and suitable produce, nor enabled them to develop their productive powers. If free trade in England, is " no part of the Sermon on the Mount", much less can it be such in India. If changed conditions of the British Empire demand a change in her system of foreign trade, much more imperatively is a change called for in India of which the conditions were never in favour of such a system.

Writers who are conversant only with the social conditions of Europe defend unrestricted competition on the ground that capital or labour, when driven from one means ot emyloyment, will find another, perhaps more suited to its conditions. This may be true in the Western countries in modern times. But, in India, it is certainly not true. In England itself the misery that overtook the weaving classes on the introduction of machinery to replace manual labour, proves that a social state can prevail when the emyloyment of labour-saving contrivances might be carried too far and might result in more harm than good to the poorer classes. In 1883, Sir John Bowring made a speech in the House of Commons, wherein he referred to the condition of 50,000 hand-loom weavers of London who had been starving without being able to find that new kind of employment, which the free-traders held out to them in the distance. "The misery of the hand-loom weavers," he said, "is the inevitable fate of all kinds of labour which are easily acquired, and which may, at any moment, be replaced by less costly means. As in all these cases, competition amongst the working people is very great, the slightest falling off in demand brings on a crisis. The hand-loom weavers are, in a certain sense, placed on the verge of human existence. One step further, and that existence becomes impossible. The slightest shook is sufficient to throw them on the road to ruin. By more and more superseding manual labour, the progress of mechanical science must result, during the period of transition, in much temporary suffering. National well-being cannot be bought except at the price of some individual evils. The advance of industry is achieved at the expense of those who lag behind, and of all discoveries that of the power-loom weighs most heavily upon the hand-loom weavers. In a great many articles formerly made by hand, the weaver has been completely ousted; but he is sure to be beaten in a good many more stuffs that are now made by hand."

In England this transition period soon come to an end, and the labourers thrown out of employment for temporary periods soon found fresh occupations and were restored to their normal standard of life. In India, for over one century and a half, the deplorable unsettlement of the old indigenous industrial system has gone on, and the culmination has not been reached yet. The unsettlement commenced with the inroads of British merchants who deliberately crushed native industries and reduced the artizans and craftsmen to the status of daily labourers. Sir John Bowring, in the same speech, referred to the revolution wrought in the condition of Indian labourers. He said, " I hold in my hand a correspondence of the Governor-General with the East India Company. The correspondence is about the weavers of the Dacca District. The Governor says in his letter : A few years ago, the East India Company received from six to eight million pieces of calico woven upon the looms of the country. The demand fell off gradually and was reduced to about a million pieces. At this moment it has almost entirely ceased. Moreover, in 1800, North America received from India nearly 800,000 pieces of cotton goods. In 1830 it did not take even 4,000. Finally, in 1800, a million pieces were shipped to Portugal ; in 1830 Portugal did not receive above 20,000. The reports on the distress of the Indian weavers are terrible. And what is the origin of that distress? The presence in the market of English manufactures, the production of the same articles by means of the power-loom. A great number of the weavers died of starvation; the remainder have gone over to other employment, and chiefly to field labour. Not to be able to change employment amounted to a sentence of death. And to this moment, the Dacca Disirict is crammed with English yarns and piece goods. The Dacca muslin, renowned all over the world for its beauty and firm texture, had also been eclipsed by the competition of British machinery. *In the whole history of commerce, it would perhaps be difficult to find suffering equal to what these whole classes in India had to submit to.*"

Thus, nearly a century ago, the displacement of the skilled manual labour of the Indians by machinery began and caused large numbers of lives to be lost by death from starvation, besides driving even larger numbers to field labour. The same terrible fate has pursued the Indian weavers down to this day, and the weavers in the obscurest corners of this vast continent are abandoning hereditary occupation for others which are less remunerative and which require less skill. The weaving industry was the first to be throttled by the raids of British imports; but a similar fate soon overtook other industries, until, at the present day, with the 26,000 miles of railways traversing every part of the country and almost annihilating the distance between the village and the sea port, every industry has been nearly killed. What is the result of this truly heart-rending spoliation? Millions of workmen who pursued hereditary occupations, which called into exercise their intelligence and imagination, and who therefore led a life of decent means and self-respect, have been reduced to a condition of abject poverty, having become agricultural labourers or day-labourers in towns. Agriculture has become the sole occupation of the great bulk of the nation, who, earning much lower wages than their forefathers did, degenerate in vitality and add to the annual mortality of the country, to the disease and suffering of the people, and to the burden of the earning classes by setting on the world at large ever-increasing numbers of weaklings, cripples, and men smitten with infirmity and disease. It is the hypocritic cry of the apologists of British rule in India that the investment of British capital furnishes means of emplyment to hundreds of thousands of labourers who would otherwise have remained a burden on the income of the villages or competed with other coolies in towns. But it seldom occurs to them to ask themselves how such a state of things has to come to pass. It is nothing but the heartless industrial vandalism of Britain that has brought it about, and to-day we are called upon to admire the feeble palliation of its effects in the factories, mines, and plantations owned by the very authors of the evil. The industrial greatness of Britain was built on the ruin of India, and the classes that have been ruined have no hope, under existing political conditions, of the advent of better times.

While this conversion of whole classes of skilled labourers into unskilled and degraded workers, continues, the prospect of native industries conducted on modern principles with the help of machinery, is indefinitely put off by the chances of indigeneous capital and credit growing in the country being minimised. How colossal the evil is can be judged from the astounding fact that twelve million and a half of adult males are without work in India all the year round. Sir James Caird first brought this terrible fact to light. "The waste of energy," he wrote in 1878, "converted into its money value at, say, 40 rupees per adult per annum, represents a loss of Rx. 82,000,000 or 82 crores—more than the whole gross revenue of the Indian empire." "In no agricultural country that I know of, are so many people to be seen stalking idly about during the hours of labour in India. The streets and court houses, and yards are always full of idlers. The roads are never empty, and the railway carriages are crammed with people. Enter a village at any hour of the day, you are surrounded by idlers. *Much of this arises from the absence of other occupations than agriculture,* and in many parts of the country from the uncertain character of land tenure." What are these poor people to do? Agriculture gives no continuous occupation for all months in the year; and, in towns, the competition of labour for employment is always so keen that there is hardly elbow room for fresh arrivals at any time.

The East India Company became the administrators of Bengal in the year 1765. Four years later, they issued an order that "the manufacture of silk fabrics should be discouraged in Bengal, that the people should produce raw silk in India to be woven in England, that the Indian silk-winders should be made to work in the Company's factories and prohibited from working outside, under severe penalties, by the authority of Government." The effect of this mandate, according to the Select Committee of the House of Commons of 1783, was to change the whole face of the country with its industries, in order to render it a field for the produce of crude materials subservient to the manufactures of Great Britain. Subsequent to the report of this Select Committee, an inquiry was made, as usual, before the renewal of the Charter in 1813. Eminent witnesses like Warren Hastings, Sir Thomas Munro, and Sir John Malcolm were examined. They were asked by the House of Commons, not how the manufactures of India could be fostered, but how they could be discouraged so as to make room for British manufactures. For it was found ,even at that date, that Indian silk and cotton goods could be sold in England at a price from 50 to 60 per cent. lower than those produced in England. What was the policy that England pursued ? She imposed a prohibitive duty which killed the Indian manufactures. The following statement was made by Joseph Ranking before the House of Commons during their enquiry of 1813 :—

" Can you state what is the *ad valorem* duty on piece goods sold at the East India House ?"

" The duty on the class called calicoes is £3. 6*s*. 8*d*. per cent. upon importation, and if they are used for home consumption, there is a further duty of £68. 6*s*. 8*d*. per cent.

"There is another class called muslins on which the duty on importation is 10 per cent.. and if they are used for home consumption, of £27. 6*s*. 8*d* per cent.

"There is a third class, coloured goods, which are prohibited being used in this country, upon which there is a duty upon importation of £3. 6*s*. 8*d*. per cent ; they are only for exportation.

"This Session of Parliament, there has been a new duty of 20 per cent, on the consolidated duties, which will make the duties on calicoes. . . . used for home consumption £78. 6*s*. 8*d*. per cent., upon the muslins for home consumption £3. 6*s*. 8*d*."

There was no thought of concealing the real object of these prohibitive duties. The same witness, Joseph Ranking, said further on : "I look upon it as a protecting duty to encourage our own manufactures."

England adopted this policy of rigid protection in the face of the theories which Adam Smith and his disciples were loudly preaching. According to these theories, England should have bought what she required where she could buy then cheapest and best. But, as a fact, as is seen from the evidence of Joseph Ranking, England not only prohibited the consumption within her boundaries of the cheap imports from India, but re-exported to the Continent the fine Indian fabrics at lower prices, contenting herself with her own inferior and more costly stuffs. As the German economist, Friedrich List, observes, "had the cotton and silk goods of India been allowed to be imported into England and consumed by her people, the English cotton and silk manufactures should have soon come to an end." The British Ministers, therefore, set aside Adam Smith's theories regarding the efficiency of exchange. Said Adam Smith : " It is the maxim of every prudent master of a family never to attempt to make at home what it will cost him more to make than to buy. The tailor does not attempt to make his own shoes, but buys them from the shoe-maker. . . . . What is prudence in the conduct of every private family can scarce be folly in that of a great kingdom." But the policy actually pursued was contrary to this " well-known maxim." England pursued exactly the policy which she is now so loud and vehement in condemning other nations for pursuing. The maxim of her statesmen was to import produce and export fabrics ; and in fulfilling this, they did not mind if the nation were obliged to use costly and coarse home made stuff, instead of cheap and fine fabrics imported from abroad. She aimed at the development of her powers of production, and at the establishment of flourishing manufactures, in which the accumulated money of her capitalists and landlords might be invested, and the products of which might be exchanged for the corn and raw materials imported from foreign countries.

The Parliamentary inquiries of 1813 brought no relief to Indian manufactures. The prohibitive duties were not reduced. The Company's investments were not stopped. On the contrary, they were distinctly sanctioned by the Committee of the whole House.

" The whole or part of any surplus that may remain of the above described rents, revenues and profits, after providing for the several appropriations, and defraying the several charges before-mentioned, shall be applied to the provision of the Company's investments in India, in remittances to China for the provision of investments there, or towards the liquidation of debts in India, or such other purposes as the Court of Directors, with the approbation of the Board of Commissioners, shall from time to time direct."

Of this peculiar system of trade, the immortal Burke wrote: " In all other countries, the revenue following the natural course and order of things, arises out of their commerce. Here, (in India,) by a mischievous inversion of that order, the whole foreign maritime trade, whether English, French, Dutch, or Danish, arises from the revenues; these are carried out of the country, without producing anything to compensate so heavy a loss." But apart from this drain, how were those parts of the revenues, not employed in the Company's own investments, disposed of? Here, again, we have Burke's description of the great injustice done to India—injustice, it may be remarked, that has continued from his time up to the present moment. " From the portion of that sum which goes to the support of civil government, the natives are almost wholly excluded, as they are from the principal collections of revenue." In regard to the army, " all the honourable, all the lucrative situations, all the supplies and the contracts of whatever species that belong to the army, are solely in the hands of the English, so that, whatever is beyond the mere subsistence of a common soldier and of some officers of a lower rank, together with the immediate expense of the English officers at their table, is sooner or later, in one shape or another, sent out of the country."

It was thus that India was brought under contribution to the manufacturing and commercial greatness of England. The foundation having been thus strongly laid, it is no wonder that England has prospered remarkably under a system of free-trade. What might have been the economic career of India, if England had not deliberately crushed her industries, it were vain to consider. But Indian opinion is entirely opposed to that of Lord Northbrook, who thinks that India has prospered under free-trade. She has not prospered. She can prosper only under a system of protection. An impoitant condition that is essential for the success of protection is fulfilled in India in the enormous variety and extent of her home markets.

Now, to go back to the subjeot of the effect of England's economic treatment of India on her labouring classes. In England there are people who believe that free-trade has not done much for these classes. It has given them cheap food no doubt, but it has counteracted this benefit by checking the rise of wages. Cheap food is no doubt a great blessing to the poor man ; but it often induces him to be content with low wages, and he is easily exploited by the capitalist. No employer will give more wages than the labourer is willing to take; and cheap food drives the latter, on account of competition among his class, to the lowest rate compatible with mere sustenance. It was recently admitted by the leader of the Free-Trade Liberals himself that, in spite of the cheap food due to free-trade, no less than a third of the whole population of Britain are living below the "poverty line," and are so wretchedly poor that even the addition of a farthing to the price of the four pound loaf is a matter of serious concern to them "Prosperity, indeed!" exclaims a Social Democratic organ. "There has been prosperity, no doubt, for the classes which have been able to extend their commerce and build up their fortunes on the cheap labour which freely-imported food gave them ; but the prosperity of the masses of the people is a hollow mockery." If the masses are prosperous, how does it happen that Sir William Anson and the Earl of Meath, and the general public in agreement with them, are alarmed at the gradual deterioration of the physique of the working classes ?

An Indian writer in Bombay recently maintained that in India free-trade has immensely benefited the poor millions. We doubt if, in making such a statement, the writer knew what he was writing about. If he would compare the condition of the working classes, including artisans and farm labourers, in the pre-British days when there was no free-trade, with the condition of the same classes at present after half a century of its prevalence, he would know how erroneous his view is. In England, free-trade has given the poor people cheap food ; in India it has done the reverse. In England wages have risen in all industries, as the result of accumulated capital and large profits, although, as will appear from above, the wages thus raised are still inadequate to maintain the physical strength of the masses. In India it is notorious that free-trade has not resulted in a rise of wages. On the other hand, it has brought prosperity to the foreign capitalist, who exploits the cheap labour of the half-starving coolie and makes large profits. Every pound of foreign capital brought into the country adds to the destruction of indigenous industries, and every industry thus destroyed drives thousands of people to field labour or to coolie work. Not only do the numbers of the labouring classes thus increase, but they all crowd into the same occupation which any man can do and which requires no particular intelligence or skill. Thus, the foreign capital, for whose abundance in this country we are indebted to free-trade, operates on the wages in two ways and reduces them to a point much below that of mere sustenance. When there are ten men competing for work which can be done by one, and when any of them, without previous training or inherited aptitude, can do it as well as another, what effect will be produced on wages can be imagined. The employer will not be slow to take full advantage of this excessive competition.

Nor should we be misled by the specious argument that free-trade means a division of labour among nations. The argument is as dishonest as the self-complacent assumption that it is the merciful dispensation of Providence that the destinies of the world should be directed by the white races as the masters with the black races as their slaves. It is the latest notion of the brotherhood of man which Christianity has taught the nations of the West. It is implied that India should remain for ever an agricultural country producing raw materials, while England makes use of these raw materials and supplies India with manufactured goods. There is no natural reason whatsoever why this should be so. As we have pointed out already India was a manufacturing as well as an agricultural country before British rule put an end to her industries. It was not the prosperity of the agricultural classes that attracted foreign nations, but the splendour and prosperity of the towns. Two centuries ago, Nature, which does not trouble itself about commerce and which favours all nations as well as individuals alike, had planted neither sugercane nor coffee plants in the West Indies. It may so happen that within a few decades no sugarcane or coffee plant will be found there. The weavers of Dacca who, from the beginning of time till British competition destroyed their industry, wove by hand, were apparently destined by Nature to that occupation. But what Nature proposed Manchester has disposed! And now field or town labour is said to be their natural destiny!

Then, who is it that has made this international division of labour? So far as India and Britain are concerned, Britain has done it, and done it in a manner so beneficial to her. All industries are not equally large or paying. One industry prevails over others and secures to the nation that monopolises it immensely wider markets. The cotton industry is such a one. If Manchester had not secured the monopoly of this industry, perhaps the world would hear much less of free-trade from British money-makers. According to a recent letter in the *Times*, about half the cotton looms in the world (650,000 out of 13,50,000) are in Great Britain. The raw cotton to supply these looms costs about £35,000,000; the price for the finished products comes to about £ 90,000,000. Of the balance of £55,000,000, the greater part goes in wages. Of the total production the consumption of the home market, according to the writer of the letter, is less than 20 per cent. The rest is exported abroad. In the commerce of the world, cotton alone has much greater importance than all the other raw materials used in the manufacture of clothing. It is obvious that the nation that gets the monopoly of the trade whose products are of every day consumption almost all over the world, must be more prosperous than other nations. Britain, having got this, proclaims that the world must accept the present division as final!

Low prices and high wages mark a prosperous condition of a people. In India the reverse is the case. Writes the *Times of India* of Bombay: "The effect of the low wages in retarding the improvement of agriculture cannot be overrated. High wages are the whip which keeps the inventor and the 'enterpreneur' always on the look out for improved means of production. It is high wages that have made the United States so formidable a producer for the world's market. We do not go so far as to say that Trades Unions alone can bring about a rise of wages, but at the same time we do not believe with Dr. Pierson that a rise of prices automatically brings about a rise of wages. In India, as we have seen, a rise of prices is not infrequently accompanied by a fall of wages. The great thing is that the labourer should know his own interests. So long as he is ignorant, he will be oppressed by those who make use of his services. Every day's experience confirms us in the opinion that a larger spread of elementary education will prove economically more beneficial to the country than many other and more ambitious schemes."

CHAPTER XIV.

Railways.

THE services of Mr. Robertson were engaged by the Government of India, as an expert, to report on the administration of Railways in this country, and he has, accordingly, in an elaborate and able report, suggested improvements which, in his opinion, are necessary to bring the Indian administration into line with that of European countries and America. He has not touched on other questions which the construction of railways in India raises. There are special features connected with it in this country which are absent in other countries. Most of the money required is borrowed in the English market, and every million added to India's foreign debt swells her drain, which is already serious. Whether, in view to this fact and to the fact of India being no manufacturing but an entirely agricultural country, the construction of fresh railways should proceed at the same rapid pace as it has proceeded for some years, deserves to be considered. In the opinion of many persons, too much attention is given to railways, while the question of increasing the facilities of irrigation and of extending the means of communication in the rural parts, receives no adequate consideration. There is also the economic aspect of railways in India. Every mile of railway carried into the interior helps the introduction of foreign imported articles which replace products of indigenous industry. In the same way, it renders easy the transport of Indian articles from the villages to the sea-ports. Railways have put an end to the native middlemen's trade, which is now monopolised by the various railways. They have tended to raise the prices to a uniform level throughout India, and already a complaint is heard that the abundance of rice which Burma used to enjoy till now she is about to lose, because of the drain to other parts of the Indian Empire. Further, there is the important question of the employment of the Indian people in the administration of railways. There is no country in the world where not only is the money required for the construction of railways borrowed from foreigners, but the agency employed in their direction and administration also is foreign. Besides, according to the present system, the interest in their economical and efficient management is divided. There is first the Government whose interest in such management is of every imaginable variety. The people who are taxed to meet the cost, for whose benefit the profits of the railways are partly appropriated, and who make use of them for purposes of locomotion and of trade, have no less important interest. Besides the Government and the people, foreign merchants and capitalists have their own interest in these railways. It is this three-fold interest that has to be represented and reconciled in the construction of railways in this country. The interest of the one is not necessarily the interest of another. The foreign capitalists and merchants who constantly press for new railways are apt to use their best endeavours to bring about a general adoption of the principle of guaranteed interest in the general policy of the Government. The Government itself, for obvious reasons, is in favour of private enterprise relying on itself. Both the Government and the private capitalists ignore the political and economic aspects in which the people are deeply concerned ; and the travelling public are apt to be exploited by the companies to increase their net earnings.

Mr. Robertson has not given his attention to these various features of railway construction in this country. He confines his recommendations to improvements in the administration of railways. Even in this limited purview, we fear Mr. Robertson has failed to bear in mind the exceptional fact that the companies administering the railways consist of foreigners whose sole object and aim is to increase the earnings, and find lucrative employmont for as many of their relations and dependants as possible. He is oblivious of the fact that, between the foreign companies and the people, an impartial third-power is necessary to protect the interest of the latter. We are for these reasons opposed to the general drift of his recommendations that the direct control of the Government over the railways should be minimised. Not only should the Government retain a full control over them, but it should also set its face against a general adoption of the system of guaranteed interest in all cases of private enterprise. If the projected railways are such as will pay, no guarantee from the Government is necessary; and if they will not pay, the Government will not be justified in throwing away public money on unremunerative undertakings. What are called protective railways, in other words, railways necessary for the protection of certain tracts against famine, are under a different category altogether. In their case, the question of remunerativeness does not arise. But such railways have all been already constructed; and what are under contemplation now and what may be projected hereafter, are commercial concerns which ought to be started and run entirely on commercial lines. It is time that the resources of the country ceased to be wasted on undertakings of doubtful prospect. The Government of India is not accustomed to afford direct help to private enterprise. It has made an exception of railways and of certain planting industries. To do so was perhaps necessary in former times, and the people have paid a heavy penalty for the haste and folly of their rulers. The aid of a Government guarantee is very much wanted in other directions. There are scores of industries which could be started and developed if only the Government would extend its helping hand to the first pioneers. This the Government has persistently refused to do; and the justice or wisdom of bribing British capitalists at the cost of the taxpayers is not so patent. British capitalists investing their money in other countries do so at their own risk, and the Indian railway promoters have enough of inducement without a guaranteed interest on their investment from the Government of India.

Mr. Robertson is inclined to favour the system of management through the agency of companies in preference to the system of direct State management. At any rate, he is positively against the present system of dual control. The Goverument should either work all railways as State railways, or should lease them all to companies to work. The latter on the whole, he considers, would be the best course for India. We are not sure that it would be so. The railways being valuable State properties as they are in other countries, there is no reason why their management should be handed over to companies of foreigners who would not only intercept a part of the profits, but would also add to alien vested interests in the country which are already powerful enough and which often operate to the detriment of those of the people. It is obvious that the direct management by the State would be more economical, and would afford better guarantee for a due protection of whatever interests the people of the country may have in the railways. The foreign company cannot be in touch with the people as the State can ; and there would be more sympathy and confidence inspired in the public mind when the management is in the hands of those whose motives are not entirely the making of profits, but the protection of public interests also.

In no country in the world are all the organised big enterprises so entirely in the hands of foreigners and the people so rigidly kept out of them as in India. In every imaginable effort involving powers of organization, large expenditure and far-reaching results, it is Englishmen that are entrusted with the entire responsibility, whereas the people themselves, who often supply the sinews of war, are given menial positions, and receive hardly any training in the exercise of their higher mental faculties or in the invaluable capacity of corporate action. The character of a nation is formed chiefly by the occupations that bring into play its mental and moral faculties. A nation consisting of petty farmers must remain simple, superstitious and poverty stricken; whereas nations like the British, German or American, by virtue of their training, are able to handle world-wide interests and to protect their own against foreign competition however strong. There is hardly one Indian throughout the country who has any experience of railway management, for the simple reason that no one has had an opportunity to learn it. The Indian people cannot for ever remain the drudging slaves that they have been to help foreign wealth-seekers to make wealth at their cost. It would be, in our opinion, a great misfortune if the management of all our railways were vested in foreign companies with no other attachment to the country than the exploitation of it for their benefit. Mr. Robertson. throughout his lengthy report, shows no appreciation of the peculiar conditions of India. He writes as if India is in the same position as other countries in this respect. Under the alien British rule, India has developed a peculiar position which renders it necessary that the great problems of her well-being should be solved, not by a reference altogether to the experience and knowledge of other countries, but by a reference to her own requirements constantly overshadowed as they are by more powerful conflicting interests.

For three successive years the Indian railways have yielded a profit. For the first time in their history they yielded the small profit of 8·72 lakhs in the year 1900 ; in the next year the profit was 115 lakhs ; and in the year 1902, this dwindled to 20·41 lakhs. Some people talk as if these profits were the gift of the British capitalists to India. Of course, the fact is entirely different. These profits represent an infinitesimally small percentage of return on the enormous borrowed capital invested in them by the State. This capital amounts to nearly 500 crores ; and what profit does a net average earning of about 50 lakhs represent on this enormous outlay? It represents no more than a profit of ·01 per cent, whereas the investment of the Government of India in the execution of irrigation works yields a net profit of 8 or 9 per cent; and in regard to certain particular works, the profit is no less than 12 per cent. The whole of the profits does not go into the public treasury of India; only what remains after the payment of interest to the foreign lenders, dividends to the foreign shareholders, and salaries to the directors and the staff in London and to the host of foreign employês on the various lines throughout India, is appropriated by the Government. If the economic condition of India were like that of other self-governing countries in the world, India would derive really more substantial profits from her railways. The expenditure on them would be more moderate, and they would benefit the country in various ways. A chief portion of the capital would be the money of Indian lenders; and though the interest might be higher than that paid on foreign capital, still there would be the enormous advantage of the amount of interest being retained in the country and fructifying in the pockets of the people. The crores of Indian money now paid to foreign lenders as interest do double injury to India. Each rupee sent out of the country represents the starvation of an Indian for more than a fortnight; and, besides, each rupee thus sent abroad adds to the savings of the foreigner who lends his savings, thus augmented at India's expense, to exploit India further. Thus, with our own money the foreign exploiter impoverishes us. Not only would the interest on the railway debt remain and fructify in the country if the system were like that of other countries, but the administration would also be entirely in the hands of Indians who would receive the salaries and acquire the experience, which are now monopolised by foreigners.

The dwindling of the profits from 115 lakhs in 1901 to 20·41 lakhs in 1902, is explained by the fact that extensive repairs and revivals effected during the year enhanced the working expenses. As this expenditure, it is ingeniously added, was in the nature of the improvement of property, it will react favourably on the receipts. This may, indeed, happen. But it may also happen that the improvement, having but made good the deterioration in the property, would only help in maintaining the normal level of the income. The chief source of income is the passenger traffic, while the receipts from the goods traffic fluctuate from year to year, according to the state of the season. In times of adversity, there is greater movement of commodities, chiefly grain, while, in prosperous years, these are retained for local consumption in the neighbourhood of the places where they are produced. It is noteworthy that though the total weight of goods transported increased by two million tons, the earnings were less by Rs. 26,000. But the *Times of India* observes: "But the phenomenon is a sign of restored economic health rather than the reverse. The country's return to normal conditions rendered necessary a smaller movement in the lower class of foodstuffs and deprived several of the railways of the long lead on a large proportion of their traffic. There was, too, litttle or no movement to the ports of rape and mustard seeds, and the railways would have fared badly if it had not been for the large increase in the exports of wheat from Karachi and Bombay, and the growth of the trade in metals, jute, wood, cotton and fodder. The most unsatisfactory feature on this side of the accounts is the decline in the exports of coal."

In other words, the prosperous or the adverse condition of our railways is in inverse relation to that of the season. The largėr the depletion of the foodstuffs, which are so badly wanted for the consumption of our half-starved millions, and the greater the diversion of agricultural industry from food crops to non-food commercial crops, the larger are the receipts. For the rest, the railway income is mostly contributed by the middle and poorer classes. Unlike the large profits which the British nation earns on its shipping trade at the cost of foreign nations, the railway receipts of our country come from no extraneous source, but from the pockets of the people themselves. This is so, of course, in other countries also. But there is this serious difference between India and other countries. Whereas in other countries the railway revenues, like revenues from other sources, are spent in the country, the same revenues in India go for the benefit of the foreigner, except an infinitesimal fraction as we have pointed out above.

Moreover, railways in other countries are constructed mainly with a view to the stimulation of internal trade and home production, whereas in this country the policy is determined chiefly by a consideration of its foreign trade. To carry the export articles from the villages where they are produced to the seaports where they are shipped off to foreign countries, and to bring the foreign imports from the coast to all parts of the interior, constitute the sum and substance of our railway policy. The increasing extension of our railway communications has become a necessary condition of British rule in India. In proportion as our foreign payments, called Home Charges, increase, the exports from India have to be increased as the only means of paying the interest due to foreign lenders and investors ; and the increase in exports means a corresponding increase in imports. Thus, the chief function that our railways discharge is to help our foreign trade, which is entirely in foreign hands. Far from stimulating internal trade or home production, the railways have had the injurious effect of crippling the scope of indigenous local trade and the business of the middlemen. They have already destroyed the indigenous industries. They have failed to stimulate agricultural production. They, no doubt, tend to raise the level of prices; but the rise is due to the increased cost of delivery at the place of consumption, and this cost being incurred by the railway companies and the ship owners, the increase in the prices representing this portion of the cost is appropriated by them and does not reach the actual cultivators.

No country in the world is in such an anomalous condition economically as India unfortunately is. The revenues of Government, instead of being spent in the stimulation of wealth production, are spent for the purpose of merely transporting goods from place to place. It is obvious that to produce fresh wealth is an object more important than the movement of what little already exists. No railway system can be in a healthy condition which depends for its financial prosperity on the transport of agricultural produce over long distances and to foreign countries, while it is necessary that such produce should be consumed in the immediate neighbourhood of the place of production. The natural restorer of the fertility of the soil is the substance of the produce returned to it in the shape of manure, and it is impossible that this can be done if the food of the people is carried off to distant foreign countries. It is an undoubted fact that the soil has deteriorated, as is proved by the difference in the yield of wheat cultivation between Akbar's and modern time. The enlightened British rulers of India would confer a more substantial boon on the people if they devote the fiscal resources of the country to the development of indigenous productive industries than they now do by devoting them to the covering of the country's surface with an ever-widening net-work of railways, which benefit foreign exploiters while impoverishing the population.

Because Indian railways have been the most paying investments for British capital, every Englishman cries in season and out of season, with little or no knowledge, that railways can save India. In the mouth of the British capitalists and statesmen, the cry is dishonest. But, in the mouth of the great majority of Anglo-Indians, it is the result of ignorance and of spurious patriotism. Because railways are an unmixed good in other countries and because they afford immense profits to investors, educated as well as uneducated Anglo-Indians echo the cry that India's salvation is in the multiplication of railways.

Almost every Englishman in this country joins in this parrot cry, and the construction of railways with about 15 crores of borrowed money every year goes on without interruption. Every mile of fresh railway constructed in India, be it remembered, brings profit to so many Englishmen that influential men are never wanting to keep ceaselessly egging on the Indian authorities to undertake fresh works every year. Occasionally we hear the voice of common sense from individual Englishmen who remonstrate againt this policy of selfish greed. The Government congratulate themselves that the railways have at last begun to pay, as if the railway revenues are derived from the profits instead of from the food reserve of the people to a great extent. "Does he (Sir Edward Law) know," asks the *Investors' Review*, "to what extent their gross receipts are swollen by freight charges upon the materials bought with borrowed money and carried inland by existing lines for railway extension, or can he tell us the amount of public revenue that has been transformed into railway gross receipts by the process of carrying Government purchased grain to the famine-stricken regions of India in recent years? We would like to have a net account, in short, of railway receipts, tracing everything to its origin, finding out who pays the charges that make their revenues, and to what extent the gross amount is swollen by Gevernment extravagance or inconsiderate outlay of loan money. No native of India has ever been given a voice in determining the projects the directors carry out wholly at India's expense and our profit." Regarding the so-called valuable assets of railways against the debts of the country, the *Investors' Review* is under no delusion. "There is a debt, to be sure", writes our contemporary, "but it is only about £22,000,000 net after allowing for assets which he (Sir Ed. Law) estimates at a commercial value of some £301,000,000. He thinks the capitalised value of the railways at 25 years' purchase of their net annual revenue amounts to £265,000,000, and adding in cash, and adding in the gold reserve, debts due by Native States, and such like, he arrives at the figure named above, while the total gross debt he puts at only £323,000,000. This is really beautiful finance, and if the money borrowed had been all, or mostly all, raised in India, we should not have had so much to say to it. But, who would buy the railways at twenty-five years' or any number of years' purchase if we put them on the market ?"

So much for the finance of the Indian railways. What about their economics, on which the advocates of endless railway construction set such value ? The advocate of the official view knows enough of political economy to lay down dogmatically that "every country should mainly produce that for which it has the greatest natural advantages." What are these "natural" advantages ? Were coal and iron natural advantages in England before the middle of the eighteenth century, when England was, as India is now, an entirly agricultural country ? Like individuals, nations also discover unsuspected advantages in the course of their development. So will the Indian nation, if only British exploiters allow it to pursue its development unhampered and untrammelled.

It is the ordinance of nature, it is said, that England must export her manufactures to India and India must export her raw materials, including food grains and oil seeds, to England. England is rich in coal and iron, while India, though possessing these advantages, has fertile plains, with brilliant sunshine, favourable to the growth of cotton, grain, indigo, etc. India must therefore be chiefly agricultural. To this we may reply that, until British competition destroyed all our industries, India could boast of numerous productive industries which made her rich and which excited the wonder of foreign purchasers. There is nothing to prevent similar industries reviving, except the unfair and State-aided competition of Englishmen. The instance of the United States, the exports of which, like those of India, chiefly consist of raw produce, is not to the point. India is not a country with a fertile virgin soil and limited population like the United States. Indian agriculture might indeed be made more productive than at present by the application of modern scientific methods. But this can be done only to a small extent; because a soil that has undergone ceaseless cultivation for ages for the support of a teeming population, cannot yield like the American, Canadian or Australian soil. India cannot possibly remain an exclusively agricultural country; she was never so before the British destruction of her industries. The United States export yearly increasing quantities of manufactures and decreasing quantities of raw produce. So is Russia trying to do. India alone *is ever to be*, but never *is*, blest. Her industrial regeneration will commence on the first day of the Greek Calends!

The railways are said to be one of the best means of mitigating the severity of famines. It is not now pretended that they will "prevent" them. Advocates of railways have grown wiser since 1878, when a Commission of experts prophesied the cessation of famines as soon as certain lines of railways were completed. But even in the way of mitigating the severity of famines, we do not know that the 26,000 miles of railways that we now have, have done much. If a few thousands of people in a limited tract suffered severely and died in the occasional famines of the pre-British period, millions now live a life of chronic famine and die the slow harrowing death of unrelieved starvation. In these days of British civilisation, what is called the normal year has become the famine year; and the famine year officially recognised is one when hundreds of thousands of people can no longer stay at home, nor escape death from starvation, without flying to the Government relief camps. The feeding of the poor directly by the State is becoming an established institution in India as it once became in Rome. While the railways have failed to prevent famine, they produce other economic evils that virtually make famine the normal condition of large sections of the population. Of these evils the greatest is the depletion of India's food resources, food resources of animals as well as men, directly helped by the railways.

The rulers of India have decided that famine will remain her normal lot so long as the Himalayas and the seas constitute her boundaries, and that to talk of the prevention of famine is as much a blasphemy as to think of "wresting the keys of the Universe from the hands of Providence." Lord Curzon is not the only statesman who, by smart, epigrammatic sayings, would solve difficult problems of human destiny. But other men of more prosaic nature, but none the less gifted with true insight, have concluded that such wresting of the keys of the Indian Universe is possible in India as it has been elsewhere. Providence himself has no such inveterate malice towards one nation and good will towards another as Lord Curzon would make out. We have referred to the delusion of the Famine Commission of 1878 who expected that railways would put an end to famine. Famine Commissions have grown wiser since. Notwithstanding 25,000 miles of railways, famine on a stupendous scale occurred in 1897, and another Commission inquired into its causes and remedies. This Commission did not go the length of reiterating the discredited prophecy of their predecessors. But while rejecting the theory that railways would prevent famine, they did not allow their faith in their economic efficacy to dwindle. If railways did not lead to the production of increased quantities of food, they would bring into the country, it was argued, enough from other countries. This complacent prediction was likewise falsified during the still more terrible famine of 1900. For no food was imported from foreign countries, except Burma. Not only was this not done, but the scanty home supply was depleted during the famine period by a brisk exportation of food grains.

This last is a serious evil, and perhaps our readers will be glad to know the views of certain Anglo-Indians on it. The late Horace Bell thus comments on the Commission's conclusion regarding the normal food supply of the country :

"On the whole, the Commission thought that the real available surplus *i. e.* in a normal year, would not be greater than what it was estimated to be by the Famine Commission of 1880, *viz.* 5,165,000 tons. It is to be carefully noted that this would represent the entire surplus *i. e.*, the amount which would have to meet an export demand. Let us see now what one year's deficiency may result in. The Commission says, in paragraph 585, that it was computed that in 1896-97 the food outturn of British India (excluding Burma) represented a deficiency of 18,000,000, or 19,000,000 tons. Would it be wrong to assume that an even greater deficiency occurred in each of the years 1898-99 and 1900? Yet in 1898-99 the export of food still went on. In the former year the export of wheat alone was nearly 1,500,000 tons, and in the latter considerably over 1,000,000 tons, while the exports of grain of all kinds and seeds in these two years were respectively, in round figures, 8,750,000 and 10,500,000 tons. Note then that the surplus including export demand, in a normal year, is only a little over 5,000,000 tons and the deficit of one not very bad year was 18,000,000 to 19,000,000 tons, and that export still went on even in such bad years as 1898-99.

" The Famine Commission (1898) admits that there was then some evidence to the effect that the export trade and general improvement of communications " have tended to diminish the custom of storing grain, as a protection againt failure of harvest, which used to be so general among the agricultural classes." They further remark that, while the price of food has notably risen of late years, the cash wages of the great bulk of the people have not risen in the last twenty years " in due proportion to the rise in the price of the necessities of lite," and that their power of resisting the difficulties of a time of scarcity seems to be increasing. They, moreover, show, as might be expected, that,in a famine, the rise of labour wages does not accompany rise in the price of food, and they might have added that normal wage may, and does, in fact, actually disappear in a bad and long-continued famine. In face of such facts and figures, and especially of the fact that the importation of food into India is practically restricted to one of limited and precarious source, can we reasonably resist the conclusion that the average normal surplus of food outturn in India may be wholly insufficient to meet the stress of a succession of years of scarcity? This evidently means that India cannot afford to export food except in abnormally good years, and moreover that the immense area now under cultivation for seeds for export should really be growing food *i.e*, the millets and pulses, which form the staple food of the people.

"I hold that we cannot allow ourselves to maintain the view that, under present conditions, famine in India is inevitable, any more than it should be in England *i e.* if we rightly estimate the effect of secondary causes, and are prepared to grapple with them. It seems to me to be quite possible that more than one of our well-known sources of food supply may, ere long, find that unrestricted export, whether of food or other things, tends towards national disaster more or less acute, and offers a problem, the solution of which may perchance be found in the direction I have indicated."

"I urge, in conclusion, that we have to allow as a fact that famine in India has not, as was expected, been prevented by our railways, for we have just gone through probably the worst one that she has ever experienced. Are we to be content to sit down and wait for the next one, meanwhile, doing no more than still further perfecting our relief measures in the light of our recent experience? Or shall we not rather devote ourselves at once to seek the radical causes of scarcity, and endeavour to prevent the trouble, instead of merely trying to alleviate it when it comes? My own idea—I may be wrong—is that, situated as India is as regards importation of food, one most obvious and necessary step is to restrict exports in the face of expected scarcity. * * * * The far-reaching effects of such an impost, or even the possibility of it, cannot, I allow, be exaggerated. It would for a time to some extent affect the balance of trade between India and Europe; it might, though imperceptibly, disturb the value of land, and in many directions temporarily affect the fiscal position of the Government, and of the railway administration. But grave as are these effects, they would seem as nothing if the restriction brought immunity from possible famine, and from the train of misery, suffering and ruin, not to mention the cost in money which this entails on the Government and on the great bulk of the people."

The late Mr. Horace Bell was a Government official. That he should have expressed views so diametrically opposed to those held by the great bulk of his fellow-officials is significant. We shall quote below the views of an Englishman who is not an official, but who is a Behar planter of more than 35 years' experience. He may be expected to know as much as any Anglo-Indian official of the conditions of the poorer classes. We refer to Mr. Donald N. Reid, who, in an able article contributed to the pages of the London Congress organ, *India*, in December, 1894, wrote as follows :—

" I know that I am diametrically opposed to many acknowledged authorities on the subject when I assert that railway construction has already been overdone in India. India is miserably poor, and if the large sum of 1,520 lakhs of rupees is available for public works, let it be spent on the extension of irrigation and, better still, in improving agriculture by arranging to supply the rayats with suitable manure for their wheat fields. The statement exhibiting the "moral and material progress and condition in India during 1892-93," gives the normal outturn of wheat per acre at only nine bushels, or say seven maunds. This average can be doubled, nay trebled, by a proper system of manuring, which is quite within the reach of cultivators if Government will only extend to agriculture one half of the attention that is now being paid to railways. It seems strange to me that it does not strike the authorities as a cruel mockery to cover the face of the country with a network of railways where the average outturn of the principal cereal crop is only nine bushels per acre. I, therefore, repeat that Indian railways have already received too much attention from the capitalists of Great Britain without a corresponding improvement being introduced in the agriculture of the country; and if England is to do any good in India, agriculture must be made the principal field on which to work improvements.

"English Free Trade principles were never intended to flourish in India, as there is a total want of enterprise in the peasantry of the country (who are completely at the mercy of mahajana grain-dealers and money-lenders), and I have always viewed with alarm the exportation of wheat and oilseeds. This is what I wrote on the subject in my Report to the Famine Commission in 1878:

"'I cannot say that Free Trade principles have improved the condition of the rayats. Being notoriously poor and improvident, they have sold their grains in season of plenty, and starved in season of scarcity. The most extraordinary feature of the Indian grain trade is the rapidity with which the prices fluctuate from cheap to famine rates. Barley may be selling to-day at one rupee per maund and six months hence it is not procurable at twice that rate. And we can rest assured that, when the price of grain is verging on famine rates, the cultivators are not the men who profit. They are the great consumers in the country, and, as, at best, they only produce enough to keep body and soul together, it is their object (if they could only act upon it) to keep their granaries full and prices low. At present the mahajan is the ruling spirit of the age, and he has grown fat at the expense of the Government reputation and the masses of the people. It is sinful the way the money-lender is allowed to deal with the people, more particularly in grain transactions, and as much as 100 per cent. profit is often made by the village grain-dealer.

" The trade in oilseeds sprang up about the time of the Crimean War, in consequence of the closing of the Russian ports, and it has made most alarming strides of late. The total trade in grain and seeds increased in value from £3,850,000 in 1857 to £13,560,000 in 1877 or about 252 per cent., and it now constitutes 23 per cent. of the entire exports. I see nothing but ruin staring India in the face from the nature of its export trade.' "

" Since these words were written in 1878, the export trade in grain and oilseeds has reached most alarming proportions, the value being Rs. 40,907,821 in season

1891-92 which constitutes 38 per cent. of the export trade of India. The country, instead of benefiting by this enormous increase in its export business, is poorer now than it ever was, and the people are thoroughly discontented.

"Quick-growing crops, such as cheena (*Panicum miliaceum*) are sown on an extensive scale in suitable fields, and the grain is gathered every day in a half-ripe condition for the evening meal. This attempt on the part of the rayats to satisfy the cravings of hunger with half-ripe grain is not an exceptional occurrence in seasons of drought, as it happens every year in Behar and other congested provinces as soon as the crops begin to ripen. The result is that diarrhœa, dysentery and other bowel complaints are particularly common among the peasants of India who have not the stamina to fight against fever and other diseases which are also too common in the country. It is sometimes surprising to me how they manage to live, and it will be gathered from all these statements that high prices for food grains in India do not mean the same thing to the agriculturists of that country as they do to the English farmers, and it would be the best thing that could happen in the interests of the rayats of the North West Provinces, Oudh, and Behar if the export trade in wheat were checked by a heavy duty. Even in the Central Provinces, where the highest density of population to the square mile only reaches 127, the average being 125, relief works have been kept open all the year owing to the partial failure of the crops in that part of the country. This shows that the people are unable to withstand the effects of one indifferent season."

No one of our great Indian administrators had wider knowledge of famine questions than Sir George Campbell. In his evidence before the Select Committee of 1878 on Indian Public Works, he said :

"Then there is another very important view which I think it necessary to bear in mind. We are very much alive to the fact that improved communications have the effect of enabling us to meet famines in a way in which they never were met before ; but we must also remember that there is another view of the question, that those improved communications lead to the export of grain and a cessation of the old native habit of hoarding grain, which was formerly a very great security against famine."

Further on he says on the same subject : "Now-a-days there is nothing so conspicuous in the recent famines as the extent to which the country has been devoid of supplies of grain by the facilities of exportation which such means of communication have afforded. In Orissa, it is actually the case that, up to the month of March of the famine year, a very active export of grain was going on, that is within six weeks of the time when the country was in the throes of the most frightful famine. The traders had miscalculated. In Bengal, during the greater part of the famine, whilst the Government were importing with one hand, the traders were exporting with the other, so that a very great drain took place. I have not the least doubt that, on general economical grounds, the result of improved communication is a very good one. It is very much better that the cheap grain of cheap years should be brought to markets in the quantities in which it is wanted, and that it should be imported in years of dearness and scarcity; but, from a financial point of view, it leaves the evil just as great as ever it was, because although it is perfectly true that the means of communication enable you to bring into a famine district in a bad year the grain which is there wanted, still that does not give the people the means of buying the grain. What has happened of recent years is that, there being no grain stores in the country where those famines have occurred, the grains being brought in through improved communication, it has been necessary to supply the grain to the people, or to furnish the means of buying the grain. And, therefore, although you may have succeeded more or less, sometimes more and sometimes less, in obviating the mortality by famine, you have done so at enormous expense, and that expense is increasing from famine to famine. . . I think this is a subject which is very necessary to work out."

There is no mention here, however, of the impossibility of importing food from outside, nor of the possible need for restricting export.

I wish to make another quotation from a very high authority. In the *Westminster Review* in 1880, Mr. W. T. Thornton penned the following paragraph, on a subject on which he was an acknowledged authority. "Thus, it is established there is a drain from India to England. What is its nature and extent? Experience, as usual deferring until too late her captious counsels, at last teaches us clearly enough how serious an oversight there has been in an important branch of the domestic policy instituted by the Government of India some twenty five years ago, and steadily pursued ever since. Every one could see that railways, which had so marvellously developed the resources of Europe, were equally desirable for India ; but neither did it occur to any practical administrator to inquire, nor did any theoretical economist volunteer to point out, how greatly the investment of English capital on Indian public works must, by necessitating the remittance to England of annual interest or profit on the investment, derange the Indian exchange, nor how grevious would be the effects of the derangement. Railways are good, irrigation is good, but neither one nor the other good enough to compensate for opening and continually widening a drain, *which has tapped India's very heart-blood* and has dried up the mainsprings of her industrial energy. So grievous an error of the past, having been at length, however tardily, detected, will scarcely be persevered in, and we may reasonably assume, therefore, that there will be no more guaranteeing of private British enterprise....There is for India just now no other public work half so urgent as the restoration of equilibrium between income and expenditure, and all the rest should be imperatively required to wait until there shall be a surplus revenue applicable to them, *unless perchance the requisite funds can be got intermediately from local capitalists to receive their interest on the spot* . . Here, then, I bring my story to a close by drawing from it the pregnant moral that *it is India's tribute which is so balefully weighing down the Indian exchange, and that the same burden threatens, unless speedily and materially lightened, to break the Indian camel's back—miracle of endurance though the animal be*" (The italics are the author's)

H. C. Irwin, author of the Garden of India, wrote as follows, regarding the economic condition of the N. W. Provinces and Oudh, in 1888 :—

"A noteworthy point is the wide variation in the amount of food which different individuals estimate as a sufficient daily ration. The most liberal estimate is that of a well-to-do Kurmi, No. 11, who said he always ate one and a half seers (3lbs). The lowest is about three-quarters of a seer for an adult male (1½lbs). I am inclined to think that this is very much a matter of habit, resulting from a long course of easy or pinched circumstances. In well-to-do families, accustomed to eat as much as they can, I dare say a man who was at work all day would eat three pounds at two meals. In hard up households, on the other hand, one and a half pounds would be the usual thing; and no one would think of eating more. One seer for a man, three quarters for a woman and half a seer for a boy of ten would perhaps be a fair average allowance.

" The poor classes don't eat a full ration of grain every day in the year. For some weeks before each harvest, they bring home from their fields bundles of green corn which they roast and eat, and this they exclude from their estimate of threshing floor totals. Again, 120 to 160 lbs of carrots may be bought for a rupee—and these when in season are largely used to eke out the food supply. The same is the case with mangoes, cucumbers, and 'quashes.' Probably a quarter of the food consumed by the poorest classes consists of such beggarly elements as these.

"To the main question—whether the poorer classes get enough to eat—a categorical answer is not easy. I believe that a great majority do in ordinary times satisfy their hunger at least once a day. That the poorer families eat as much as would be good for them, I very much doubt. Hunger, as already remarked, is very much a matter of habit; and people who have felt the pinch of famine—as nearly all the poorer households must have felt it—get into the way of eating less than wealthier families and less than they could assimilate with physical advantage to themselves.

"The more one looks into the condition of the Indian cultivator and labourer, the nearer, it seems to me, one must be impressed by the narrowness of the margin between him and destitution. The upper class of tenant, the man worth from five to ten acres of land and upwards, should, in average times, and with ordinary industry, be well above the pressure of actual want. But the small cultivators, *i e* the large majority, must be always on the brink of want of food though the services of the *mahajan* generally save them from going further than the brink. * * *"

"I must plead guilty to holding the heroic heresy that the exportation of grain from Indian ports should be stopped when prices in any large portion of the country reach a certain point. It is true that the grain exported is chiefly wheat, and that wheat is not the food of the poorest classes. Still, the effect of keeping wheat down below starvation prices would be obviously to reduce the intensity of the demand for the coarser grains. This, however, is of course a remedy for exceptional scarcity only and one which no one would advocate in normal times."

Mr. Irvine is somewhat frightened by the heroism of this heresy. If the export of not only wheat, but of all exported food grains, were taxed in all years, it is obvious that these grains would become cheaper, with the result that the classes that now subsist on wheat, rice, jawar, bajri, wheat flour, &c, would have more quantity available for their consumption in ordinary years; and in years of dear prices, there would be less rush than at present on the coarser grains. The poorer classes should be given every help to enable them to consume more healthy and nutritious food than they do at present.

CHAPTER XV.

Where India Should Borrow.

THE question of railway extension in India raises the other important question—where should the required money be borrowed, in London or at home? I have already referred to one weighty consideration in favour of the latter course. There are other reasons to which it is necessary to refer here. In an article I contributed to the columns of *India*, the London organ of the Indian National Congress, in the year 1897, I wrote: "The result of borrowing in London has not been at all encouraging during the last quarter of a century. Though the rates of interest have been reduced, still the rupee has so fallen in value that the saving from reduced rates of interest has been more than counterbalanced by the increase in the cost of exchange. The amount of interest on the sterling loan has grown during the last eighteen years from $2\frac{1}{2}$ millions to nearly $3\frac{3}{4}$ millions. In 1896 the Government resolved to borrow nearly 30 crores of rupees more for the construction of railways. Of these 30 crores, about ten are to be borrowed in India, the rest being raised in London, and this will add another half-a-million sterling to the amount of interest. When "the 20 crores are raised in London, the total amount of sterling loan will be 125 millions roughly speaking. If the Government of India were to make up its mind to repay this whole loan, it would have to find nearly 17½ rupees for every pound sterling, that is to say, nearly 2,200 crores of rupees. But this impossible task the Government has no intention of trying. No provision is made in the Indian Budget for a sinking fund every year for the repayment of the foreign loan. So that the four millions paid as interest will be a perpetual yearly charge on the revenues of India. Nobody can maintain that such an unceasing drain is desirable. On the other hand, if all further growth of this charge could be stopped and all loans were raised in India, limiting the annual amount to what the Indian money market can safely supply, not only would the increasing drain be arrested, but the Indian capitalists would be benefited in proportion. The Government has estimated that about 5 crores of rupees can be annually borrowed in India; and to be on the safe side, and in order that the capital available for local industry and trade may not be encroached upon, we may put this figure as 3 crores. If to this amount a crore from the current revenue of the Government were added, it would give 4 crores every year for the extension of railway communication; and with this amount, whatever might be the consequence, the Government should rest content. During recent years, Indian borrowing at home has been beneficial. The price of rupee paper has been steadily rising, and Government has been able to borrow at lower and lower rates. The 4 per cent. rupee paper was converted first into 3½ per cents, and subsequently to 3 per "cents. Even if the Government has to pay a higher rate of interest in the Indian market than in the London market, it would be, for reasons already stated and for those which I shall briefly refer to below, more advantageous, on the whole, to borrow in the home market. Strangely, our financial authorities lose sight of the fact that the fall in the gold value of the silver is exaggerated by the Secretary of State's offering for sale every year an increasing number of Bills in London. But the question should not be looked at entirely from the point of view of Government's finance; it should also be considered in respect of the effects on the people of India. If the loans were raised in India instead of in London, the interest would be paid to people resident in India. Supposing ten crores of rupees were borrowed in India at 3 per cent., the interest paid to those that lent thc money would be 30 lakhs a year, and along with all the benefits to the trade and industry and the education of the people which would result from the railways built with the money thus borrowed, the 30 lakhs would remain in the country and fructify in the pockets of the people. Such a policy steadily pursued by the Government would be a great inducement to the habit of economy and prudent investment among the people. If the ten crores were not lent to Government, that money, or most of it, would have been spent in the households, in the making of ornaments, on marriage and other ceremonies, or in more or less unproductive ways. But, lent to the Gcvernment, it would yield an income of 30 lakhs a year, which would probably be spent in new productive investments."

Mr. T. Lloyd, writing to "*India*", in June 1895, on the subject of Home Charges, observes:

"If India were to borrow at home instead of in London, there would be no further growth in the interest on debt in London. There would, of course, be a growth in India. But the payments would be made in silver and, what is still more important, they would be made in the country itself. Let us suppose that India were to borrow such a sum as would involve the payment of interest amounting to a quarter of a million sterling every year. It would be a matter of very great importance whether the quarter of a million sterling was sent altogether out of the country or was paid in the country. In the former case there would be a drain from the country. In the latter case the money that would be taken from the tax-payers would be paid to the creditors, and there would be a quarter of a million sterling every year which the creditors might use either in business or in increasing their comforts. In either event they would give employment to more labour and would stimulate industry. It would, therefore, be possible immediately to reduce the Home Charges by about one-fifth, and it would gradually become possible to reduce them perhaps by as much more by ceasing to borrow in London whenever possible, and by altering the arrangements which have hitherto been in force with regard to officials. The official mind is naturally indisposed to changes of this kind. They are, it is said, too sweeping; they disturb the course of business; and they throw people out of employment. But the Royal Commission on Indian Expenditure ought to be above such considerations as these. It ought to look to the interests of India alone, and it ought to recommend whatever, upon full enquiry, it finds to be conducive to those interests."

The fact that the item of "cost of exchange" has been eliminated in the accounts of the Government, does not affect the force of the above observations. Whatever the Government have saved under this item by an artificial enhancement of the value of the silver rupee, is paid by the Indian producer. The saving in interest on sterling obligations is only apparent, and the disregarded advice of the Currency Committee to the Government of India that "they should husband the resources at their command, exercise a resolute economy and restrict the growth of their gold obligations," is as sound at the present moment as it ever was.

CHAPTER XVI.

The Foreign Trade of India—In Ancient Times.

IN the most ancient period of their history, the people of India showed great aptitude for commerce, and the fact that, notwithstanding the facilities for trade that modern civilization, under the auspices of British rule, has introduced, they should have lost their ancient habits of trade, their enterprise and desire for wealth, is a melancholy commentary on the blighting effects of continued foreign dominion. In modern times we are accustomed to associate trade with railway and telegraphic communications and with steam and electric power. In the rivalry between nations to seize the best portion of the world's wealth each for itself, time and space having become intolerable impediments, they have been annihilated by the service of Science. A few nations are accumulating colossal wealth at the expense of other nations. That international commerce scatters peace and prosperity among all communities of the world is the fiction started by England and maintained by other European nations who grow rich by exploiting every country unable to protect itself. The discovery of the Cape of Good Hope and the opening of the Suez Canal have placed at the disposal of three or four nations of the world the hidden as well as the developed resources of the world, with the result that to-day Asiatic countries are poorer than they were two hundred years ago and their wealth is being rapidly transferred to Western Europe and to America. Where this process will end, whether the "dying" races will be dead in a century and, when they are dead, the "living" nations will begin their process of dying, having lost the sustenance derived from the "dying" races, none can say. If the gentler species of animals in the forest were all to become extinct, or to become so lean as to cease to afford meat to their destroyers, the latter must either swallow one another or starve to death.

Meanwhile, it is doubtful whether the nations that are carrying away to their capitals the wealth of Asia and Africa and other outlying parts of the world, are themselves the better for their organised militant spoliation. Modern civilisation is only a process which perpetually creates wants and tries to supply them. Often the wants are real, while the efforts to supply them are delusive. If the average wealth of the individual has increased, his wants also have increased. Hardly is one new want partially or fully supplied when other wants grow, and the activity of the individual and the nation is strained to the utmost to have these latter supplied. Germany, England and America are now the wealthiest nations in the world, and their wealth is rapidly growing. But it is significant that each of these denies that the others are really making progress. Fully one-third of the population of Britain, according to Messrs. Booth and Rowntree and Sir Henry Campbell-Bannerman, are below the line of tolerable poverty. In Germany, the poorer classes are becoming more and more discontented, while, in America, the working man spends more because he earns more. After all, wealth is a means to an end, the end being happiness, understanding it in its grosser sense, the satisfaction of physical wants. Philosophers from the very beginning of time have concluded that the satisfaction of physical wants cannot make man happy, because wants never cease, but always grow. If happiness is the result of the moral or spiritual perfection of human nature, it is doubtfulwhether wealth helps this process. On the other hand, material prosperity and moral elevation have been, in numerous instances of individual and national career, found to be incompatible with each other. Excessive wealth contains within itself seeds of demoralisation and decay; and while in our ordinary experience the wealthy man is not found to be always the moral man, in the history of the world there are several instances of a nation which, having reached a very high state of material prosperity, deteriorated and decayed in consequence of the effeminacy and pride engendered by wealth.

We do not here propose to enter into a disquisition on the relation between wealth and happiness. We have made the above observations with a view to lay stress on the lesson taught by history that, in the case of a nation any more than in the case of individuals, wealth is not the cause or the criterion of happiness. Because in former times the Indian people had not the help of steam power and electricity to advance their commerce and did not make large accumulations of wealth, it would be wrong to conclude that they were then more unhappy than modern nations or their faculties were attenuated from want of sufficient scope for exercise. We are by no means advocating in this place the ancient Hindoo ideal of renunciation. We are as alive to its evils as we are to those of the modern craze for wealth. The history of the mediæval Hindoo race furnishes, we think, a most happy illustration of the superiority, from every human point of view, of moderate wealth and of its even distribution among the different orders of society, over the modern tyranny of wealth at one end of society, and the abject misery of poverty at the other.

To the mind of many a wise man, the modern militant commercialism, with its basis of over-crowded industrialism, has no particular attractions. Its vulgar aggressiveness, its ceaseless competition, its sordid, unscrupulous, unremitting and cruel struggle for wealth as the supreme object of human effort, point with an unerring warning voice to other ideals towards which the progress of humanity should march. Whether it will be diverted towards such ideals as it passes through its future stages of evolution, it would be too bold a prediction to make. As practical men we have to fix our attention on the fact that the stage through which human evolution is now passing is dominated by ideals imperfect and erroneous as we have indicated above; and as the nations who lead the world are addicted to them, the weaker nations of the world have no choice but to follow their lead and march behind them along the paths that they lead. India, China, Persia, Egypt—these ancient countries with their own hoary civilisations and established social systems, can no longer pursue their own separate destinies in continuity with their past history. As Japan has done, these countries should imbibe the spirit of the West and partially transform their institutions, if they are to retain their independence. Resistance to the forces of the material ideals of the West means death to the East, and in this predicament do all the countries of Asia find themselves at the present moment.

A the very dawn of history, India carried on a profitable trade with Western as well as Eastern countries. " The industrial genius of her inhabitants", writes the late Sir W. W. Hunter, " even more than her natural wealth and her extensive sea-board, distinguished her from other Asiatic lands." Greeks, Romans, Persians, Arabs and Moors were successively the chief Western nations that carried on a profitable trade with the Eastern coast of India. The enterprising Chinese nation, on the other hand, first by the land route across Tibet and other mid-Asiatic lands down to Karachi, and subsequently *via* Ceylon to the Malabar coast, maintained for centuries an unbroken trade with India. No Asiatic country, not the Arabian Peninsula on the West, the Malayan Peninsula on the East, nor the fertile Empire of China, maintained, as India did, a continued active intercourse with European countries. The precious cargoes of

Solomon's merchant ships came from the coast of ancient Malabar; the wealth of India induced Alexander to open up communication between his Persian dominion and India on the one hand,and along the Red Sea and Alexandria on the other; it was the commander of a ship engaged in the Indian trade, that was driven by the regular periodical winds of the Arabian Seas to the West coast of India, and discovered the Indian *Monsoons'* a most important discovery of ancient navigation; it was the silk *sarees* of India that adorned the classic frame of the Roman ladies; the mediæval Republics of Rome grew rich with the profits of their Indian trade; and finally, it was the hope of participating in this trade that stimulated Columbus to the discovery of America, and Vasco de Gama to the circumnavigation of the Cape of Good Hope The Cape of Good Hope was replaced by the Suez Canal, which, within the last forty years, has brought India next door to Europe,and which,in the 300 millions of the Indian inhabitants living in peace, order and security under the *pax Britannica*, has opened for her manufactures a vast and growing market such as is found in no other part of the world.

For nearly eighteen centuries, from the days of the Ptolemies, almost until the Portuguese rounded the Cape of Good Hope, Alexandria was an emporium and half-way station of the sea-borne trade. The Roman Emperors spared no pains to monopolise the commercial navigation of the Red Sea ; and their jealousy of the merchants of Palmyra, who were diverting the stream of Eastern traffic into an overland route from the Persian Gulf to

Syria, is said to have been one reason why they destroyed the flourishing city. It is true that, when the Arab conquest had overflowed Egypt and Syria, Constantinople became for a time the chief storehouse of the Levant, and the main current of trade with India and China took the line across Central Asia to the Black Sea, avoiding the countries recently over-run by the Mahomedans. The commerce of Europe centred at Constantinople in the eighth and ninth centuries more completely than it has ever done since in any one city. But, as Constantinople declined, Venice and Genoa, the cities of the inland sea which lay beyond the desolating range of Asiatic conquest, rose into splendid prominence. They soon became the principal agents for the importation into Europe of the precious commodities of Asia; in so much that in the fifteenth century the Venetians appeared literally "to hold the gorgeous East in fee," for they were not far from possessing the whole of this enormously profitable business*

The foreign trade of India in those ancient times was not like her foreign trade in these days of quick communication with the help of electricity and steam. These have placed in the hands of European nations most powerful weapons to crush non-European countries; and they have forced a system of unrestricted competition—the very mockery of the boastedfreedom of the present day civilisation—on these nations. The result is what is beheld in India. India is fast becoming the "dumping" ground of the world.

* Rise of British Dominion in India, by Sir Alfred Lyall.

The manufacturers of Britain, Germany, Austria Belgium and America make for the special benefit of the poor people of India cheap trumpery articles, and with the help of cheap shipping on the sea and of ubiquitous railways inland, convey them to the obscurest village, and from the obscurest village take away every possible agricultural and raw produce that can be turned to account. It was not so in those days. All articles of the nature of necessaries were retained mostly in the places of their production, or were sold in the markets of the neighbouring town. But luxuries like spices, drugs, dyes and rare woods ; fabrics of silk and cotton ; jewels, and gold and silver and precious stones, were carried from the interior over long distances to the coast, where numerous cities that had sprung up, exchanged these valued articles for the imports with which foreign ships arrived laden. Throughout these ancient times, there existed numerous well-known trade routes along which a constant succession of caravans, led and guarded by professional guides, carried their merchandise in carts or on the backs of animals without serious molestation.

Foreign critics sometimes construe the absence of regular made-up roads in former times in India as a proof of her commercial inactivity. The facilities for intercourse were not, as a fact, so small as might be supposed from the analogy of European countries. In a climate where the rainfall is limited almost entirely to one season of the year, and in a country the greater part of which is a level plain, the absence of well-made roads, or of roads of any kind, does not mean the same lack of facilities that it would mean in cold countries. For three months in the year commerce might be slack, but during remaining months it could go on uninterruptedly. The large rivers were crossed by ferries or boat bridges; the small ones could be easily forded. Any track served for a road, and the worst inconvenience experienced was the slowness of the journey, an inconvenience which, in those times when living had not become too quick even for electricity and steam, did not matter much. The huge Indian armies during the wars of the most warlike British pro-consuls in the Company's time, moved across the country along such rude natural tracks. Nor, as a fact, was the utility of roads for purposes of inter communication neglected by the rulers in peaceful times. It is said that the great Buddhist Emperor, Asoka, took particular care in maintaining roads and providing comforts for the travellers. "Roads were maintained by the royal officers, and pillars were erected on the principal highways to serve as mile-stones at intervals of about an English mile and a quarter. Examples of similar pillars (*Kos Minar*) erected many centuries later by the Moghul Emperors still exist. Asoka prided himself on having further consulted the comfort of the travellers by planting shady trees and digging wells at frequent intervals along the main roads."* Mohamed Toglak constructed a road from Delhi to Doulatabad, a forty days' journey, laid it out with infinite care, bordered with trees all the way like an avenue in a park, with frequent inns and rest houses. † The Grand Trunk Road, running up-

---

* Asoka—Rulers of Indian Series by Vincent A. Smith.

† "Mediæval India" by Stanley Lane Pool.

the entire valley of the Ganges from Calcutta to the North-West frontier, was first planned as a highway for armies in the 16th century by the Afghan Emperor Sher Shah, and was brought up to completion under the administration of Lord William Bentinck. During the Moghul rule the whole of India was intersected by a number of trunk roads of several hundreds of miles in length. The great Hindu institution of religious pilgrimage which kept thousands of Hindus on travel for the greater part of the year, rendered necessary some sort of tracks, well-known among the people, more or less protected against dangers and provided with comforts.

Professor Rhys Davids, in his admirable volume on 'Buddhist India' gives an account of the trade routes in Northern India in the sixth century B.C. The Aryan system was founded on village communities which comprised the great mass of the people. They were well-to-do peasantry or handicraftsmen, mostly with land of their own, ruled over by local headmen of their own selection. Each community was self-contained and supplied its own wants. Under such a social system it would be supposed that there was little scope for the development of trade. But such was not the case. There were monarchs, wealthy nobles, priests enjoying rich grants, a few millionaire merchants, and a considerable number of lesser merchants and middlemen, all in the few towns that flourished in the country. There were merchants who carried their goods from one part of the country to another, along routes that were in general use.

The internal trade of India expanded and grew as the population grew and different parts of the country were occupied. The accounts given of the wealth and magnificence of the capital cities of the dynasties that established themselves in different parts and, after reaching a state of striking prosperity, disappeared either by absorption by a more powerful neighbouring kingdom or by the destruction of a vindictive and ferocious conqueror, prove the prevalence of a wide and elaborate system of trade, with guilds and companies, middlemen and bankers, and laws to regulate trade and contract. Even while anarchy prevailed at the centre of the ruling power, trade pursued its usual course without serious impediment or molestation. Political anarchy is not incompatible with the general prosperity of arts and trade as is shown by the condition of the Italian republics in the mediæval times.

In the earlier centuries of the Christian era, we come across frequent allusions to the condition of trade in India. Woollen and cotton cloths, fabrics woven with silk and covered with wool, as also silken stuffs and fabrics made of fibres are spoken of. The cultivation and manufacture of indigo prevailed. Sage Yajnavalkya lays down rules under which companies were formed to carry on commercial transactions. Mr. R.C. Dutt, in his 'History of the Ancient Civilisation of India' extracts the following two rules laid down by this sage: "The profits and losses of merchants who work in concert for profit, shall be determined according to their shares, or according to agreement previously made. The loss which is incurred by violating a rule (of the company), or by acting without the permission (of the company), or by negligence, shall be made good by the party who caused the loss. The party who saves an amount from loss is entitled to one-tenth of the amount saved." There is also mention of laws against merchants combining to unduly enhance the value of commodities, or to unduly lower the prices of imports. When commodities are sold immediately after purchase(i.e. when interest on the capital does not enter into the calculation), merchants are told to be satisfied with a profit of ten per cent. on imports and of five per cent. on home manufactures. The King is required to fix the prices of commodities on principles stated above. These rules seem crude in these days of free trade and free competition ; but, as Mr. Dutt remarks, such and worse rules prevailed in Europe until a century or two ago.

Professions formed themselves into guilds of trades such as those of weavers, druggists, corn-dealers, oil-manufacturers &c. Dr. Bhandarkar, in his invaluable 'History of the Dekhan' gives a brief description of the organisations that prevailed in those days : "Their organisation seems to have been complete and effective, since they received permanent deposits of money and paid interest on them from generation to generation. Self-government by means of such guilds and village communities has always formed an important factor of the political administration of the country. *A Nighama Sabha* or town corporation is also mentioned in one of Ushvadâtas Nasik inscriptions, which shows that something like municipal institutions existed in those early days." "The prevailing rates of interest varied from five to seven and a half per cent. per annum. It (the rate of interest) depends on the degree of security and bears an adverse ratio to the efficiency of government It appears that the country was well-governed notwithstanding political revolutions. To this result the efficient local organisation spoken of above, which no changes of dynasties ever affected, must no doubt have contributed in a large measure."

In the sixth century A. D., the following passage from Mr. Dutt's work already quated from, gives an idea of the condition of trade in the celebrated Kingdom of Magbada,

" Under the shadow of the royal power dwelt the peaceful merchants and bankers in the exchange or merchants' quarters, *Sreshti Chatvara* as the poet calls it. Quiet and unostentatious as Hindu merchants were these banker merchants probably had their branch firms in the great towns all over Northern India, carried on extensive operations in silks, jewels, and valuable goods, and concealed in their dark vaults in crowded and narrow lanes enormous treasures and money which Kings and Emperors did not disdain to borrow in times of need. Ostentatious only in their charity and religious works, they no doubt beautified the town with many a graceful temple, fed and supported priests and Brahmins and earned a name among their fellow-citizens by their good works. To the present day the Shets and merchants of Northern India are respected for their wealth and their pious acts, and build many a holy temple where Jaina and Hindu worship are performed day by day. Jewellers and artists flocked to the vicinity of merchants. In the words of the poet, " skilful artists examine pearls, lopazes, sapphires, emaralds, rubies, the lapis lazuli, coral and other jewels; some set rubies in gold, some work gold ornaments on colored threads, some string pearls, some grind the lapis lazuli, some pierce shells and some cut coral. Perfumers dry the saffron bags, shake the musk bags, express the sandal juice, and compound essences." These artists found a market all through the known world, and the products of their skill were appreciated in the court of Harun al Raschild in Baghdad, and astonished the great Charlemagne and his rude barons, who, as an English poet has put it, raised their visors and looked with wonder on the silks and brocades and jewellery which had come from the Far East to the infant trading marts of Europe."

In the series of articles contributed recently by Mr. S. N. Saldanha to the *Madras Review*, we have most valuable materials for an estimate of the commerce of ancient India, and to him we acknowledge here our indebtedness for much of what is said in the following pages. The Empire of Alexander was dismembered by the inroads of the Scythians who carried their conquests in India as far south as the Dekhan and whose settlements were in the southern delta of the Indus. Their capital was Minagar (the city of the Mins or Scythians) afterwards Patala, now Tatta, a small municipal town in the District of Sind. In the 12th century A. D., Minagar was dependent on Multan and enjoyed great commercial prosperity. Mr. N. S. Saldanha writes: "The trade of the country must have been very lucrative as appears from the presents brought to the sovereign to ensure his protection : plates, musical instruments, handsome girls for the harem, the best wines and the finest perfumes. Pliny wrote of this trade that every pound laid out in India produced a hundred at Rome. Egyptian ships imported into Tatta woollen cloth of a light fabric, linen in chequer work, precious stones and some aromatics unknown on the coast, coral, sorax, glass vessels, some wrought silver, money and wine. In return for these they received spices of various kinds sapphires and other gems, silk stuff, silk thread, cotton cloth and black pepper." When Nader Shah entered Tatta at the head of his army in 1742, there were in the city 40,000 weavers, 20,000 other artizans, and 60,000 dealers in various trades.

In the earlier centuries of the Christian era there were two great capitals in the Peninsula, Ujjani in Central India, the capital of the Imperial Sakhas, and Paithern on the Northern bank of the Godavari in the modern district Aurangabad, the capital of the Salivahanas. Broach on the Narbada was the port of these two great cities. During the time we are referring to, Broach was the most important seat of trade and attracted the traffic from all quarters of Northern and Southern India. "Down the stream of the Narbada," says Mr. Saldana, "or by land carriage from the city of Tagron (or Devgar or Daulatabad) across high mountains the productions of the interior country were conveyed to it. Onyx tones, porcelain, muslins, ordinary cotton in large quantities, and even the aromatic spikenard from distant Kabul came to Ujjani which passed them on to Broach for export to the Western world. From this port, the markets of Arabia and Persia were regularly supplied with Indian products. Among the imports of Broach are mentioned Italian, Greek and Arabian wines, brass, tin, lead, girdles or sashes of curious texture, melilot, white glass, red arsenic, black lead, and gold and silver coins. Later on the foreign trade of Guzerat centred more and more in Surat until it was absorbed in Bombay.

The Mahomedan city of Chaul was an important sea-port whose prosperity can be traced to the latter half of the 14th century and is said to have continued throughout the two succeeding centuries. It carried on trade with Persia and the shores of the Red Sea by which route all the Indian traffic to and fro was conducted. The city was famous for its weavers of silk and as a market for horses. "The supply of horses," says Mr. Saldanha, "was a matter of the highest importance to the Kings of the Dekhan, and every endeavour was made by them to maintain the traffic in horses from the ports of the Red Sea and the Persian Gulf. This fact is borne out by the history of the Portuguese trade; for stipulations as to the importation of horses find a place in every treaty of the Portuguese with the Kings of the Dekhan." Chaul was also a well-known centre of silk manufacture. It is said that the quantity brought out in this city alone was enough to supply all the Indian markets. The raw material was obtained from China and was worked into the finest clothes in the Mahomedan settlement. In the century of war that ensued between the Mahomedan rulers of India and the Portuguese settlers, the city declined and was finally destroyed by the Mahrattas.

Modern scholars are agreed that there was a well-established commercial intercourse between Dravidian India and Babylonia or Chaldea during the pre-Aryan period. The learned author of 'Vedic India' in the 'Story of the Nations' series, in concurrence with various other well-known authorities, states that the Dravidians of Northern and Western India and the Babylonians belonged to the same Turanian stock ; that these people maintained relations with one another before the Aryan immigration ; that teak wood which grows in Malabar was exported in those days to Persia ; that the sandalwood, ivory, apes and peacocks which King Solomon's ships brought him, were the products of Malabar; that the manufacture of muslin was an Aryan home industry ; that this industry was flourshing in Northern India in pre-Vedic days; that at that time the Dravidians were enterprising traders; and that the muslins of Northern India found their way to the ports of the West Coast, and were exported thence to Babylon. Caranganore and Quilon were among the most flourishing ancient commercial towns on the Malabar Coast. According to Mr. Saldanha, Caranganore owes its fame as much to the settlements of the Jews and the Christians as to its having been the Western capital of Kerala and the first emporium of trade in India. Tradition points to the arrival of the first Syrian colony at Caranganore in the 4th Century A. D. with the permission of " Cheruman Perumal." Its decay did not commence till the arrival of the Portuguese, and its fort was finally destroyed by Tippu Sultan. The Laccadives and the Maldives were known under the collective title of the Divi islands, which were dependent on Ceylon. They were inhabited and produced precious stones and pearls. A brisk trade in cowries, amber and coir was carried on. Mr. Saldanha gives a full and interesting account of the trade between India and China. The intimate relation brought by Buddhism between China, Ceylon and India, led to important commercial intercourse between these countries. According to Mr. Saldanha, the Christian missions that went from Caranganore and Quilon to China, stimulated this commercial intercourse. The latter was the most important emporium of Chinese trade in India. Between the Chinese port, Canton, and the mouth of the Euphrates *via* numerous ports in Cochin-China and the Molucas, in Ceylon, on the Western coast, of India, at the mouth of the Indus, Chinese ships carried on a regular exchange of commodities. On their voyage to and fro the larger Chinese ships found a safe harbour at Quilon. The traffic between India and China appears to have been considerable. Towards the close of the ninth century strangers from India are spoken of as having been established in the Eastern provinces of China. In the year 1282 envoys were sent by the King of Quilon to the Emperor of China, who responded by dispatching a mission to that King. A roaring trade was kept up in brazil wood, indigo, ginger, and pepper, which were exchanged for copper, gold, silver and cloths of silk. After an uncontested monopoly of the Indian trade during two centuries, the Chinese began to be molested by the Moors, who in 1341 had seized a portion of the trade in Quilon. The Zamorin favoured the Moors and the people too were more friendly to them. When in the year 1498 Vasco de Gama arrived in India, the Chinese traders had abandoned all their posts West of Sumatra. The Moors themselves were driven away by the Portuguese.

CHAPTER XVII.

The Foreign Trade of India—In Mediæval Times.

At the end of the 15th century two memorable events in the annals of the world's commercial and political history, occurred suddenly and almost simultaneously: the discovery of America and the doubling of the cape of Good Hope, the former under the auspices of Spain and the latter by the unflinching enterprise of Portugal. It was then that the Pope Alexander Borgia issued his Bull dividing the whole undiscovered non-Christian world between Spain and Portugal, under which, while the Western hemisphere was declared the possession of Spain, Africa and Asia were awarded to Portugal. Both the countries combined a keen commercial ambition with the most savage proselytism, and the Portuguese proceeded with ruthless energy to put down their Mahomedan rivals of Alexandria and Constantinople, and establish fortified settlements on the Indian coast. From the cities on the shores of the Mediterranean and the Black Sea to the powerful maritime States of Western Europe was the rich trade of India with Europe now transferred. For a time the trade was monopolised by Portugal which added the ferocity of religious fanaticism to the greed of unscrupulous aggrandisement. But her prosperity was short-lived. She was annexed by Spain in 1580, and Spain neglected the Eastern trade in favour of the gold and silver of the West. Still, she claimed that "the Indies, East and West, are our house, privately possessed by us for more than 100 years; and no one has a right to enter without our permission." But these pretensions did not prevail on other maritime states of Europe, on Holland and England. Holland preceded England in establishing commercial settlements in the East, and in spite of the threats of Spain and in spite of the offer of the Spanish King in 1607 to renounce his claim over the United Provinces (the Netherlands) if the Dutch would, on their side, abandon their navigation to the East Indies, the latter so thoroughly understood the importance of the Eastern trade that they insisted on their right to trade freely with these parts, and Spain had to give way. The success of Holland stimulated the enterprise of English merchants, and between the two, throughout the seventeenth century, the same jealousy prevailed as is witnessed in modern times between rival nations. It is true that Portugal on recovering her independence in 1640, made some feeble attempts to recover her lost position in the East; but she was obliged to sign a treaty which confined her to Goa and some minor ports on the West coast of India, while, on the other hand, all the conquests of Holland in Asia were recognised by the peace of Munster. The Dutch gradually annexed all the Portuguese possessions and asserted paramount European power in all the Asiatic seas and islands.

The career of the English East India Company in the years that followed is generally well known, though it is not equally well-known that so early as in 1689 the Company resolved to consolidate their position in India on the basis of territorial sovereignty to enable them to meet the opposition of the India powers. "The increase of our revenue is the subject of our care," they said,"as much as our trade; 'tis that that must maintain our force when twenty accidents may interrupt our trade; 'tis that that " makes us a nation in India." It is not, therefore, a fact as some writers allege, that the East India Company had at firstno ambition ofpolitical power, but were actuated entirely bycommercial pursuits The politicalcondition of India at the time that the East India Company felt its ground secure was such as to incite their ambition of territorial sovereignty in the earliest stage of their career. The country lay prostrate without a responsible central power to guard it against its going to pieces, and not only every adventurer that could collect a band of depredators to follow him tried to help himself to the status of a dynastic ruler, but also the great European enemy of Great Britain in those times, France, was making vigorous efforts to establish an Empire in India and oust the Britain altogether from her shores. After the downfall of Spain and Holland as chief maritime powers, France and England began a long contest for colonial expansion, and throughout the eighteenth century the wars between the two great nations were wars directed towards this end. Their rivalry extended to India also; and the pivot of the British policy in India throughout this period was to defeat the ambition of France and her collusion with the Native States for its fulfilment. The Peace of Paris in 1763 put an end to the rivalry of the maritime European powers for supremacy on the seas, and thence forward England was left alone in India in its contest with the native powers.

We have related the circumstances under which the Portuguese became the first European power to open a sea-borne trade with India. They were actuated by the double object, religious peoselytism and commerce, and in the attainment of it they did not hesitate to adopt the most barbarous means. Like the English East India Company in later times, the Portuguese forced the Indian Rulers to exempt their vessels from dues and permit them to exact a revenue from the local customs tariff. Calicut, Cochin and Quilon were the chief Portugese settlements on the Malabar coast. Besides these, four other important sea ports further up, Goa, Bassein, Daman and Diu, were turned into Portuguese settlements. Of these, in later years, Goa was the most prosperous. In the years from 1641 to 1648, Tavernier regarded it as one of the best harbours in the world. A most powerful fleet was employed in the maintenance of the Portuguese trade. Between 1497 and 1612, no fewer than 806 ships were thus employed. Besides the ships from Europe, vessels of the hardest teak were built in the dockyards of Goa and Daman. The annual fleet which took the Indian cargoes home numbered, in the palmy days of the Portuguese commerce, twenty sail. Regarding the value of the trade we take some facts from Sir W.W. Hunter's History. The first cargo brought home by Vasco de Gama, was reckoned to have repaid the whole cost of the expedition sixty-fold. Cabral returned to Lisbon in 1501, with a freight of precious spices, perfumes, porcelain, pearls, rubies and diamonds. In 1504 Albuquerque similarly followed with " forty pound of pearls and four hundred of the small, a diamond of wonderful bigness," and other costly articles The gains of trade were augmented by the profits of piracy—for every Moslem or Heathen ship was a fair prey. A single Calicut vessel in 1501 yielded, among other treasure, 1500 costly pearls. In 1503, another capture contained an idol of gold weighing thirty pounds, with emeralds for eyes, a huge ruby on his breast, and part of him covered with a cloak of gold set with jewels." In return for gems, and for the pepper, ginger cinnamon, came nutmegs, cloves, drugs, porcelain, perfumes, carved work, art products and textile marvels of the East, the main commodity sent from Portugal, as from the old Roman Empire, was silver. But she also exported woollen fabrics to a large extent woven from English fleece on Flander's looms, linens, red cloth of state, Genoa velvets, cutlery, metal work, hardware, corals, glass, mirrors, and chemicals. Goa carried on a lucrative horse trade. It imported the fine breed of the desert in Arab vessels and resold the animals at a great profit to dealers from the inland courts of India. The rapacity, the cruelty, the intrigue, and fanaticism of the Portuguese in India, it is out of the scope of this work to describe at large; but it is these that first made the name of Christian (Feringi) a word of terror—until the strong rule of the Moghul Empire turned it into one of contempt. It was these characteristics of their rule in India, combined with the political vicissitudes of Portugal in Europe, that brought about the ultimate extinction of their power.

England, after making vain attempts to discover a North Western route to India, resolved on contesting the claims of Portugal, Spain and Holland for absolute supremacy in the ocean highways to India. Her quarrels with Holland ended in the disastrous massacre of Englishmen by the Dutch at Amboyna in 1623, and in the latter planting their chief commercial establishments on the coast of India. We need not say that the profits of the Company during the earlier years of their adventure were fabulous. Their capital was £466,1791, and the profits ranged between 95 to 234 per cent. During some years the profits were even 87½ per cent. A writer in the *Hindustan Review* for March 1903, under the pseudonym of "A Mercator" gives an idea of these profits in the following statement:

INDIAN GOODS CONSUMED IN ENGLAND IN 1614.

	Cost on Board in India. £.	Selling price in England. £.
250,000 lb pepper	26,042	208,333
150,000 ,, cloves	5,626	45,000
150.000 ,, nutmegs	2,500	18,750
50,000 ,, mace	1,666	15,000
200,000 ,, indigo	11,667	50,000
107,140 ,, silk	37,499	107,140
50,000 ,, pieces of calico	17.500	50,000
Total	102,500	494,223

These enormous profits naturally excited jealousy and suspicion and the Company began to be denounced as being inimical to national interests. It was charged with causing the impoverishment of the country by exporting the treasures of the United Kingdom in exchange for the Indian spices and cloves, with the destruction of timber by the building of ships and with bringing about a decline of employment among the mariners. These charges look ridiculous to modern minds. England did not throw away her treasure in the Indian trade; but she got back many times its worth in the shape of commodities. In the building of ships timber was put to a most reproductive use, and, far from a decline in the employment of mariners, the voyages of the East India Company afforded a professional and general training which was of invaluable service in later times.

In a brochure entitled "Discourses on Trade" published as far back as 1670 by Sir Joshua Child who was one of the early chairmen of the Board of Directors, are enumerated the many advantages which England gained from Indian trade in the following propositions :—

1. That from 25 to 30 merchant vessels, of a semi-belligerent type, remain fully employed, with about 3,000 mariners on constant wages.

2. That saltpetre, so necessary for warlike operations, is being cheaply and extensively brought.

3. That the kingdom is supplied with pepper, indigo, calicoes, and other drugs and spices for domestic consumption of the value of £180,000 per annum.

4. That it is instrumental in supplying materials for trade with Turkey, France, Japan, Italy and Guinea.

On the above, "A Mercator" comments: "The same economic phenomenon on which learned controversies are now carried on was also then beheld. There were alarmists in those days who could not view without apprehension the excess of imports over exports from India forgetting that the former included a hundredfold and two hundredfold profit over the value of the original exports. Thus the world of commerce revolves, and thus every century presents its own special features which to the impartial seeker of the economic facts are most valuable. At the same time, those who thought that the considerable importation of silks from India were injuring their trade, began to murmur, till their murmur rose to tumultuous proportions. The guild of the silk mercers complained that Indian silks and calicoes were worn by all sorts of persons in greater quantities which curtailed the sale of indigenous stuffs. They were so far enraged at the East India merchant-men that they attempted to take the law into their own hands by seizing a consignment of treasure in the docks. But let us pass over these early ebullitions of trade jealousy which in reality were the premonitory indications of heavy and crushing protective tariffs later on, which, inch by inch, killed the profitable trade in those articles which the home weavers produced."

From the commencement of the 18th century up to 1733-4, fully 353 vessels, with an aggregate tonnage of 14,298, sailed for the East Indies. This gives an average of 406 tons for each ship. These vessels carried from Great Britain 3 million pounds in merchandise and 12 millions pounds in bullion or a total of 15 millions. Twenty ships were lost on their return voyage during the period ; and yet the goods they took back were valued at 337½ millions ! So that the profits equalled well-nigh 125 per cent. By 1765-66 the British had established their first firm foothold in India. It will be interesting to compare the volume of exports and imports from 1708-9 to 1733 with the period from 1734 to 1765.

	Exports from England. Merchandise.	Bullion.	Total.	Imports from India & China.
	£	£	£	£
1708-9 to 1733-4.	3,064,744.	12,189,147	15,253,921.	33,571,709.
1734-5 to 1765-6.	8,434,769.	16,081,496	24,516,625.	64,452,377.

Thus, as the British power extended, the trade increased. While the average per annum during the first period of 26 years came to 1·30 million sterling, that during the second amounted to 2·15 million, that is to say, the increase in value was 65 per cent.

It seems, however, that owing to war and other causes the trade declined. In 1765-66 the exports from England, merchandise and treasure, equalled £737,452 for which the imports from India and China were valued at £2,789,952. After a spasmodic rise in 1769 and 1770, it fell to £4C5,442 in 1788. Thereafter it swelled over a million and a quarter pounds on an average till 1792-93. The imports from India, however, steadily rose till in that year they were valued at 6¼ millions. The condition at the end of the eighteenth century was as follows :—

1799-1800	merchandise and treasure from Great Britain	£	1, 976, 824
Do	imports from India to	Do	2, 792, 833

CHAPTER XVIII.

The Foreign Trade of India—During the Time of the East India Company.

THE eighteenth century was a period of changing ideas in England in regard to trade. The theory of the "Bullionists" first prevailed; then the "Mercantalists" followed them. The "Bullionists" regarded as an evil the draining of a country of its treasure, whereas the "Mercantilists" admitted that this was an extreme theory, that the transmission of money was essential in certain trades, and that the mercantile well-being was assured if the country maintained a favourable "balance of trade". According to the former older view, the East India Company's trade with India was opposed to the true prosperity of England. It was argued that the East India trade needed the export of bullion and that the goods imported were either unthrifty commodities, such as spices, which were not necessary, or manufactured silks or cottons, which displaced English woollens, and were also extravagant. But the trade was too profitable to be given up in accordance with these views, and its supporters urged that it not only encouraged shipping, but that it did not really drain away money, because it was possible to sell the goods from the East again to foreigners at such a profit that money was replaced. Over this point a violent controversy was carried on, until the "Mercantilists" triumphed. It then became the prevalent belief that, so long as exports exceeded imports, there was a "balance of trade" in favour of England. If the excess of exports over imports was large, the country was supposed to grow rich ; if the reverse was the case, then it was supposed that the country was losing more than it gained, or was on the way to bankruptcy. The object to be aimed at was to amass treasure by means of excess exports, so that the country might be powerful. "It was then under the influence of the policy of power, as applied to shipping, agriculture, industry and treasure that England was governed until far on in the eighteenth century. The policy did not indeed completely disappear until the nineteenth century, when the last relic of it, the corn-laws, was destroyed by Peel. But for some time before that it was moribund; the central idea of the importance of money had been given up earlier, and the restrictions had taken the place of indiscriminate protection given to all English industries against the foreigner."

In pursuance of the theory that treasure was the true test of the country's industrial prosperity, the export of gold was prohibited and its import was encouraged ; the export of goods was likewise encouraged, while all imports except the raw materials of industry were discouraged. Systems of tariffs and regulations were devised as the machinery to carry into effect this policy, out of which grew up the protective system.

In course of time, the encouragement of manufactures became a more deliberate aim, and the system was pursued with the object of maintaining the prohibition of foreign finished goods, of directing consumption at home, and of stimulating new home industries. The principles which directed the commerce of the eighteenth century embodied in a large degree the chief doctrines of protection as it has been advocated in the present century, and the arguments then advanced in its defence are commonly repeated in the proposals of to-day. Indeed they find a most powerful advocacy in the controversy now raging round Mr. Chamberlain's proposals for England's fiscal reform.

When the maritime nations of Western Europe acquired colonies, they applied to them the principles of restriction that they practised in their trade with one another. By the "Mercantilist" statesmen the colonies were treated as the property of the nations which gained them, and their markets and products as the exclusive monopoly of the sovereign nation, and they were allowed no commercial intercourse with foreign nations. The industries of the colonies were so regulated as not to compete with the market for goods which they produced for the home industries, their shipping was controlled, and ships built in the colonies were even required to be equipped with sails from England. Ireland and America were included in the system. Ireland was ruined, but America rebelled and declared her independence. On Ireland, however, a time of prosperity and contentment is dawning. But India, the worst of the victims to this pernicious colonial system of England, has endured for one hundred and fifty years the relentless process of bleeding, to what end Heaven alone knows!

The Free Traders of modern England may ridicule the "Mercantilist" statesmen of the eighteenth century, but they did exactly what the conditions of those times rendered necessary. If they had not pursued what was called the "national policy" of strength to suit the spirit of the age, the nation that hesitated would have been crushed by the stronger and more energetic nations. Such a policy was a necessary stage in the growth of the English nation, and is found to be an equally necessary stage in the growth of all modern nations, even the United States of America, in these days. It is understood as such by the British colonies who mock their professions of consanguinary attachment to the mother-country by heavily taxing the imports from the latter and by refusing to contribute their share of cost incurred in the defence of the common Empire. Herr Schmoller, a representative of the historic school of economists in Germany, states this view in his valuable monograph on Mercantilism.

He says:—"The statesmen who put into form their theories gave the economic life of their people its necessary basis of power, and a corresponding impulse to its economic movement, and they furnished

Quoted by Principal Armitage Smith in his "The Free Trade Movement and its Results."

the national striving with great aims. At a time when most advanced nations were carrying on the collective struggle for existence with the harshest colonial egoism, with all the weapons of finance, of legislation, and of force, with navigation laws and prohibitive laws, with fleets and admiralties, with companies, with a trade under state guidance and discipline, those who would not be hammer would assuredly be anvil."

India is the anvil on which beats ruthlessly the hammer of England. To my mind there is not much difference between England's Mercantilism of the eighteenth century and the so-called Free Trade she has forced on India. Unrestricted commercial competition between two such countries as England and India, England politically the dominant and commercially the more wealthy and advanced of the two, and India politically dependent and commercially yet in the medieval stage, is no freedom, but is only a mockery of it. Handicap is a well known practice in redressing the inequality of advantage between two competing animals, and in the absence of such handicap, weaker India is being crushed by stronger England. The "Mercantilist" statesmen regarded the colonies as the property of the nation that had acquired them; so is India now regarded. We hear the hypocritic cry that India is designed by nature to be an agricultural country and can never be a manufacturing country, although, at every stage in the history of her ancient trade that I have attempted to trace in the preceding pages, proofs abound to show the prosperity of her manufactures. This prosperity distinguished the country until Britain established her political supremacy and began to employ that supremacy to build her own industrial prosperity on the ruin of the industries of India. A species of false patriotism now deters Englishmen from admitting the great economic evils that have followed the establishment of their supremacy in this country. That supremacy has conferred on India invaluable political advantages; but from the point of view of the peoples' material well-being, British rule has been a dismal failure. Anglo-Indian statesmen of the eighteenth century and of the first half of the nineteenth, frankly admitted this melancholy fact. Their opinions were not based on abstract deductions from theories; nor were they those of the Viceroys and Secretaries of State of the modern day who survey from a balloon the ground below and indent on their imagination or on the notes of their Secretaries for their facts. On the other hand, Anglo-Indians of those times spoke out what they saw with their own eyes and learnt from the mouths of the people. We shall proceed to quote the opinions of a few of these, for which we are indebted to the laborious but most convincing writings of that veteran and devoted patriot, the greatest patriot that modern India has produced, Mr. Dadabhai Naoroji.

Year 1787. Sir John Shore: "The Company are merchants as well as sovereigns of the country. In the former capacity they engross its trade, whilst in the latter they appropriate the revenues. The remittances to Europe of revenues are made in the commodities of the country which are purchased by them. Whatever allowance we may make for the increased industry of the subjects of the State, owing to the enhanced demand of the produce of it (supposing the demand to be enhanced), there is reason to conclude that the benefits are more than counterbalanced by evils inseparable from the system of a remote dominion. Every information from the time of Bernier to the acquisition of the Dewani, shows the internal trade of the country, as carried on between Bengal and the upper part of Hindustan, the Gulf of Moro, the Persian Gulf and the Malabar coast, to have been very considerable. Returns of specie and goods were made through these channels by that of the foreign European Companies, and in gold direct for opium from the Eastward . . . . A large proportion of the rents of the country are paid into the Company's treasury, and the manufactures are applied to remit to England the surplus which remains after discharging the claims on this Government, and *to augment the commerce and revenue of Great Britain*. (The italics are throughout these quotations mine).

1790. Lord Cornwallis: "The consequences of the heavy drain of the wealth from the above causes (viz., large annual remittances to Europe, assistance to the Treasury at Calcutta, and the demands of other Presidencies) with the addition of that which has been occasioned by the remittances of private fortunes, have been for many years past, and are now, surely felt, by the great diminution of the current specie and by the languor which has thereby been thrown on the cultivation and the general commerce of the country."

1816. Mr. Montgomery Martin: "The annual drain of £ 3,000,000 on British India has amounted in 30 years, at 12 per cent. (the usual Indian rate) compound interest, to the enormous sum of £723,900,000. . . . . So constant and accumulating a drain even in England, would soon impoverish her. How severe then must be its effects on India, where the wage of a labourer is from two pence to three pence a day."

1837. The Hon'ble Mr. Frederick Shore: "But the halcyan days of India are over; she has been drained of a large proportion of the wealth she once possessed, and her energies have been cramped by a sordid system of misrule to which the interests of millions have been sacrificed for the benefit of the few. . . . . The gradual impoverishment of the people and country, under the mode of rule established by the British Government, has hastened their (old merchant princes') fall".

1837. Mr. Suville Marriot on the condition o Bombay: "For many years past, I have, in common with many others, painfully witnessed their decline (the peoples'), and more especially that part of the community which has emphatically been styled the "sinews of the State,"—the peasantry of India. It is not a single, but a combination of causes that has produced this result. Some of these are, and have been, from the beginning, obvious to those who have watched with attention the development of the principles of our rule in relation to such as have been superseded became blended with our system or are opposed to it in practical effect. Others are less apparent, and some complex; whilst another cause of the decline may be possibly invovled in obscurity." Mr. Marriot quoted the chairman of a Court of Proprietors held on the 25th February 1815 as follows: " India paid to the mother-country, in the shape of Home Charges, what must be considered the annual tribute, 3,000,000 sterling; and daily poured into the lap of the mother-country a continual stream of wealth in the shape of private fortunes."

1849. Mr. Robert Knight on Guzerat. "Many of the best families in the province, which were rich and well to-do when we came to Guzerat in 1807, have now scarcely clothes to their backs......Our demands in money on the Talookdars are more than three times what they originally paid, without one single advantage gained on their parts. Parties from whom they have been compelled to borrow at usurious rates of interest enforced their demands by the attachment of their lands and villages; thus they sink deeper and deeper in debt, without the chance of extricating themselves. What, then, must become of their rising family? What indeed? After two generations of steady deterioration, the peasantry and land-owners of Guzerat were overtaken by an appalling famine, which has nearly ruined this fertile and once wealthy province "

1854. Mr. Bourdillon of Madras: " Now it may certainly be said of almost the whole of the ryots, paying even the highest of these sums, and even of many holding to a much larger amount that they are always in poverty and generally in debt. A ryot of this class, of course, lives from hand to mouth. He rarely sees money. His dwelling is a hut of mud walls and thatched roof—far ruder, smaller, and dilapidated than those of the better classes of ryots above spoken of, and still more destitute, if possible, of anything that can be called furniture. His food, and that of his family, is partly thin porridge made of the meal of grain boiled in water, and partly boiled rice, with a little condiment; and generally the only vessels for cooking and eating from, are of the coarsest earthenware, much inferior in grain to a good tile or brick in England, and unglazed. Brass vessels, though not wholly unknown among this class, are rare."

About the labourer he says :—"As respects food, houses and clothing, they are in a worse condition than the class of poor ryots above spoken of. It appears from the foregoing details that the condition of the agricultural labourer in this country is very poor In fact, almost the whole of his earnings must necessarily be consumed in a spare allowance of coarse and unvaried food, and a bare sufficiency of clothing. The wretched hut he lives in can hardly be valued at all. As to anything in the way of education or mental culture, he is utterly destitute of it."

CHAPTER XIX.

The Foreign Trade of India—Since the Abolition of the E. I. Coy.

Such are some of the opinions regarding the pitiable condition of the country as directly due to the system of government "a sordid system of misrule," as the Hon'ble Mr. F. Shore observed, the opinions of those great administrators of earlier years who knew the people intimately by personal intercourse as none of their successors of these days know. These opinions relate to the earliest period of British rule, from 1769 to about 1850. The Mutiny of 1858 introduced important political changes, but did not affect the trade. The opening of the Suez Canal in November 1869, was of a most serious consequence to India's foreign trade. The exports and imports of India between 1835 and 1872, that is till the year when the above event began to bear fruit, may be stated as follows: (I take the figures from Mr. Dadabhai Naoroji's work, "the Poverty of India," a book which must be in the hands of every student of Indian politics).

Exports	... ...	£ 1,120,000,000
Imports	... ...	£ 943,000,000
Balance	... ...	£ 177,000,000

Now, according to the theory of "Mercantilism", which we considered in previous pages, this balance of trade will return to India either in the shape of money, or in the shape of commodities which can be re-sold to other countries and converted into money or which can be consumed in India. Then India would be benefited. But this does not return to India, but is absorbed in the tribute which she pays annually to the ruling country. It would, however, be a mistake to suppose that this balance is all the tribute that is extorted from this country. Mr. Naoroji calculates the real value of the tribute as follows: "The exports being £1,120,000,000, the imports with an addition of 15 per cent. to exports for profits (of about £ 168,000,000) should be about £ 1,288,000,000. Besides this India has incurred to foreign countries debt of about £50,000,000 for the public debt and about £ 100,000,000 for railways during the same period. Now on the other hand, in return for exports, *plus* profits, of £ 1,288,000,000, and £ 150,000,000 of the loans, India has actually imported, during the last 38 years, from 1835 and 1872 (not, as would be the case in a normal condition, £ 1,430,900, but) only about £ 943,000,000 leaving a balance of about £ 500,000,000 which England has kept back as its benefit, chiefly arising from the political position it holds in India. Towards this drain, the net opium revenue contributed by China amounts to about £141,000,000. The balance of about £360,000,000 is derived from India's own produce and profits of commerce. The profits of commerce are, say about £ 168,000,000. Allowing then the whole opium revenue and the whole profits of commerce as having gone towards the drain, there is still a deficiency of nearly £200,000,000 which must have gone out of the produce of the country. Deducting from this £ 200,000,000 the interest on Railway loans remitted to England, the balance still sent from the very produce of the country is about £ 144,000,000. Strictly speaking the whole £ 200,000,000 should be considered as a drain from the very produce of the country, because it is the exhaustion caused by the drain that disables us from building our rail roads &c. from our own means."

As I have said, the transfer of the Government of India to the British Parliament, though it introduced important political changes, effected no change in the economic results of foreign dominion. On the other hand, it has since been greatly aggravated, its full magnitude being now experienced in the rapidly recurring famine which lays desolate extensive regions of the country and kills millions of people, besides leaving a permanent legacy of the most lamentable deterioration in the stamina and the earning capacity of the poorer classes. The drain of India's wealth between the years 1850 and 1869, the year when the Suez Canal was opened, was as follows:

	£
1850-54	7,458,000
1855-59	7,730,000
1860-64	17,300,000
1865-69	24,600,000

The drain during the five years ending 1869 would have been represented by a higher figure, had not an exceptionally large amount of treasure been imported into India to pay for the Mutiny. During that period £11·27 million worth of treasure was imported against £4·79million in the previous quinquennium.The average import of treasure during the ten years ending 1869 was 17·34 millions against 11·27 millions of the previous period and represented the price of the cotton sent to Manchester during the American War. During the same period India borrowed enormous amounts, including 40 millions to meet the cost of suppressing the Mutiny and the amounts required for lavish expenditure on military public works and on railways and other means of communication.

The opening of the Suez Canal and the rapidity with which railway construction was pushed, and has been pushed till the present moment, imparted a great stimulus to India's foreign exports. The import duties, which were yielding a large income to the Indian Treasury without pressure on the people, were also abolished in deference to the wishes of British manufacturers, more especially of the cotton manufacturers of Lancashire. In January 1886, Sir Auckland Colvin as Finance Member of the Government of India thus described the various causes that had contributed to the growth of India's foreign trade:

The value of imports of manufactured goods, treasure and Government imports apart, which in the ten years before 1878-79 averaged £35,000,000, was in 1884-8› £53,000,000. The average of the four years from 1878-79, when the first duties were remitted, to 1881-82, the year before the final abolition, was £47,000,000 ; the average of the three years from 1882-83 to 1884-85 has been £51,000,000. The percentage of increase from 1878-79 to 1881-82 was 28 ; from 1878-79 to 1884-85 it has been 45. If we remember that during this period prices have been steadily falling and that these figures represent value, not quantities, the real increase will be much greater. I am not so foolish as to suppose that the great growth of our imports since 1878-79 is due solely or mainly to the abolition of the import duties. It is due to a variety of causes ; it is partly due to the increase in our exports; it is partly due to the cause to which so much of the increase of our exports is due—namely, to the extension of our railways, and to the consequent improvement in the distribution and cheapening of commodities ; it is due to the forcing of accumulated stocks, owing to the fall of prices in England, upon the Indian market ; it is very largely due to the fall of prices in England ; but, unquestionably, it is also partly due to the abolition of import duties".

The first serious remission of duty on cotton manufactures was made in March 1879. In the four years preceding that date, the average annual value of the imports of cotton goods was Rs. 18,760,000. In the four years following the complete abolition of the duty, and ending in March 1886, it was Rs. 24,690,000, and in the five years ending 1892-93 it was Rs. 29,718,000. The prices of cotton goods fell greatly after the remission, and the increase in the quantities imported was more striking than the increase in value.

The foreign trade of India, both exports and imports, with the exception of a small duty on the export of Burmese rice, continued under a system of Free Trade more perfect than in any other country, until March 1894. Then, the Government of India, in consequence of financial pressure caused by the fall in the gold value of the rupee as well as by their extravagant increase of the Home Charges, were driven to resort again to import duties to strengthen their financial position. The tariff of 1875, under which, with the exception of the precious metals, almost everything imported into India was subject to a duty of 5 per cent., was with some modification restored. Two important changes were made. Silver bullion was included among dutiable articles, and cotton goods were exempted. This exemption lasted, however, for a short time only. In December 1894 a 5 per cent. import duty was imposed on cotton goods, and a countervailing excise duty of 5 per cent. *ad valorem* was imposed on cotton fabrics manufactured at power mills in India. In February 1896, these duties were again revised, and cotton yarns were exempted from duty. A duty of $3\frac{1}{2}$ per cent. *ad valorem* was imposed on cotton manufacturing goods imported from abroad, and a corresponding excise duty at the same rate was imposed on goods manufactured at mills in India.

CHAPTER XX.

Mr. Chamberlain's Fiscal Reform and India.

WHAT will be the position of India in any scheme of Imperial fiscal reform such as is proposed by Mr. Chamberlain, remains to be seen. Those that object to Mr. Chamberlain's proposals introduce India in the controversy having in view the effectual obstacle she would present in case England should adopt a system of Protection. The so-called scheme of Imperial Reciprocity is only a scheme of Protection thinly disguised, and once England converts her fiscal policy from Free Trade to Protection, she would, it is argued, lose the right to force Free Trade on her dependency as she does now. India having no manufactured articles to export, her exports mainly consisting of food grains and raw materials, no preferential duties of the mother-country on Indian exports can benefit this conntry. The true interest of India demands that wheat and rice, and other agricultural produce, like oil seeds etc, should be consumed in India and not exported. An export duty on these articles would make them cheaper to the home consumer and bring large revenues to the state. On the other hand, if the Indian corn, cotton and other produce were taxed at the ports of foreign countries, their prices would rise and would be injurious to the Indian people. If India's exports were taxed at the ports of Germany or America, India would have the right, under the proposed scheme of fiscal reform, to tax the imports from these countries. Or, if the foreign countries were to retaliate on Britain by taxing Indian imports for preference shown to the colonial produce, then too India could tax the foreign imports at her ports. In both cases the same result would follow, namely, increase in prices. The fact that British imports would be free would not affect the situation, because of the well-known principle of the impossibility of two prices in the same market. English articles would be sold at as dear prices as those of Germany, Austria, Belgium, or America. Thus the result of Mr. Chamberlain's scheme being made applicable to India also, would be to enhance the Indian prices all round, on the necessaries of life as well as on luxuries. Such enhancement would operate with extreme hardship on the poorer classes. Even in the United Kingdom, great fear is entertained as to the effect which these proposals might have on prices. According to the highest authorities, there are a vast mass of people in that country who can scarcely be said to have any fixed or regular employmer nd who are able and only just able, to earn su to gain a livelihood. " In spite of our natior .th", said the Duke of Devonshire, "in spit .e prosperity of the people employed i our great industries, there are to-day millions for whom the margin between themselves and famine is very slender." What a rise of price in food means to these people, who cannot afford to spend a single penny thoughtlessly without serious consequences, can be imagined. England depends on foreign countries, as udia depends on the rains, for her food supply, and if this supply breaks down, the slender margin to which the Duke of Devonshire refers, will become more slender. A rise in prices virtually means a decrease in wages, and when the same wages can purchase less food, the classes that are constantly on the verge of famine must increase. These considerations which are urged against dear food in England, hold good with increased force in this country.

We have said that preference shown for Indian wheat would not help India. The quantity of wheat sent from this country to England is comparatively insignificant, and the price of wheat in London is determined by the supply from the United States. Of all British colonies and possessions, Canada is the only one that sends to England a substantial quantity of wheat, being about 9,500,000 cwts. against 2,900,000 cwts. from India and 1,480,000 from Australia. Canada is increasing her wheat area with great rapidity, and Canadian enthusiasts say that in five or ten years' time the Dominion will be able to supply the full demand of the United Kingdom. If this be so and if the United States also continue to export undiminished quantities of wheat, the prices may actually go down instead of rising. Great Britain is the only great market for American produce, and the competition of the United States against the Colonies might neutralise any effect that preferential duties in favour of the colonies might produce. That the Indian produce of wheat should be stimulated is much to be wished, but not for the sake of foreign but of domestic consumption. Mr. Chamberlain's choice of Indian pr oducts is unfortunate. We do not see that in any way Indian indigo would benefit by preference, because, there is no competitive import of the same article from other countries, and therefore no favour shown to Indian indigo would operate as a stimulus to indigo cultivation or would improve its prospects. Tea would benefit no doubt from a preferential duty. The Indian tea-planters would derive increased profits and would extend their cultivation. But tea is a special industry, entirely in the hands of Englishmen, and any advantage conferred on it would not benefit the great bulk of the people.

Thus if India accept the proposals made in the name of fiscal reform by Mr. Chamberlain, the result will be to her,—as it is apprehended will be to Great Britain,—a probable increase of prices all round and worse suffering and starvation to millions of people. If wheat and rice become dearer than they are now, what would be the result ? The poorer classes would resort to inferior grains and subsist, even more largely than at present on unhealthy roots, fruits, and leaves, which can be had cheaply or for nothing. This latter evil is already serious and is telling most injuriously on the physical stamina of the working classes. This happens even in ordinary seasons ; but as the occurrence of famine and scarcity has become a regular feature in our economic condition, in such times the mortality among the poor would be more appalling and would be a greater discredit to British rule than it is at present. A policy of true enlightenment and benevolence requires the causation of two-fold results, namely, a reduction in prices and a rise in wages. The advocates of Free Trade claim these results in the United Kingdom, and their opponents, the advocates of Protection and modified Protection, claim the same result for their policy. In India alone the anomalous system of forced Free Trade has had the effect of raising the prices and keeping the wages stationary. Instead of a system of Free Trade, if India follows a policy of Protection such as the colonies follow, the prices will become cheaper and wages will rise, and the millions that now "die like musquitoes," during recurring famines from chronic starvation and disease and that leave behind a sickly, deformed and stunted progeny will live less unhappy lives and confer on their country the great boon of a well-fed, healthy and contented class of labourers and artisans.

Thus neither Free Trade nor a system of preferential duties in favour of Indian exports will be beneficial to this country. What is wanted in the best interests of its material well-being is exactly what the British colonists insist on doing, that is, to develop their manufacturing industries by a system of high Protection against imports from all foreign countries including

Great Britain. The colonies are as much dependent on England as India is; they are in many ways as much indebted to the mother-country as is this great dependency. Still, the colonies follow their own policy in entire regard to their own interests. They are great agricultural countries and export articles of food to England. The population being still thin when compared to the area, the colonies have large surplus agricultural products to export, and they do so. India also is an agricultural country, but she has a teeming population to support and cannot therefore export much surplus articles of food. Still, by great temptations offered to the producer and under partial indirect coercion from the State, a substantial amount of agricultural produce, including food and raw materials, is exported to England. But here the resemblance between the colonies and India ceases. The former are not content to remain agricultural countries. They wish manufacturing industries to develop, and their policy is directed towards this end. They have imposed protective duties on foreign imports, including British goods, in order that their own industries might grow. British Free Traders wish that the colonies had never adopted protective measures in their desire to foster their own manufactures. If they had not done so, they would be supplying Great Britain a much larger proportion of her wants in food and raw materials. For, with free play and open competition, the Free Traders argue, it would have been worth the while of the colonies to develop only such industries as were profitable without the aid of protective duties. Their natural course of development is in the direction of agriculture and mining, and, if they would follow it, they would increase their exports to the mother-country. In other words, Great Britain would be glad and would applaud the wisdom of the colonial statesmen if they had done exactly what has been done in India under her rule. But the colonies are no more prepared to receive lessons on their industrial policy from Great Britain that Great Britain is prepared to be dictated to by her daughter-countries in the same matter. Whether the first overtures for a preferential system came from Great Britain or from the colonies, it is certain that the colonies are not prepared to go beyond a certain point in favour of the mother-country. They will not sacrifice their industrial future in order that Great Britain may continue to hold her commercial ascendency in the world.

There are already important manufactures in existence in the colonies, specially in Canada and Australia; and as Professor W. J. Ashley says, whether it is wise or no for these two great countries to protect these manufactures, "it must be distinctly understood that no colonial ministry would think for a moment of granting such terms to Great Britain as would seriously endanger them." It is a vain dream of some English Imperialists that in the colonies will be found markets for all the manufactures of their country. It is probable that they will make an all-round deduction of duty in favour of British goods. But they will, quite certainly, says the same writer who is a Chamberlain protagonist, to protect if necessary their large industries, previously raise the general rate on particular goods to an equivalent extent, so that on those goods the deduction will be meaningless.

The question is whether the colonies---besides the preference of British to foreign goods—will consent, in return for adequate reciprocal concession from Great Britain, to abstain for a time from entering upon such branches of manufactures as they have not yet undertaken. In other words, "will they consent to a certain slackening in their manufacturing development?" This seems to be a rather impertinent question for England to ask; but considerations are urged, from the point of view of the mother-country, to justify the colonial statesmen in consenting to such a policy. These considerations consist in the fact that great Britain and the other European countries which have rushed into the path of manufacturing activity have not reaped such unmixed success as to encourage unlimited imitation by the colonies. A policy of protected manufacturing development carried to the same extreme as by the United States, will produce in Canada and South Australia the same evil of the desertion of the rural areas and the overcrowding of the towns. The wise policy of these countries lies in the distribution of the population over the land and the maintenance of its physique by rural life, while its intelligence is heightened by education and improved means of communication. The English statesman that advises the colonies as above, no doubt, protests that he is honestly convinced that his suggestion is the wisest course for the colonies to adopt. But the colonies know their own minds and are determined to follow their own course. In fact, both Canada and Australia have plainly said so.

We have dwelt on the policy that guides at present the inter-Imperial relations mutually between the mother-country and the colonies, in order to draw attention to the fact that what England would persuade the colonies to do by appealing to their own future interest, that she already coerces India to do. England will not help India to develop her manufactures, but will do everything possible to exploit her as a producer of her food and of the raw materials required for her manufactures. But there is no reason why India should not look at this great question from her own standpoint as the colonies do. India is ambitious, as the colonies are, of becoming a manufacturing country and will be glad to foster her nascent industries by Protection. Such fostering is more needed in India than it is in the colonies. The nations of these countries are young and their vast and fertile lands yield them enough to maintain themselves in a healthy and contented condition. It will take a century before Canada or Australia can contain a population which will press on the resources of the land and render a multiplicity of manufacturing industries necessary India, on the other hand, occupies an entirely different position. Her teeming population is an increasing burden on the produce of the soil, and not only is a variety of industrial occupations imperatively needed, but this need is aggravated by the disappearance of the old industries which maintained millions of people.

To bring into existence a variety of non-agricultural occupations is the most paramount want of the country, and this can be done, as the history of nations shows, by the adoption of a policy of Protection, against England as well as against other countries that imported articles which can be produced in India and which she is now prevented from producing by the two-fold cause of the unfair competition of the Western countries and of the attitude of indifference and secret antipathy adopted by the rulers. The British nation must be told frankly that the Indian people have no doubt whatever in their own minds that, so long as the present so-called Free Trade and unequal competition continue, India has no hope of a future which will be distinguished by material prosperity. India is doomed to ruin under the present system of the helpless exploitation of her agricultural resources by every nation in the world and of her being compelled to take almost every manufactured article for ordinary and daily use by the millions of her population from foreign countries. To preserve the food grains and raw materials that she produces for consumption in her own domestic markets, by taxing their export, and to prevent the import of competitive manufactures by protective duties in view to the growth of indigenous industries—this is the policy that alone will save India.

CHAPTER XXI.

Exports and Imports of India—Are They Evidence of Prosperity?

THE export of Indian manufactured goods has grown from 60 to 263 million rupees in value, while the total trade, import and export, is now valued at 2,503 million rupees compared with 1,381 million rupees in 1880-81. On these facts, Mr. R. E. Enthoven, Director-General of Statistics to the Government of India, thus comments in the latest volume on 'Financial and Commercial Statistics of British India:' "This is not the place to draw inferences from these facts; but they do not seem entirely in harmony with some recent theories of the gradual impoverishment of the country owing to the pressure of Home Charges, the ravages of agricultural distress, or other adverse infleunces." In the opinion thus expressed Mr. R. E. Enthoven echoes that of a great majority of British Indian officials and merchants, who are content to apply to the conditions of India, in spite of their special character, theories popularly accepted in European countries. Mr. Enthoven who refers to "some recent theories" considers them to be sufficiently disproved by his citation of the total trade, import and export, as if those that adopt these theories are not aware of this total and of the official inference from it, and as if this inference has not been repeatedly proved by them to be erroneous. In the first place, it is not difficult to see that the aggregate quantity of the import and export trade is a misleading proof of a country's prosperity. Two amounts of wealth exchanged between two countries cannot constitute the measure of the prosperity of either country. The true measure is the balance of the foreign trade rather than the import or export or the two trades taken together. The imports of a country may partly consist of goods from foreign countries intended to be re-exported abroad; or the exports of that country may consist partly of the products of foreign enterprise there, in which case they will represent only in a partial sense the prosperity of the country or they may partly indicate foreign indebtedness as it does in India; or, again, as is the case with Japan, the exports and imports may exceed each other by turns, and the increase in the total, instead of indicating prosperity for the time being, may indicate a reverse state of things. The total, absolutely considered, may be a very big figure, but when taken in relation to the population, it may not signify much. Critics of Indian administration on the side of the Government do not advance the controversy towards a satisfactory solution by an attitude of absolute self-confidence like that of Mr. Enthoven. If the object is the establishment of correct opinions on these important matters, officials should fully examine the grounds on which their pessimist opponents base their theories.

A substantial portion of the imports represents the loan which India takes every year from England. For the prosecution of public works and for administrative purposes, India borrows largely from the ruling country which, instead of sending specie, sends merchandise and treasure. On the other hand, a similar portion of the exports of India represents the interest paid by the country on the amounts borrowed as above. Of these two items, the accumulating annual amount of interest being larger than that of the amount of the loan in a year, the excess is represented by a corresponding excess of exports over imports. There is, then, India's political drain, the tribute that she pays as the price of the blessing she derives from the overlordship of Great Britain. Thirdly, the manufactured goods exported from India represent only to a small extent the capital and skill of the people of the country; they mostly represent those of British capitalists who bring their capital here and make profitable use of the raw materials and cheap labour abounding in the country. According to Mr. Enthoven, the value of the total manufactured and partly manufactured goods exported to India is a little over 26 crores of rupees, nearly one fifth of the value of the total export trade. But even of this small total, the proportion representing industries that bring to the people profits consumed by them, is fractional. If we next consider the imports, they are not goods which are mainly consumed by the bulk of the people. They are chiefly intended to meet the wants of the Government, of the railways, of the frontier territories, of the European residents of the chief cities, of the native princes and nobility, and of the Anglicised inhabitants of the urban population. If allowance were made for consumption under these heads, the balance bought and consumed by the great bulk of the people, by the eight-tenths of the total population of British India, would be hardly worth mention. If the total trade has increased, since 1880, the population too has increased, and if we look into the figures, we shall see that, while exports have steadily increased, chiefly from political causes, the increase in the imports has been insignificant, and not at all what the increasing wants of a growing and, according to official theory, prosperous, population, and the strenuous efforts made by the State to increase the foreign trade of the country, might suggest. "Let the Government give us correct information," writes Mr. Dadabhai Naoroji, in his invaluable book on 'Poverty and Un-British Rule in India,' "about these particulars, and then we shall be able to know how insignificant is the commercial benefit England derives from her dominion over British India." There are 16,877 miles of railway needing new rails, new rolling stock, with ever new railway extensions; an army of 334,193 officers and men continually requiring fresh armaments; public works carried on on an extensive scale needing materials from England; a population of 168 thousand Europeans requiring articles for personal wear, as also furniture and food, for consumption from oversea, and with, at the outside, two millions of Europeanised Indians who have more or less learnt the wants of Europeans in their personal and domestic habits. If these factors were eliminated from Indian consumption of foreign imports, the consumption of the great bulk of the people would be represented by a few pence.

Increasing imports are not absolutely a cause or result of prosperity. Even in England, the controversy about fiscal reform now fiercely raging there, has brought to the front a number of eminent men who argue that the British system of free imports is doing serious harm to the economic prosperity of that country. In India, which has not many manufactured goods to export, this system is doing serious harm to the well-being of the people. On the other hand, the bulk of our imports consist of manufactured goods and it is obvious that every increase in an imported article or every fresh article imported, far from indicating any increase in the purchasing power of the consumer, only results in accelerating the extinction of the few indigenous industries still lingering. While the imports of cotton-goods, for instance, have been increasing for years past, we know as a matter of fact that hundreds of the weaving classes have been deprived of their means of livelihood and obliged to resort to manual work to earn a daily wage. "The process of such displacement" (of indigenous industries), said the Hon'ble Mr. Gokhale in March last in the Viceregal Legislative Council, "is not yet complete, but the large and progressive totals of our import trade only show that the transition of the country from the partially industrial to the purely agricultural phase of economic life is going on at a rapid pace, and that the movement has already reached an advanced stage. There is at present hardly a country in the world which has become so preponderatingly agricultural, or sends abroad so much of its food supply and raw material for manufacture abroad as British India. When the disastrous transformation is completed—and this is only a question of time, unless remedial measures on an adequate scale are promptly undertaken—it will reveal a scene of economic helplessness and ruin before which the heart of the staunchest optimist will quail. No doubt there are here and there signs of an awakening to the dangers of the situation, but the first condition of this awakening producing any appreciable pratical result is that the fact of our deep and deepening poverty and the real exigencies of the economic position should come to be frankly recognised by the Government of this country. And, my Lord, it is a matter for both surprise and disappointment that a few paltry increases in revenue under certain heads should be accepted by the Finance Minister of this country as conclusive evidence of our growing material prosperity when most important indications point just the other way."

Referring to the same figures which drew from Mr. Enthoven the half-sneering allusion "to some recent theories," the late Sir William Hunter said in 1880, "these figures are so great and the material progress which they indicate is so enormous that they elude the grasp of the imagination." They may do so in the case of these gentlemen who are in the main responsible for the present state of things and who are pledged to support it. But there are impartial Englishmen who, after a careful study of the question, conclude that there is another and dark side. Mr. Samuel Smith M. P. for instance sees this other side, and acknowledges that "the people of India require to export a large portion of the produce of the soil in order to buy their clothing and utensils, and another large portion to liquidate the "Home Charges" and private remittances made to England. *When thus analysed, it will be seen that it is futile to reckon increase of foreign trade as equivalent to increase of wealth*; it is rather a substitution of foreign for domestic exchange. The food and raw produce are exchanged against the cloth and hardware of England, instead of the produce of innumerable small makers at home."

Then there is the question of the political drain or of the tribute which India is forced to pay to England every year to the extent of 25 millions. The financial difficulties of India, which reached almost the acute stage of an impending bankruptcy in 1894, are due to the demands on India for sterling expenditure in England, which up to 1872 was disguised by payments of railway capital in that country and since then by annual loans taken in London. These withdrawals of Indian revenues and resources without affording a commercial return, constitute the predominating adverse factor, as Mr. Martin Wood said in his evidence before the Currency Committee, in India's monetary, industrial and commercial condition, and, besides being a direct unrequited outlay, force India to exchange her produce for the foreign commodities she receives on less advantageous terms, as was pointed out by J. S. Mill in a well-known passage. Critics like Mr. Enthoven, when they extract from India's exports and imports a proof of prosperity, should remember that the economic facts of India have to be discussed from points of view which do not occur to writers in European countries where industry and commerce are not subject to direct and indirect politicial influences as they are in this country.

CHAPTER XXII

The Condition of India at the Eve of the Establishment of British Rule.

IN this chapter I quote below some contemporary opinions* on the condition of different parts of India at the eve of the establishment of British supremacy. These opinions expressed by perfectly impartial critics, who could have had no motive whatever to exalt the merit of Indian rule, ought to suffice to disprove completely the views disseminated by Anglo-Indian writers that British rule redeemed the people of India from a state of anarchy and destitution.

We have the following interesting account of the state of the Mahratta Territory from the pen of Anquetil du Perron :—

"On February 14,1758, I set out from Mahé for Goa, in order to proceed to Surat, and, in all my routes, I took care to keep specimens of the money of all the States I passed through, so that I have examples of every coin that is current from Cape Comorin to Delhi.

"From Surat, I passed the Ghats, the 27th of March the same year, about ten in the morning, and when I entered the country of the Mahrattas, I

* The passages containing these opinions are reproduced with omissions here and there from Mr. Dadabhai Naorogi's book.

thought myself in the midst of the simplicity and happiness of the golden age where nature was yet unchanged, and war and misery were unknown. The people were cheerful, vigorous, and in high health, and unbounded hospitality was a universal virtue. every door was open, and friends, neighbours, and strangers were alike welcome to whatever they found. When I came within seven miles of Aurungabad, I went to see the celebrated pagoda of Ellora."*

Hyder Ali bequeathed to his son, Tippoo Sultan, an overflowing treasury, which he had filled; a powerful Empire, which he had created; an army of 300,000 men, that he had formed, disciplined, and inured to conquest; and a territory which, as contemporary historians and eye-witnesses assure us, had in no way deteriorated under the sway of his successor.

"When a person, travelling through a strange country, finds it well cultivated, populous with industrious inhabitants, cities newly founded, commerce extending, towns increasing, and everything flourishing, so as to indicate happiness, he will naturally conclude it to be under a form of government congenial to the minds of the people. This is a picture of Tippoo's country, and this is our conclusion respecting its government. It has fallen to our lot to tarry some time in Tippoo's dominions, and to travel through them as much, if not more, than any other officer in the field during the war; and we have reason to suppose his subjects to be as happy as those of any other sove

* Extracted from page 376 of the *Gentleman's Magazine* of 1762, "Brief Account of a Voyage to India, by M. Anquetil du Perron."

reign; for we do not recollect of any complaints or murmurings among them; although, had causes existed, no time would have been more favourable for their utterance, because, the enemies of Tippoo were in power and would have been gratified by any aspersion of his character. The inhabitants of the conquered countries submitted with apparent resignation to the direction of their conquerors; but by no means as if relieved from an oppressive yoke in their former government; on the contrary, no sooner did an opportunity offer than they scouted their new masters and gladly returned to their loyalty again."* "Whether from the operation of the system established by Hyder, from the principles which Tippoo adopted for his own conduct, or from his dominions having suffered little by invasion for many years, or from the effect of these several causes united, his country was found everywhere full of inhabitants and apparently cultivated to the utmost extent of which the soil was capable, while the discipline and fidelity of his troops in the field until their last overthrow were testimonies, equally strong, of the excellent regulations which existed in his army. His government, though strict and arbitrary, was the despotism of a strict and able sovereign, who nourishes, not oppresses, the subjects who are to be the means of his future aggrandisement, and his cruelties were, in general, inflicted only on those whom she considered as hi enemies."†

* Moore's "Narrative of the War with Tippoo Sultan," p. 201.

† Dirom's "Narrative," p. 249.

It would be a great mistake, however, to suppose that all this prosperity was created either by Hyder or his son. Their sway, which did not last for half a century, was too short for such a work. The foundation of it was laid by the ancient Hindoo dynasty which preceded them—the constructors of the magnificent canals by which Mysore is intersected, and which insure to the people certain and prodigal returns from its fertile soil.*

The British Government and their great rival, Hyder Ali, appeared on the political stage of India nearly at the same moment, and in the year that Hyder established his sway over Mysore, by usurpation from its legitimate sovereign, Bengal—the brightest jewel in the Imperial Crown of the Moghuls—came into our possession. Although still suffering from the scourge of a recent Mahratta invasion, Clive described the new acquisition as a country "of inexhaustible riches,"† and one that could not fail to make its new masters the richest corporation in the world. "In spite," says Mr. Macaulay, "of the

* "The watercourses in Mysore, in magnitude rather resembling navigable canals, which, issuing from the embankments, are conducted with admirable skill along the slope of the hills, and occasionally across ravines, with a fall barely sufficient for the flow of the water, fertilise the whole of the intermediate space between their course and the river. These works are of great antiquity, the last in order of time, which supplies Seringapatam, having been completed in the year 1690 by Sheik Deo Raj Ovdaar, to whom the country is also indebted for some of its most useful civil regulations."—Wilke's "Mysore," vol. ii.

† "Life of Clive."

Mussulman despot and of the Mahratta freebooter, Bengal was known through the East as the Garden of Eden—as the rich kingdom. Its population multiplied exceedingly; distant provinces were nourished from the overflowing of its granaries; and the noble ladies of London and Paris were clothed in the delicate produce of its looms." From another authority * we have an account of the people of Bengal under its Native sovereigns, which we should be disposed to regard as fabulous if it did not come from one who had been long resident in the country, and who spoke from an intimate acquaintance with his subject. "In truth (says Mr. Holwell), it would be almost cruelty to molest this happy people; for in this district are the only vestiges of the beauty, purity, piety, regularity, equity, and strictness of the ancient Hindostan Government. Here the property, as well as the liberty of the people, are inviolate. Here no robberies are heard of, either public or private. The traveller, either with or without merchandise, becomes the immediate care of the Government, which allots him guards, without any expense, to conduct him from stage to stage; and these are accountable for the safety and accommodation of his person and effects. At the end of the first stage he is delivered over, with certain benevolent

* "The enormous amount of capital in the hands of individuals at this time may be inferred from the fact that in the Mahratta invasion of 1742 the banking firm of Juggat Sett, of Moorshedabad—then the capital of Bengal—was plundered to the extent of two and a half millions sterling."—Duff's "History of the Mahrattas," vol. ii. page 12.

formalities, to the guards of the next, who, after interrogating the traveller as to the usage he had received in his journey, dismissed the first guard with a written certificate of their behaviour and a receipt for the traveller and his effects, which certificate and receipt are returnable to the commanding officer of the first stage, who registers the same and regularly reports it to the Rajah.

"In this form the traveller is passed through the country; and if he only passes he is not suffered to be at any expense for food, accommodation, or carriage for his merchandise or baggage; but it is otherwise if he is permitted to make any residence in one place above three days, unless occasioned by sickness, or any unavoidable accident. If anything is lost in this district, for instance a bag of money or other valuables, the person who finds it hangs it on the next tree, gives notice to the nearest chowkey, or place of guard; the officer of which orders immediate publication of the same by beat of tomtom, or drum."*

"By the prudent administration of a system of sound policy and humanity, the rich province of Dacca was cultivated in every part, and abounded in everything requisite for the comfort and gratification of its inhabitants. Justice was administered with impartiality, and the conduct of its administrators, Gholab Aly Khan and Jeswunt Roy, gained great credit to their principal, Sarferaz Khan. Jeswunt Roy had been educated under the Nawab Aly Khan,

*Holwell's Tracts upon India.

whose example he emulated in purity, integrity, and indefatigable attention to business; and in framing his arrangements for the government of the province, he studied to render them conducive to the general ease and happiness of the people; he abolished all monopolies, and the imposts which had been laid upon the grain."*

Such was the state of Bengal, when Alivardy Khan, the predecessor of Surajah Dowlah, a nominal Lieutenant of the King of Delhi, assumed its government.

Nor was it in British territory alone that the evil of the Company's misrule was felt. It spread into the dominions of Native rulers. From the Company's first connection with the Nabob of Oudh, his kingdom was made a carcass for it to prey upon. "I fear," said Mr. Hastings,† when still vested with the supreme rule over India, and describing a state of things which he had been a party in producing, "I fear that our encroaching spirit, and the insolence with which it has been exerted, has caused our alliance to be as much dreaded by all the powers of Hindostan as our arms. Our encroaching spirit, and the uncontrolled and even protected licentiousness of individuals, have done more injury to our national reputation than our arms and the credit of our strength has raised it. Every person in India dreads a connection with us, which they see attended with mortifying humiliation to those who have availed

* Stewart's "History of Bengal," p. 430.

† Gleig's "Life of W. Hastings," vol. ii.

themselves of it." And as a signal example of this feeling, and of measures which awakened it, he adduces our dealings with the Nabob of Oude.

We have seen that when the Governor-General, Lord Cornwallis, was pronouncing the Kingdom of Bengal to be in a state of rapid decay, the Kingdom of Mysore, under the rule of Tippoo, was upon the evidence of eye-witnesses in a state of high prosperity; that its prosperity had in no way diminished many years afterwards under the regency of Poorneah, we have, amongst many others, the testimony of the great Duke, who, speaking from his own observation, pronounced the government of Mysore to be in every respect entitled to applause, and, as a mark of his approbation and esteem, made the Dewan Poorneah a present of his picture.*

"Every trait," says the British Resident of that day,† "in the character of Poorneah marks him as an extraordinary man. . . . . To a mind of singular vigour he added an extensive accquaintance with the resources of the country, and an intimate knowledge of characters. The revenue of Mysore has been raised to its present amount by the superior management of Poorneah; by his attention to the repair of tanks and watercourses, and the construction of roads and bridges: by the encourgement which he has given to strangers to resort to and settle in Mysore, and his general endeavours to improve the agricul-

* Colonel Wilkes.

† Duke of Wellington's Despatches, vol. 1.

ture of the country and the situation of the people under the Government of the Rajah."*

Contemporary with Poorneah, and in no ways inferior to him, was Nana Furnawese, who for a quarter of a century administered the territory of the Pieshwah during the minority of Bajee Rao. "To attempt a character of this great statesman would be to detail a history of Mahratta politics for the last twenty-five years, during which he discharged the duties of Minister with abilities unequalled. During the long and important period of his administration, by the force and energy of his single mind, he held together his vast Empire—composed of members whose interests were as opposite as the most anamalous elements—and by the versatility of his genius, the wisdom and firmness and moderation of his government, he excited this mass of incongruities to one mutual and common effort. With that wise and foreseeing policy which, strong in its own resources, equally rejects the extremes of confidence and despair, he supplied from the fertility of unexhausted genius an expedient for every possible event."†

The state of the territory which has been so long administered by this distinguished man was visited not many years after by the late Sir John Malcolm, who thus describes its condition :—

"It has not happened to me ever to see countries better cultivated, and more abounding in all produce

---

* Official Report on Mysore, 1805 ; Asiatic Annual Register, 1805.

† Asiatic Annual Register, vol. v., p. 70 ; Miscellaneous Extracts.

of the soil, as well as in commercial wealth, than the southern Mahratta districts, when I accompanied the present Duke of Wellington to that country in the year 1803. I particularly here allude to those large tracts near the borders of the Kistnah. Poonah, the capital of the Peishwah, was a very wealthy and a thriving commercial town, and there was as much cultivation in the Deccan as it was possible an arid and unfruitful country could admit."*

And of another large portion of the Mahratta territory, Malwa, now and formerly under the sovereignty of the Holkar family, and of the character of some of its rulers, we have the same favourable testimony from the same distinguished witness :—

"With respect to Malwa, I saw it in a state of ruin, caused by the occupancy for a period of more than half-a-century of that fine country by the Mahratta armies, the Pindarries, and, indeed, the assembled predatory hordes of all India. Yet, even at that period, I was perfectly surprised at the difference that exists between a distant view of such countries and a nearer examination of their actual condition. I had ample means afforded to me as the person appointed to occupy that territory, and to conduct its civil, military, and political administration, to learn all that the records of Government could teach, and to obtain from other sources full information of this

* Evidence before Committee of Commons, 1833, p. 41.

country; and I certainly entered upon my duties with the complete conviction that commerce would be unknown, and that credit could not exist in a province which had long possessed, from its position, the transit trade between the rich provinces of Western India and the whole of the North-West Provinces of Hindustan, as well as the more eastern ones of Saugor and Bundlecund. I found, to my surprise, that in correspondence with the first commercial and moneyed men of Rajpootana, Bundlecund, and Hindostan, as with those of Guzerat, dealings in money to a large amount had continually taken place at Oogein and other cities, where soucars or bankers of character and credit were in a flourishing state, and that goods to a great amount had not only continually passed through the province, but that the insurance offices which exist through all parts of India, and include the principal moneyed men, had never stopped their operations, though premiums rose, at a period of danger, to a high amount. The Native Government of Malwa, when tranquillity was established through our arms, wanted nothing but that which the attachment of the Natives of India to their soil soon supplied them with, a return of the inhabitants. And I do not believe that in that country the introduction of our direct rule could have contributed more, nor indeed so much, to the prosperity of the commercial and agricultural interests as the re-establishment of the efficient rule of its former Princes and chiefs, who, though protected from attack, are quite free in their internal administration from our interference. With respect to the southern Mahratta districts, of whose prosperity I have before spoken, if I refer, as I must, to their condition before the last few years of Bajee Row's misrule, I do not think that either their commercial or agricultural interests are likely to be improved under our rule, except in that greatest of blessings, exemption from wars which, while under our protection, they equally enjoy, and I must unhesitatingly state that the provinces belonging to the family of 'Putwurden,' and some other chiefs on the banks of the Kistna, present a greater agricultural and commercial prosperity than almost any I know in India. I refer this to their system of administration, which, though there may be at periods exactions, is, on the whole, mild and paternal; to the knowledge and almost devotion of the Hindoos to all agricultural pursuits; to their better understanding, or, at least, better practice than us in many parts of the administration, particularly in raising towns and villages to prosperity from the encouragement given to moneyed men, and to the introduction of capital; and, above all, to Jāgheerdars (Kandownos) residing on their estates, and these provinces being administered by men of rank, who live and die on the soil, and are usually succeeded in office by their sons or near relatives. If these men exact money at times in an arbitrary manner, all their expenditure, as well as all they receive, is limited to their own provinces; but, above all causes which promote prosperity, is the invariable support given to the village and other Native institutions, and to the employment, far beyond what our system admits, of all classes of the popula tion."*

Equally favourable testimony to the condition of the dominions of the Rajah of Berar, another member of the great Mahratta confederacy, was given by eye-witnesses :—

"The thriving condition of the province, indicated by the appearance of its capital (says a European traveller) and confirmed by that of the districts which we subsequently traversed, demands from me a tribute of praise to the ancient Princes of the country. Without the benefit of navigation (for the 'Nerbudda is not here navigable) and without much inland commerce, but under the fostering hand of a race of good Princes, a numerous people tilled a fertile country, and still preserve in the neatness of their homes, in the number and magnificence of their temples, their ponds, and other public works; in the size of their towns, and in the frequency of their plantations, the undoubted signs of enviable prosperity. The whole merit may be safely ascribed to the former government, for the praise of good administration is rarely merited by Mahratta chieftains, and it is sufficient applause to say that the Chief of Saugor in twenty years, and the Rajah of Berar in four, have not much impaired the prosperity which they found."†

* Sir John Malcolm.

† Journey from Mirzapore to Nagpore 1798, by a Member of the Asiatic Society. Asiatic Annual Register, vol. 8; Miscellaneous Tracts p. 32.

"We now," says another traveller in Berar, "continued our journey through a fine champaign country, abundantly watered with rivulets that issue from the neighbouring mountains. It was entirely free from jungle, full of villages, and beautifully varied with tufts of trees and pools of water. It is more easy to conceive than express the delight we experienced in changing the difficulties of the former part of the journey. The Mahratta Government being well established in this part of the route, we experienced very civil and hospitable treatment, and found plenty of every kind of grain, which this highly-cultivated country produced at a very cheap rate;" and although inland commerce derives very little encouragement from the Government, which pays no attention to the public roads, yet the whole exports in seasons of plenty are said to employ a hundred thousand bullocks. *

From the Mahratta we pass to the Rajpoot States; and here again we bring the evidence of an eye-witness to bear upon their conditions:—

"As compared with the cultivation of the King of Oude's dominions, it has always struck me that there was a marked superiority in the appearance of the British territory. At the same time, it is but fair to state that I have beheld small independent States, governed by Hindoo Rajahs, where the cultivation appeared superior to that of the Company's provinces, and where the independent aid of the pea-

* Miscellaneous Tracts, Asiatic Annual Register, vol. ii, p. 166.

santry announced a greater security of rights. In the year 1810, when a large force marched beyond the British territory, the division halted for nearly two months within the dominion of the Rajah of Tihree, the flourishing condition of which excited the admiration of the whole army." †

"In passing through the Rampore territory, ‡ we could not fail to notice the high state of cultivation to which it has attained, when compared with the surrounding country; scarely a spot of land is neglected: and although the season was by no means favourable, the whole district seems to be covered with an abundant harvest. As we have no reason to conclude from the description we had received of the present Regent that this state of prosperity had been produced by any personal exertions on his part, we were solicitous to trace its source, and to discover whether, in the nature of the tenures, the mode of arrangement or otherwise, there were any peculiar circumstances which it might be useful for us to advert to in the course of executing the duty entrusted to us. The management of the Nawab Fyz-oolah Khan is celebrated throughout the country. It was the management of an enlightened and liberal landlord, who devoted his time and attention and employed his own capital in promoting the prosperity of his country. When works of magnitude were required,

† White's "State of British India," 1822.

‡ Report from Commissions upon the North-West Provinces, 1808.

which could not be accomplished by the efforts of the individual, the means of undertaking them were supplied by his bounty. Watercourses were constructed, the rivulets were sometimes made to overflow and fertilise the adjacent districts, and the paternal care of a popular chief was constantly exerted to afford protection to his subjects, to stimulte their exertions, to direct their labours to useful objects, and to promote by every means the success of the undertaking.

"If the comparison for the same territory be made between the management of the Rohillas and that of our own government, *it is painful to think that the balance of advantage is clearly in favour of the former.* After seven years' possession of the country, it appears by the report that the revenue has increased only by two lacs of rupees, or £ 20,000. The papers laid before Parliament show that in twenty years which have since elapsed, the collective revenues of Rohilcund, and the other districts forming the ceded provinces of Oude, had actually declined £ 200,000 per annum.

"We could not fail, however, to observe the singular difference which the application of greater capital and greater industry is capable of producing in the state of contiguous lands. While the surrounding country seemed to have been visited by a desolating calamity, the lands of the Rajahs Diaram and Bugwant Sing, under every disadvantage of season, were covered with crops produced by a better husbandry, or by greater labour. It should here be explained that the neighbouring lands alluded to in the report *consisted of British territory, already five years in our occupation.*" *

And even after all the abuse that has been lavished upon Oude and upon its sovereigns, we find upon unexceptionable testimony that neither the state of the country nor the character of its sovereigns is so black as it is represented by our own officials.

"I was pleased and surprised (says Bishop Heber),† after all I had heard of Oude, to find the country so completely under the plough, since, were the oppression as great as is sometimes stated, I cannot think that we should witness so considerable a population and so much industry; yet that sufficient anarchy and misrule exists, the events of yesterday afforded sufficient reason for supposing."

The same high authority testifies to the prosperous condition of the State of Bhurtpore under the Native Sovereigns:

"The country, though still bare of wood, has more scattered trees than we had seen for many days back; and notwithstanding that the soil is sandy, and only irrigated from wells, it is one of the best cultivated and watered tracts which I have seen in India. The crops of corn now on the ground were really beautiful; that of cotton, though gone by, showed marks of having been a very good one. What is a sure proof of wealth, I saw several

* Appendix to Political Report, 1882. pp. 36-37.

† Bishop Heber's "Journal," vol. ii. pp. 77-79.

sugar mills, and large pieces of ground where the cane had just been cleared; and, contrary to the usual habits of India, where the cultivators keep as far as they can from the highway, to avoid the various molestations to which they are exposed from thieves and travellers, there was often a narrow pathway winding through the green wheat and mustard crops, and even this was crossed continually by the channels which conveyed water to the furrows.

"The population did not seem great; but the villages which we saw were apparently in good condition and repair, and the whole afforded so pleasing a picture of industry, and was so much superior to anything which I had been led to expect in Rajpootana, of *which I had seen in the Company's territories* since leaving the southern parts of Rohilcund, that I was led to suppose that either the Rajah of Bhurtpore was an extremely exemplary and parental governor, or that the system of management adopted in the British provinces was in some way or other less favourable to the improvement and happiness of the country than some of the Native States."

To the high character of Pertab Sing—the first Rajah of Sattara—as a ruler, and to the prosperous condition of his territory, we have the emphatic testimony of the British Government itself:—

"We have been highly gratified by the information, from time to time transmitted to us by our Government, on the subject of your Highness's exemplary fulfilment of the duties of that elevated situation in which it has pleased Providence to place you.

"A course of conduct so suitable to your Highness's exalted station, and so well calculated to promote the prosperity of your dominions, and the happiness of your people, as that which you have wisely and uniformly pursued, while it reflects the highest honour on your own character, has imparted to our minds the feelings of unqualified satisfaction and pleasure. The liberality also which you have displayed in executing, at your own cost, various public works of great utility, and which has so greatly raised your reputation in the eyes of the Princes and people of India, gives you an additional claim to our approbation, respect, and applause.

"Impressed with these sentiments the Court of Directors of the East India Company have unanimously resolved to transmit to you a sword, which will be presented to you through the Government of Bombay and which we trust you will receive with satisfaction, as a token of their high esteem and regard."*

And whilst thus congratulating this Rajah on the prosperity of his dominions, and the happiness of his people, the condition of some thirty millions of Native British subjects, who have been under British rule for almost a century, is thus described by an unimpeachable witness†:—

"No one has ever attempted to contradict the fact that the condition of the Bengal peasantry is

* Letter of the Court of Directors, Par. Pa. A.D. 1843. No. 569. p. 1268.

† Dr. Marshman, *Friend of India*, April 1st, 1852.

almost as wretched and degraded as it is possible to conceive, living in the most miserable hovels, scarcely fit for a dog kennel, covered with tattered rags, and unable, in too many instances, to procure more than a single meal a day for himself and family. The Bengal ryot knows nothing of the most ordinary comforts of life. We speak without exaggeration when we affirm that if the real condition of those who raise the harvest, which yields between three and four millions a year, was fully known, it would make the ears of one who heard thereof tingle."

Appendix.

English Economists and India.

THE economic interests of India and the conditions under which they have to be safeguarded being different in many essential respects from those of European countries and of America, many of the leading principles of the orthodox economic science, as expounded in English text-books, have to be modified when applied to the conditions of this country. This fact is not, as a rule, borne in mind by those responsible for our industrial progress. Indeed, it is doubtful if there is any code of economic principles consistently kept in view by our rulers. These seem to change in accordance with the needs and convenience of certain vested interests. Sometimes our statesmen sneer at the theories of the West; sometimes they take refuge under them to justify particular measures. Definite and rational conceptions of the duty and scope of the State in the direction of the industrial interests of the nation are it is obvious, absent, the determining force on given occasions being certain sectional interests dominant for the time being. Great economic problems are approached in this extremely narrow frame of mind. The transition state of India is, nowhere, in the multifarious branches of her life, fraught with more serious consequences—consequences affecting literally the life and death of the nation—than in her industrial life. It is in the power of our British rulers to make or mar our industrial future. They can make India a rich country, industrially independent and flourishing; they can make India a poor and decaying country whose teeming population, having lost all industrial status and all aptitude for industrial enterprise, are being reduced to a condition of servitude to British capitalists. British capitalists, with the help of their infinitely superior and efficiently organised resources and aided by their political status as belonging to the ruling class, have ousted—and are ousting—the natives of the country from all positions of advantage.

Great problems have been bequeathed by the nineteenth century to its successor, and these problems as they obtain in the West, are confronting the rulers of a country which is struggling to rise from its theocratic social basis to one of industry as organised and led in the twentieth century. Industrially speaking, the condition of India at the present moment is to be compared to the condition of Europe in mediæval times rather than to its condition in any later period. Custom instead of competition still forms the basis of the interdealings of society ; caste binds down the capital and labour of the country to a state of comparative immobility; the industrial system still rests on a domestic and individual basis; manual labour is yet to give place to the employment of labour-saving machinery; an industrial life is still held in comparative contempt; the influence of priests is still dominant; new ideas do not easily take root. A spirit of nationality, co-operation, sacrifice of the present for the future, thrift, enterprise, knowledge of the outside world, national self-consciousness, all these are yet more or less to be acquired Still, the natural wealth of the country is immense, and such as, under capable direction, will, in a comparatively short time, plant wealth and opulence, and all the higher qualities which a rich, complex industrial life invariably developes, where, at present, growing poverty, universal depression, and a melancholy pessimism in regard to life and life's interests, keep down the people.

It is in a field of this description that our British rulers are making experiments in the application of Western Principles of Political Economy. We have said that the teachings of European Economic Science are not always followed in this country; nor indeed are they discarded. In abolishing in 1882 the last vestige of import duties on Manchester goods, Lord Ripon spoke reverentially of his life-long conviction regarding the immutable truth of free-trade principles. But the present Viceroy, Lord Curzon, in imposing an import duty on foreign sugar, spoke in contempt of "the mutterings of the high priests" of free-trade. Still, it may be stated that the bias of British statesmen is in favour of the teachings of the orthodox science as expounded by their own writers, and, as a fact, India's economic interest considerably suffers from a too blind adherence to the doctrines of Ricardo and Mill on the part of our rulers. Departures are exceptional, and are taken, not in view to the general upheaval of India's industry, but, too often, to uphold and protect the interests of the ascendant class. The two exceptions to principles of free-trade in this country, the excise duty on Indian cotton goods and the import duty on sugar, were prompted by no regard for the good of the people. It is to be wished that these exceptions were more numerous and were taken to protect and advance Indian rather than other interests. As we have said, the truths of economic science are not universally applicable, irrespective of particular stages of national growth and of peculiar environments and conditions. If free-trade is good for England, it does not follow it is good for India too. Nor are protective duties, bounties and subventions, State restriction and control, if they are evils in England, necessary evils in other countries. Similarly, in regard to the relation between landlord and tenant, factory legislation, usury, organisation of rural credit, expenditure of foreign borrowed money, and so forth, what procedure on the part of the State in Western countries may prove beneficial, may not necessarily prove beneficial in a country like India, whose civilization is fundamentally different and, in many respects, still backward.

The evil is aggravated by the absence of suitable training on the part of the persons on whom rests the responsibility of directing the economic destiny of India. The bulk of our bureaucracy receive no training in the science of political economy, and the experts that are now and again sent out to India to preside over our economic affairs are birds of passage, the result being that we miss any bold and far-sighted policy designed to promote our interests and to protect them against the unresisted inroads of powerful alien rivalry. "If India is to prosper," said Professor Marshall, of the Cambridge University, who, as such, is in contact with candidates for the Indian Civil Service, "the difficult economic problems of the Gov-"ernment must be solved mainly by the Government. "But English officials in India have plenty of occupation "for their strength in doing the day's work and, if they "have not learnt to separate the apparent from the real in "the action of economic forces before they go out to India, "they can hardly do so in India. It seems, therefore, ur-"gently needed that some half-a-dozen of the young men "who go out to India every year, should take with them "a good grounding in economics, and have already got to "understand the main bearings of those modern economic "forces which are revolutionising the West and are mak-"ing great changes in the East." The Governments of Western countries are aided by the advice and criticism of a large number of able business men competent to consider the broader problems of economics as well as the details of their special trades; and there is nothing in the condition of India which makes this assistance and criticism less indispensable.

In the absence of such trained and competent advice, it is found to be the easiest course to follow expediency for the time being, or to adopt the theories of the old orthodox economics and base on them our legislative measures. The political economy of Europe has undergone steady changes in its conceptions, theories, and practical applications, since the dissolution of mediæval times. At the present day, the most approved theories as enunciated by American, French and German economists, are as different from those that fo undfavour with Turgot, as modern Indian conditions are from those of Europe in the seventeenth century. Still, if Adam Smith's ideas had prevailed in Turgot's time, or if modern German theories had prevailed in Cobden's time, the economic history of Europe would have been different to what it has been. The given conditions of society and the prevailing conceptions regarding its future and contemporary interests, determined the economic ideas that received the approbation of thinkers and the acceptance of statesmen. Modern Political Economy no longer contemplates man as a money-earning machine, as an isolated unit, entirely selfish, devoid of social obligations and beyond the reach of responsibility for the collective well-being of the society to which he belongs. Nor, on the other hand, is the State looked upon as an organization with the sole function of collecting taxes and maintaining order and peace. The latest school of economists "recognises the State not merely as an institution for the maintenance of order, but as the organ of the nation for all ends which cannot be adequately effected by voluntary individual effort. Whenever social aims can be attained only or most advantageously through its action, that action is justified. The cases in which it can properly interfere must be determined separately on their own merits and in relation to the stage of national development." When the history of British India in the past is subjected to a test of this kind, we see in vain that any such conception of the functions of the State ever guided the councils of the rulers. Yet, they are the conceptions that have dominated the direction of the economic destinies of the most powerful and progressive countries of the West, of Germany, France, Italy and America. England herself, in departing, under the pressure of new ideas born of new conditions, from her old faith, is yielding to the conclusions of foreign thinkers. Modern States call upon the people to make more sacrifices than were made in former times for the honour, freedom and independence of the country, and the people have, therefore, a right to invoke the direct intervention of the State, not only for the redress of individual wrongs, but also for raising the social status of the nation as a whole and enabling it to protect itself against foreign cupidity or unequal competition. It is India's future prosperity and greatness that such theories of economics as may command the faith of our rulers should be calculated to bring about, but not the further enrichment of Britain by India's resources being freely opened for foreign exploitation and by her latent possibilities being crippled by her subjection to the unsympathetic domination of alien interests.

On the spontaneous decomposition of the mediæval system,* when the kings of Europe had no other means of accomplishing their military and political ends than a wide system of taxation, industry became a permanent interest of Government. No other form of wealth was understood than money, and how to attract the largest quantity of precious metals from other countries became the anxious endeavour of statesmen. Each country must seek to export the largest possible quantity of its manufactures, and import as little as possible of those of other countries, receiving the difference of the two values in gold and silver. This difference was called the balance of trade, and the balance was considered favourable when more money was received than was paid. Government must resort to all possible expedients—prohibition of, or high duties on, the importation of foreign wares, bounties on the export of home manufactures, restrictions on the export of the precious metals—for the purpose of securing such a balance. Cromwell, the Great Protector, who destroyed the carrying trade of Holland by his Navigation Act, and Colbert, the celebrated French Minister, who based

* This and the subsequent articles are an abridgment of the article on "Political Economy" in the Encyclopædia Britannica.

on this system his whole economic policy, domestic and international, were its two chief representatives. But about the end of the seventeenth century, new ideas were growing, which condemned and eventually overcame this mercantile system, and which, while denying that a favourable balance of trade was the true object of Government's efforts, emphasised the importance of procuring for the whole nation, in the fullest measure, the enjoyment of the necessaries and conveniences of life. With this object, the freedom of industry was insisted upon. The impoverished condition of the agricultural population, the oppressive weight and unequal distribution of taxation, and the unsound state of the public finance, had produced a general feeling of disquiet, and led several distinguished writers to protest strongly against the policy of Colbert and to demand a complete reform.

The school of economists that advocated these ideas were called the Physiocrats. According to their general political doctrine:

" Society is composed of a number of individuals all having the same natural right. If all do not possess equal capacities, each can at least best understand his own interest; and is led by nature to follow it. The social union is really a contract between these individuals, the object of which is the limitation of the natural freedom of each; just so far as is not inconsistent with the right of the others. Government, though necessary, is a necessary evil; and the governing power, appointed by consent, should be limited to the amount of interference absolutely required to secure the fulfilment of the contract. In the economic sphere, it implies the right of the individual to such natural enjoyments as he can acquire by his labour, and, therefore, freedom of exchange should be ensured and competition in the market should be unrestricted, no monopolies or privileges being permitted to exist."

" Only those labours are " productive" which add to the quantity of raw materials available for the purposes of man; and the real annual addition to the wealth of the community consists of the excess of the mass of agricultural products (including, of course, metals) over their cost of production On the amount of this net produce depends the well-being of the community, and the possibility of its advance in civilization. The manufacturer merely gives a new form to the materials extracted from the earth; the higher value of the object, after it had passed through his hands, only represents the quantity of provisions and other materials used and consumed in its elaboration. Commerce does nothing more than transfer the wealth already existing from one hand to another; what the trading classes gain thereby is acquired at the cost of the nation, and, it is desirable that its amount should be as small as possible. The occupations of the manufacturer and the merchant, as well as the liberal professions, and every kind of personal service, are " useful" indeed, but they are " sterile," drawing their income, not from any fund which they themselves create, but from the superfluous earnings of the agriculturist. "Laissez faire, laissez passer" should therefore be the motto of Governments. The revenue to the State which must be derived altogether from this net product, ought to be raised in the most direct and simplest way,—namely, by a single impost of the nature of a land-tax."

This " Physiocratic system," after exercising some influence in France and in continental countries, soon ceased to exist as a living power, and was absorbed by the sounder and more complete construction of the celebrated English economist, the author of the "Wealth of Nations." But between Adam Smith and his predecessors, the Physiocrats, there were more points of fundamental agreement than those of difference. The principal task he set before himself was to discredit and overthrow the economic system then prevalent, and to demonstrate the radical unfitness of the existing European Governments to direct the industrial movement. In pursuit of this task, he demolished many errors and prejudices and cleared the ground for truth, but left his successors a permanent possession, in the judicious analyses of economic facts and ideas, the wise practical suggestions, the luminous indications of all kinds, with which his work abounds. Still, it is considered by his modern critics, that his conception of the social economy is essentially individualistic, the individual being treated as a purely egoistic force, working uniformly in the direction of private gain, without regard to the good of others or of the community at large. He assumes that every one knows his true interest and will pursue it, and the economic advantage of the individual coincides with that of society. By this reduction of every question to one of individual gain, he is led to a too exclusive consideration of the exchange-value as distinct from wealth in its proper sense, and leaves himself no room for a consideration of production and consumption of wealth. He tends too much towards a glorification of non-government, and a repudiation of all social intervention for the regulation of economic life. He does not keep in view the moral destination of our race, nor regard wealth as a means to the higher ends of life. His system does not sufficiently recognise the fact that man, as a member of society, is a child of civilization and a product of history : it takes no account of the different stages of social development as implying altered economic conditions and calling for economic action, or even involving a modification of the actor. These criticisms, it should be observed, are not exclusively applicable to Smith's construction of economics, but also, chiefly the last, to many of the later English economists. Smith lived at a time when the invention of steam power produced a revolution in the industrial system, and introduced glimpses of modern socialism as an expression of the protest of the working classes and their aspiration after a better order of things

This latter question was first effectually brought before the mind by Thomas Robert Malthus (1766-1834), not however under the impulse of a sympathy with the now disturbing forces, but in the interest of a conservative policy. He brought into prominence the law of diminishing returns from land, and involving as it does, though hypothetically, the prospect of a continuously increasing difficulty in obtaining the necessary sustenance for all members of society; it is this law that has given importance to the question of population as an element in the discussion of economic questions. But he exaggerated the operation of this law. He assumed that it was universal, under conditions favourable as well as unfavorable to the unrestricted growth of population He omitted from his consideration the great counteracting force of moral restraint. " If the inherent energy of the principle of population is measured by the rate at which numbers increase under the most favourable circumstances, surely, the force of less favourable circumstances, acting through prudential or altruistic motives, is measured by the great difference between this maximum rate and those which are observed to prevail in most European countries. Under a rational system of institutions, the adaptation of the numbers to the means available for their support, is effected by the felt or anticipated pressure of circumstances and the fear of social degradation, within a tolerable degree of approximation to what is desirable. To bring the result nearer to the just standard, a higher measure of popular enlightenment and more serious habits of moral reflexion ought, indeed, to be encouraged. But it is the duty of the individual and not any vague notions as to the pressure of the national population on subsistence, that will be adequate to influence conduct." We may, however, add that this latter consideration of national interest is not altogether incapable of influencing the conduct of the individual, though its influence can only be more or less indirect and remote.

David Ricardo (1772-1823) was the next conspicuous figure among the economists of his time. The principal problem to which he addressed himself was that of distribution,—that is to say, the proportions of the whole produce of the country which would be allotted to the proprietor of the land, to the capitalist, and to the labourer—proportions in which important variations take place in the progress of society. "His real services in connection with questions of currency and banking naturally created a prepossession in favour of his more general views. But, apart from those special subjects, it does not appear that, either in the form of solid theoretic teaching or of valuable practical guidance, he has really done much for the world, whilst he admittedly misled opinion on several important questions."

Then came Mill (1848), and Cairnes (1857), whose conception of the science, though it has not met with general approval from modern writers, still introduced important modifications in the extravagant pretensions of their predecessors The deductions of Smith and others were based, as we have said, on the assumption of the existence of the so-called "economic man," a being influenced by two motives only: that of acquiring wealth and that of avoiding exertion, and they laid down that, only so far as the premises framed on this conception correspond with facts can the conclusions be depended upon in practice. Besides, Mill and Cairnes laid strees on the essential difference between economic Science and economic Art—"the former ascertaining truth relating to the laws of economic phenomena, the latter preserving the right of economic action. Action can, no more, in the economic world than in any other province of life, be regulated by considerations borrowed from that department of things only; economics can suggest ideas which are to be kept in view, but standing alone, it cannot direct conduct—an office for which a wider prospect of human affairs is required."

The writings of Mill and Cairnes mark the conclusion of what is called the "orthodox school" of political economy. The subsequent fresh conceptions and the modernisation of the science are mostly the work of German and French writers.

At the beginning of the nineteenth century, the influence of French and German economists began to dominate economic thought in general. They regarded the exposition of the science as too narrow, attaching too much importance to the well-being of individuals and not taking sufficient account of the material and moral well-being of the nation, for whose collective benefit the individual is, in these days, called upon to make increasing self-sacrifice. The well-known French writer, Sismondi (1773-1842), took objection to the dominant doctrines and was dissatified that the science, as commonly understood, studied too exclusively the means of increasing wealth, and not sufficiently the use of this wealth for producing general happiness. The practical system founded on it tended, he believed, not only to make the rich richer, but to make the poor poorer and more dependent; and he desired to fix attention on the question of distribution as by far the most important, especially in the social circumstances of recent times. To the subject of population he devotes special care, as of great importance for the welfare of the working classes. So far as agriculturists are concerned, he thinks the system of what he calls patriarchal exploitation, where the cultivator is also proprietor and is aided by his family in tilling the land—a law of equal division among the natural heirs being apparently presupposed—the one which is most efficacious in preventing an undue increase of the population. The father is, in such a case, able distinctly to estimate the resources available for his children, and to determine the stage of sub-division which would necessitate the descent of the family from the material and social position it had previously occupied. When children beyond this limit are born, they do not marry or they choose amongst their number one to continue the race. This is the view which, adopted by J. S. Mill, makes so great a figure in the too favourable presentation by that writer of the system of peasant proprietors.

Henry Charles Carey (1793-1879), son of an American citizen who had emigrated from Ireland, is another representative of a reaction which arose against the dispiriting character which the Smithian doctrines had assumed in the hands of Malthus and Ricardo. His aim was, while adhering to the individualistic economy, to place it on a higher and surer basis, and fortify it against the assaults of socialism, to which some of the Ricardian tenets have exposed it. Inspired with the optimistic sentiment natural to a young and rising nation with abundant undeveloped resources and an unbounded outlook towards the future, he seeks to show that there exists, independently of human wills, a natural system of economic laws, which is essentially beneficent, and of which the increasing prosperity of the whole community, and especially of the working classes, is the spontaneous result,—capable of being defeated only by the ignorance or perversity of man resisting or impeding its action. He rejects the Malthusian theory of population, maintaining that numbers regulate themselves sufficiently in every well-governed society, and that their pressure on subsistence characterises the lower, and not the more advanced, stages of civilisation. He rightly denies the universal truth, for all stages of cultivation, of the law of diminishing return from land.

The so-called Ricardian theory of rent is a speculative fancy, contradicted by all experience Cultivation does not in fact, as that theory supposes, begin with the best, and move downwards to the poorer soils in the order of their inferiority. The light and dry higher lands are first cultivated, and only when population has become dense and capital has accumulated, are the low-lying lands, with their greater fertility, but also with their morasses, inundations, and miasmas, attacked and brought into occupation. Rent regarded as a proportion of the produce, sinks like all interest on capital, in process of time, but, as an absolute amount, increases. The share of the labourer increases, both as a proportion and an absolute amount. And thus the interests of these different social classes are in harmony.

But, Carey proceeds to say, in order that this harmonious progress may be realized, what is taken from the land must be given back to it All the articles derived from it are really separated parts of it which must be restored on pain of its exhaustion. Hence the producer and the consumer must be close to each other ; the products must not be exported to a foreign country in exchange for its manufactures, and thus go to enrich as manure a foreign soil. In immediate exchange value the landowner may gain by such exportation, but the productive powers of the land will suffer. And thus Carey, who had set out as an earnest advocate of free-trade, arrives at the doctrine of protection. The "co-ordinating power" in society must intervene to prevent private advantage from working public mischief. He attributes his conversion on this question to his observation of the effects of liberal and protective tariffs respectively on American prosperity. This observation, he says, threw him back on theory, and led him to see that the intervention referred to might be necessary to remove (as he phrases it) the obstacles to the progress of younger communities created by the action of older and wealthier nations. But it seems probable that the influence of List's writings added to his own deep-rooted and hereditary jealousy and dislike of Engligh predominance, had something to do with his change of attitude.

A distinct note of opposition to the Smithian economics was sounded in Germany by two writers, Adam Müller and Friedrich List. Adam Müller (1779-1829) was undoubtedly a man of genius. It is possible that the political and historical ideas which inspire him, his repugnance to contemporary liberalism, and his notions of regular organic development, especially in relation to England, were in some degree imbibed from Edmund Burke, whose *Reflections on the Revolution in France* had been translated into German by Friedrich Gentz, the friend and teacher of Müller. The association of his criticisms with mediæval prepossessions ought not to prevent our recognizing the elements of truth which they contain.

He protests against the doctrine of Smith and against modern political economy in general, on the ground that it presents a mechanical, atomistic, and purely material conception of society, that it reduces to nullity all moral forces and ignores the necessity of a moral order, that it is at bottom no more than a theory of private property and private interests, and takes no account of the life of the people as a whole in its national solidarity and historical continuity. Exclusive attention, he complains, is devoted to the immediate production of objects possessing exchange value and to the transitory existence of individuals; whilst to the maintenance of the collective production for future generations, to intellectual products, powers, possessions, and enjoyments, and to the State with its higher tasks and aims, scarcely a thought is given The truth is that nations are specialized organisms with distinct principles of life, having definite individualities which determine the course of their historical development. Each is through all time one whole; and, as the present is the heir of the past, it ought to keep before it constantly the permanent good of the community in the future. The economic existence of a people is only one side or province of its entire activity, requiring to be kept in harmony with the higher ends of society, and the proper organ to effect this reconciliation is the State, which, instead of being nearly an apparatus for the administration of justice, represents the totality of the national life. The division of labour, Müller holds, is perfectly developed by Smith, who makes it to arise out of a native bent for truck or barter; whilst its dependence on capital—on the labours and accumulations of past generations—is not duly emphasized. Nor is the necessary counterpoise and completion of the division of labour, in the principle of the national combination of labour, properly brought out. Smith recognizes only material, not spiritual, capital; yet the latter, represented in every nation by language, as the former by money, is a real national store of experience, wisdom, good sense, and moral feeling, transmitted with increase by each generation to its successor and enables each generation to produce immensely more than by its own unaided powers it could possibly do. Again, the system of Smith is one-sidedly British; if it is innocuous on the soil of England, it is because in her society the old foundations on which the spiritual and material life of the people can surely rest are preserved in the surviving spirit of feudalism and the inner connection of the whole social system,—the national capital of laws, manners, reputation and credit, which has been handed down in its integrity in consequence of the insular position of the country. For the continent of Europe a quite different system is necessary, in which, in place of the sum of the private wealth of individuals being viewed as the primary object, the real wealth of the nation and the production of national power shall be made to predominate, and along with the division of labour, its national union and concentration—along with the physical, no less the intellectual and moral, capital, shall be embraced. In these leading traits of Muller's thought there is much which foreshadows the more recent forms of German economic and sociological speculation, especially those characteristic of the "Historical" school.

Another element of opposition was represented by Friedrich List (1798-1846), a man of great intellectual vigor as well as practical energy, and notable as having powerfully contributed by his writings to the formation of the German Zollverein. Though his practical conclusions were different from Muller's, he was largely influenced by the general mode of thinking of that writer and by his strictures on the doctrine of Smith. It was particularly against the cosmopolitan principle in the modern economical system that he protested, and against the absolute doctrine of free-trade, which was in harmony with that principle. He gave prominence to the national idea, and insisted on the special requirements of each nation according to its circumstances and especially to the degree of its development.

He refuses to Smith's system the title of the industrial, which he thinks more appropriate to the mercantile system, and designates the former as "the exchange value system." He denies the parallelism asserted by Smith between the economic conduct proper to an individual and that to a nation, and holds that the immediate private interest of the separate members of the community will not lead to the highest good of the whole. The nation is an existence, standing between the individual and humanity, and formed into a unity by its language, manners, historical development, culture and constitution. This unity is the first condition of the security, well-being, progress, and civilization of the individual; and private economic interests, like all others, must be subordinated to the maintenance, completion, and strengthening of the nationality. The nation having a continuous life, its true wealth consists—and this is List's fundamental doctrine—not in the quantity of exchange values which it possesses, but in the full and many-sided development of its productive powers. Its economic education, if we may so speak, is more important than the immediate production of values, and it may be right that the present generation should sacrifice its gain and enjoyment to secure the strength and skill of the future. In the sound and normal condition of a nation which has attained economic maturity, the three productive powers of agriculture, manufactures and commerce should be alike developed. But the two latter factors are superior in importance, as exercising a more effective and fruitful influence on the whole culture of the nation as well as on its independence. Navigation, railways, all higher technical arts connect themselves specially with these factors; whilst in a purely agricultural state there is a tendency to stagnation, absence of enterprise, and the maintenance of antiquated prejudices. But, for the growth of the higher forms of industry all countries are not adapted—only those of the temperate zones, whilst the torrid regions have a natural monopoly in the production of certain raw materials; and thus between these two groups of countries a division of labour and confederation of powers spontaneously takes place. List then goes on to explain his theory of the stages of economic development through which the nations of the temperate zone which are furnished with all the necessary conditions, naturally pass, in advancing to their normal economic state. These are (1) pastoral life, (2.) Agriculture, (3) Agriculture united with manufacturers: whilst in the final stage agriculture, manufactures and commerce are combined.

The economic task of the State is to bring into existence through legislative and administrative action the conditions required for the progress of the nation through these stages. Out of this view arises List's scheme of industrial politics. Every nation, according to him, should begin with free trade, stimulating and improving its agriculture by intercourse with richer and more cultivated nations, importing foreign manufactures and exporting raw products. When it is economically so far advanced that it can manufacture for itself, then a system of protection should be employed to allow the home industries to develop themselves fully, and save them from being overpowered in their earlier efforts by the competition of more matured foreign industries in the home market. When the national industries have grown strong enough no longer to dread this competition, then the highest stage of progress has been reached. Free-trade should again become the rule, and the nation be thus thoroughly incorporated with the universal industrial union. In List's time, according to his view, Spain, Portugal and Naples were purely agricultural countries; Germany and the United States of North America had arrived at the second stage, their manufactures being in process of development. France was near the boundary of the third or highest stage, which England alone had reached. For England, therefore, as well as for the agricultural countries first named, free-trade was the right economic policy, but not, for Germany or America. What a nation loses for a time in exchange values during the protective period, she much more than gains in the long run in productive power,—the temporary expenditure being strictly analogous, when we place ourselves at the point of view of the life of the nation, to the cost of the industrial education of the individual. The practical conclusion which List drew for his own country was that she needed for her economic progress an extended and conveniently bounded territory reaching to the sea-coast both on North and South, and a vigorous expansion of manufactures and commerce, and that the way to the latter lay through judicious protective legislation with a customs union comprising all German lands, and a German marine with a Navigation Act. The national German spirit striving after independence and power through union, and the national industry, awaking from its lethargy and eager to recover lost ground, were favourable to the success of List's book, and it produced a great sensation. He ably represented the tendencies and demands of his time in his own country; his work had the effect of fixing the attention, not merely of the speculative and official classes, but of practical men generally, on questions of political economy; and he had without doubt an important influence on German industrial policy. So far as science is concerned, the emphasis he laid on the relative historical study of stages of civilisation as affecting economic questions, and his protest against absolute formulas, had a certain value; and the preponderance given to the national development over the immediate gains of individuals was sound in principle; though his doctrine was, both on its public and private sides, too much of a mere chrematistic, and tended in fact to set up a new form of mercantilism, rather than to aid the contemporary effort towards social reform.
